THE ETHICS OF WAR

THE ETHICS OF WAR

Essays

Edited by

Saba Bazargan-Forward and Samuel C. Rickless

OXFORD
UNIVERSITY PRESS

OXFORD
UNIVERSITY PRESS

Oxford University Press is a department of the University of Oxford.
It furthers the University's objective of excellence in research, scholarship,
and education by publishing worldwide. Oxford is a registered trade mark of
Oxford University Press in the UK and in certain other countries.

Published in the United States of America by Oxford University Press
198 Madison Avenue, New York, NY 10016, United States of America.

Library of Congress Cataloging-in-Publication Data

Names: Bazargan-Forward, Saba, author.
Title: The ethics of war : essays / Saba Bazargan-Forward and Sameul Rickless.
Description: New York : Oxford University Press, 2016.
Identifiers: LCCN 2016023720| ISBN 9780199376148 (hardcover : alk. paper) |
  ISBN 9780190614553 (epub)
Subjects: LCSH: War—Moral and ethical aspects. | Just war doctrine.
Classification: LCC U22 .B39 2016 | DDC 172/.42—dc23 LC record available at
https://lccn.loc.gov/2016023720

1 3 5 7 9 8 6 4 2

Printed by Sheridan Books, Inc., United States of America

For Peter Lewis
who made this all possible

CONTENTS

ACKNOWLEDGMENTS

This collection originates in a conference on the ethics of war held at UC San Diego on March 1–2, 2013. The vast majority of the contributors to this volume either presented or commented on papers at that conference. We are deeply grateful to all of the conference participants, including UC San Diego philosophy faculty, staff, and graduate students, for their efforts at making the conference the success that it was. We single out, for special thanks, the then chair of the department of philosophy, Don Rutherford, and the then dean of Arts and Humanities, Seth Lerer, for their unwavering support. And our deepest thanks go to our friend and benefactor, Peter Lewis, who made the conference, and hence this volume, possible.

We would also like to thank Peter Ohlin, Emily Sacharin, and Andrew Ward at Oxford University Press for shepherding the volume from conception to production, and the OUP reviewers for their constructive comments and helpful suggestions.

INTRODUCTION

Since the writings of the scholastics and jurists of the late Renaissance and Early Modern periods (from roughly the sixteenth through the nineteenth centuries), two precepts have underwritten accounts of the morality of war. First: war is perspicuously described as a relation not between individuals but between states (or, at least, as a relation between a state and a collective with aspirations of attaining—or undermining—statehood). Second: the rules governing conduct in war should proceed independently of whether the war fought is just or unjust. These precepts form the basis of what is known as "Just War theory," which today informs the judgments of ethicists, government officials, international lawyers, religious scholars, news coverage, and perhaps most important, the public as a whole. The influence of Just War theory is as vast as it is subtle; many are inclined to identify the criteria of Just War theory, once made explicit, as common sense. Indeed, according to David Rodin, Just War theory is "one of the few basic fixtures of medieval philosophy to remain substantially unchallenged in the modern world."[1] The most modern and compellingly articulated formulation of this theory is Michael Walzer's influential book *Just and Unjust Wars* written in 1977,[2] which has become a sine qua non for those interested in the morality of war.

Since the turn of the century, however, a small but growing chorus of philosophers and legal theorists has critically analyzed Just War theory. Some of them, led chiefly by David Rodin and Jeff McMahan, challenge the Walzerian framework by criticizing the paradigm dominating how we have morally evaluated wars since the late Renaissance. In doing so, they have subjected the pair of fundamental precepts underwriting the legalistic paradigm to withering criticism. From these ashes a 'revisionist' account of the morality of war has sprung, emphasizing an individualistic, self-defensive paradigm for evaluating the morality of war. On this view, wars are best characterized as relations between individuals

---

1. David Rodin, *War and Self-Defense* (Oxford: Clarendon Press, 2002), 189.

2. Michael Walzer, *Just and Unjust Wars* (New York: Basic Books, 2000).

rather than states. Certainly the number of individuals is great, the organizational relations among them are intricate and often obfuscatory, and the kinds of threats these individuals together impose and face are complex and uncertain; though these conditions make it more difficult to ascertain the relevant empirical facts, they do not undercut the fundamental principles grounding individual morality. Accordingly, the morality of war is, for these revisionists, of a piece with the morality of everyday life. In keeping with this view, these revisionists maintain that the rules governing conduct in war depend on the moral status of the war being fought. Consequently, individual soldiers who participate in an unjust war cannot absolve themselves of responsibility for what they do by adverting to their role as 'instruments' of the state. This revisionist account has, accordingly, come to be known as "reductive individualism."

The essays herein include contributions from 'first-wave' revisionists (viz., David Rodin and Jeff McMahan) as well as from 'second wave' members. Some of the second wave (viz., Richard Arneson, Victor Tadros, and Kai Draper) see reductive individualism as fundamentally correct but much in need of refinement; others (viz., Larry May, François Tanguay-Renaud, Mattias Iser, and Seth Lazar) argue that the pendulum has swung too far in the direction of reductive individualism; they raise challenges for the self-defensive paradigm dominating revisionist thought. Still others (viz., Andrew Altman, Adil Haque, and Nancy Sherman) raise issues in the morality of war that pertain to both traditional and revisionist accounts. In what follows, we further detail and connect these novel contributions to the recent resurgence of thought on the morality of war.

Part I—Proportionality in War

Much of the revisionist literature on the morality of war since the turn of the century focuses on how to weigh the lives of enemy combatants fighting an unjust war, which is a necessary task for determining whether a war satisfies the constraint of proportionality. This constraint prohibits wars (and acts in wars) that inflict harms so great that they cannot be justified by the evils that inflicting those harms averts. But how should reductive individualists weigh the life of soldiers in the proportionality calculus? Whether a soldier (or a civilian, for that matter) is morally liable to be killed depends on what she does and whether she is responsible for it, rather than simply on what group she is a member of. But this commitment to individualism raises problems. A single individual wrongly threatening the life of an innocent is morally liable to be killed if necessary to save that innocent. If this is correct, it seems we are forced to say that when many individuals together lethally threaten one innocent, each and every such wrongful threatener is morally liable to be killed (if necessary to save the innocent's life). Some find this conclusion unproblematic; but it becomes harder to accept when we stipulate that each of the wrongful threateners is only 'minimally responsible' for her own wrongful contribution. At some point, the number of minimally responsible wrongful threateners reaches a point at which it is morally preferable to allow their innocent target to be killed than it is to kill all the wrongful threateners. Yet reductive individualism, as articulated by Jeff McMahan, seems incapable of grounding this desideratum. Rodin, however, in his contribution to this volume, adds an important resource to the reductive individualist's conceptual arsenal that, he argues, enables its proponents to aggregate the lives of minimally responsible threateners in ways that avoids the conclusion that we can kill countless many to prevent them from killing a single innocent. This resource, specifically, is a novel moral concept, which he calls the 'lesser evil obligation.' It functions as the mirror image of the well-known 'lesser evil justification.' Whereas the lesser evil justification allows us to permissibly transgress an individual's rights in order to avoid a substantially greater evil (impersonally construed), the lesser evil obligation enjoins us to refrain from exercising a right that we have, on the grounds that doing otherwise will yield a substantially greater evil (impersonally construed). So though an innocent individual has the right to defend herself (or another innocent) from countless threateners who are together wrongly attempting to kill her, the lesser evil obligation requires that she refrain from exercising that right, since doing otherwise would have morally catastrophic consequences. So like the lesser evil justification, the lesser evil obligation adverts to consequences as a basis for the claim that the rights an individual has are not absolutely dispositive of what we may or should do. This novel moral category explicates, Rodin argues, our intuition that we cannot kill countlessly many minimally responsible threateners in a way preferable to the method that McMahan provides in this volume—and it does so in a way that he believes will substantially enhance our increasingly sophisticated understanding of the relationship between deontic obligations to respect rights and the consequentialist obligations to avoid bad consequences.

But some, such as Larry May, argue that such a view does not go far enough in protecting the rights of enemy combatants. He notes that international humanitarian law, which establishes the rights of combatants in wartime, is far more permissive than international human rights law, which establishes the rights of persons qua persons. The former permits any combatants to target and kill almost any enemy combatant (medics and religious personnel excluded, as well as those who are disabled or in enemy hands) even if such combatants are not presently posing a threat. This stands in contrast with international human rights law, which holds the right to life inviolable. To reconcile the two norms, some have argued that humanitarian law should give way to the more progressive strictures of human rights law. May is one such proponent. In his essay 'Human Rights, Proportionality and the Lives of Soldiers,' he points out that, historically, the lives of enemy combatants received no weight in the constraints of necessity and proportionality. This is morally tantamount, he argues, to treating them as cannon fodder. May argues in favor of adopting a human rights model of the morality of war, which requires those initiating and implementing a war to take account not only of civilian causalities, but of the casualties of enemy combatants as well, since they qua persons (in accordance with human rights law) have the right to life. May presents a picture of what the proportionality and necessity constraints would look like if, in his words, "the human rights perspective were taken more seriously than it has in the past." Some, however, have argued that combatants fighting in furtherance of an unjust cause forfeit their right against being killed. Accordingly, the weight their deaths receive in the 'costs' column of the proportionality constraint *should* be substantially diminished (if not eliminated). This would vindicate a version of international humanitarian law. May responds to this sort of challenge by arguing that though fundamental rights can be lost in certain limited contexts between very restricted sets of people—as when one individual culpably and wrongly attacks another—combatants, as a general class of people, cannot be plausibly regarded as having forfeited their right to life by virtue of their state's decision to wage an unjust war. He thus finds the self-defensive paradigm of reductive individualism largely inapplicable to war. May also responds to legal theorists who have argued that the domain of humanitarian law is *lex specialis*—that it effectively trumps human rights law. He explores various ways that human rights law and humanitarian law might occupy overlapping legal terrain. May ends by considering the relationship between the necessity constraint and the proportionality constraint from the perspective of human rights law. He argues that taking the necessity constraint seriously—which is what a human rights perspective requires us to do—proscribes conduct traditionally thought to be legally (if not morally) unproblematic. For example, he argues that that we must exhaust (or show to be ineffective) all non-lethal alternatives to achieving a military goal, including alternatives that make use of non-lethal or less-lethal means. He acknowledges that giving prominence to human rights in the way he suggests moves us toward contingent pacifism—a conclusion May urges us to take seriously.

Part II—Responsibility in War

According to reductive individualism about the morality of war, how we weigh the lives of those killed in war depends largely on what those individuals do and the degree to which they are responsible for what they do. It is no surprise, then, that much of the literature on reductive individualism—both for and against—has focused on the role that personal responsibility plays in one's liability to be killed. But reductive individualism has been criticized on the grounds that its precepts about the relevance of responsibility to liability do violence to our firmest convictions about who is targetable in war. In particular, some have argued that reductive individualists are forced to abandon the view, established in law and common-sense morality, that it is morally permissible for combatants to aim fire at enemy combatants, and morally impermissible for combatants to aim fire at noncombatants. This is because reductive individualists maintain that almost all enemy combatants fighting in furtherance of an unjust cause have forfeited their right not to be killed. The problem, though, is that (as Larry May argues in this volume) it is not clear that combatants fighting for an unjust cause have indeed forfeited their right not to be killed. After all, among combatants ignorance and coercion are commonplace; these mitigate their responsibility for killing in an unjust war (though perhaps duress justifies rather than excuses—see Victor Tadros's contribution to this volume). To make matters worse, typical combatants contribute only minimally to the war effort; this is problematic since (it might be thought) a causal contribution to a wrongdoing must be substantial in order for it to ground lethal liability. So it seems virtually all wars—including those fought for a just cause—will violate the constraint of proportionality, since many or most of the combatants intentionally targeted will be non-liable. This risks a version of contingent pacifism. In response to this, we might reduce the threshold of liability so that merely foreseeably contributing minimally to an unjust cause suffices to forfeit the right against being killed; that way the vast majority of combatants who fight in an unjust war will indeed be liable. But this criterion seems to cast the net too widely: it equally allows many noncombatants to be targeted since each of us contributes if only minimally and nonculpably to the wars fought by our government. So it seems reductive individualists are caught in dilemma: they must either accept a version of contingent pacifism, or admit that many civilians are morally liable to be killed. Seth Lazar developed this line of argument and called it the "Responsibility Dilemma."[3] Richard Arneson, in his contribution to this volume, defends the reductive individualist by arguing in favor of the more permissive horn of the dilemma. He maintains that morality does not categorically and unconditionally forbid the killing of noncombatants in war. The distinction between combatants and noncombatants is merely pragmatic, in that enshrining it in policy and international law tends to diminish unjustified bloodshed. We should not infer from this fact that there is any deep moral importance to the distinction. At the level of fundamental moral principle, "no version of the

3. Seth Lazar, "The Responsibility Dilemma for *Killing in War*: A Review Essay," *Philosophy and Public Affairs* 38 (2010): 180–213.

distinction between combatant and noncombatant plays a substantial role in determining who is a permissible object of violent attack." The Responsibility Dilemma, he argues, assumes otherwise; once we recognize that the distinction between combatants and noncombatants is morally operative only at the level of policy and law and not at the level of fundamental morality, the Responsibility Dilemma disappears.

Whereas Arneson seeks to defend reductive individualism, François Tanguay-Renaud challenges it. He contends that if, as some have forcefully argued in the last decade, a state can qualify as a group agent, we have to consider whether such a state can be liable to defensive violence qua group agent. In the same way that an individual can be liable to defensive violence should that individual engage in certain kinds of wrongful conduct, a state qua group agent might be so liable as well. Tanguay-Renaud provides reasons for thinking that states can indeed bear corporate liability: in the same way that a state egregiously violating the fundamental rights of its own citizens might have no justified "sovereignty-based" complaint against various types of external interferences aimed at thwarting those violations, it might also have no justified sovereignty-based complaint against certain kinds of external interferences aimed at countering the state's unjust threats to foreign populations. Tanguay-Renaud argues that the corporate liability of a state can affect the calculus determining the permissibility of the resort to war. He concedes, however, that cases in which corporate liability is morally determinative are likely to be rare, partly because we cannot robustly infer individual liability from corporate liability—and any violent actions aimed at a state are likely to adversely affect many individuals. Nonetheless, Tanguay-Renaud's investigation reveals a constellation of related issues pertaining to the connection between individual and corporate liability in the context of warfare (such as whether individual participation in corporate wrongdoing aggravates their individual liability) that any account of the morality of war—including those wedded to reductive individualism—must address.

Victor Tadros, like Arneson, is largely supportive of reductive individualism. His contribution to this volume focuses on exploring how we should morally evaluate the conduct of soldiers who act under duress, given that reductive individualism is true. He notes that for many conscripts, the very act of participating in a war is done against threats of fines, incarceration, or worse. Legal and moral scholars have typically assumed that duress does not justify an otherwise wrongful act—rather, it merely excuses it. That is to say, the act committed is still wrongful, but we should not blame its perpetrator for the wrong of committing it; she is thereby partially or fully excused. Whereas McMahan and Arneson in this volume discuss the liability of partially excused combatants, Tadros argues that at least sometimes duress justifies the apparently wrongful act; in such cases the perpetrator is blameless, not because there are mitigating circumstances diminishing her responsibility for what she does, but because what she does is not wrongful in the first place. This occurs, Tadros argues, in circumstances where the coercer threatens to inflict a catastrophic wrongful harm (such as death) on the coercee should the latter refuse to accede to the former's demand to inflict a much smaller wrongful harm (such as a severed finger) on an otherwise uninvolved innocent. Provided that there is nothing the coercee can do to prevent the coercer from fulfilling her threat, the right thing to do, all things considered, is to accede to the demand—not because the coercee has a permission to give special weight her own well-being, but because from an impersonal standpoint a broken finger is preferable to a lost life. Thus acceding to the coercer's demand is not simply excused, but justified. But to show that participating in an unjust war under duress can be justified, it is necessary to show that *killing* under duress can be justified. Tadros argues even if duress does not justify participating in a war that lacks a just cause, it may sometimes provide a justification for participating in wars that violate the proportionality constraint. Tadros also considers a variety of other cases in which killing under duress arguably justifies rather than excuses. They have in common that in each case acceding to the demands is the lesser evil relative to a refusal. But in some of these cases, it is not simply the lesser evil that justifies acceding. Suppose you are told to kill on pain not only of *your* death but also of those whom you are told to kill. In such a case, they have a reason to *authorize* you to kill them, since sparing them is not only worse impersonally considered but is also no better *for them*. It might be said, though, that in all these cases, that you are not merely engaged in killing when you accede to a threat; you are, moreover, acting as the coercer's agent, thereby fulfilling his malign intentions, which makes it more difficult to justify that killing. This worry is especially salient given the hierarchical command structure of war. Tadros argues, though, that at least sometimes it is permissible for you, acting as someone's agent, to carry out an instruction that it was wrong for your director to issue. He ends by considering one more challenge: that acceding to threats involves manipulative killing, which is, again, harder to justify that nonmanipulative killing. Tadros concedes that killing in duress is manipulative, but argues that it does not have other problematic features present in standard cases of manipulative harming. The upshot is that we should not assume that participating and thereby killing in an unjust war under duress is always wrongful.

Part III—The Law of War

Revisionists have largely abandoned the legalistic paradigm for the moral evaluation of war (in which morality plays second fiddle to the law). But this has only deepened the exchange between the literature on the morality of war and on the law of war, as evidenced by Altman's, Haque's, and Draper's contribution to this volume.

In "Targeting al Qaeda: Law and Morality in the US 'War on Terror,'" Andrew Altman challenges both the legality and the morality of the US policy of targeted killings, whether through drone strikes or manned military operations, as part of the implementation of the Authorization to Use Military Force against al Qaeda and its affiliates in the wake of the attacks of September 11, 2001. Altman explains that although the law of war has evolved over time, first to take account of armed conflict not preceded by declarations of war and second to implement rules governing anti-colonial guerrilla warfare, it has not yet developed a clear, concrete doctrine governing armed conflict between a state and a non-state party (such as al Qaeda, or, in more recent days, the Islamic State). Generally speaking, it would be presumptively unjust to prosecute and punish those who acquire a license to kill under the law of war. But, Altman argues, the necessary conditions for the acquisition of such a license have not been met in the war on terror. The main (legal and moral) argument used by the United States to justify targeted killings relies on the principle of collective self-defense, which, as usually understood, licenses the use of violence as a necessary means to avert an imminent threat to the life of innocents. President George W. Bush attempted to modify the principle of self-defense to permit the use of lethal preemptive measures to prevent a threat from becoming imminent. But, Altman claims, there is no international consensus on making the Bush Doctrine a part of international law. In his first term, President Barack Obama argued that imminence should be just one of several factors to be weighed in the balance in determining the legality and morality of self-defensive aggression. Altman argues that this does not represent the articulation of an adequately determinate (legal or moral) norm. In his second term, President Obama argued that three conditions must be met in order to justify lethal self-defensive action to avert a continuing threat: imminence, near certainty of no noncombatant casualties, and the absence of other governments to address the threat. Altman argues that such a principle, even if defensible, does not justify the significant number of drone strikes and other attacks on foreign soil designed to kill enemy militants and degrade their ability to pose a threat to United States citizens. This is because the claim that each and every strike, among the hundreds that have been launched, was designed to avert an imminent threat of harm to innocents is dubious. Moreover, in the aggregate, these strikes have imposed a significant risk of serious harm to innocents abroad, notwithstanding the Obama administration's claim to the contrary. Altman recognizes that the principle of self-defense might be replaced by a principle of necessity (such as one articulated by Seth Lazar[4]), according to which lethal attacks to avert a threat are

---

4. Seth Lazar, "Necessity and Non-Combatant Immunity," *Review of International Studies* 40 (2014): 53–76.

justified only if, given available evidence, any less harmful response to the threat would pose an excessively high risk of unjust harm. But even such a principle, argues Altman, would not justify the targeted killings launched by the United States, given that the risk of harm to non-US citizens posed by drone strikes and the like has not been adequately weighed. Altman concludes by calling for the development of a principle that fairly and adequately distributes risks to innocents when the use of force is considered as a means to avert serious danger posed by an aggregation of threats from non-state actors.

From the moral and legal status of drone strikes and military intervention against non-state actors on foreign territory, we move to another aspect of *jus in bello*, namely the moral and legal status of using imprecise weapons (such as biological agents and cluster munitions) in warfare. In "Killing with Discrimination," Adil Ahmad Haque argues that the use of weapons that are more likely to kill civilians than they are to achieve military objectives is inherently, and not merely instrumentally, morally impermissible, and that consequently there should be an absolute *legal* prohibition on their employment. Haque notes that there is a moral norm grounding a legal prohibition on inflicting intentional, unnecessary, or disproportionate harm on civilians. Granted, he argues, most uses of imprecise weapons violate (one or more aspects of) this norm. More generally, it might be possible to justify banning particular sorts of weapons indirectly, on the grounds that such a ban would be the most effective means of implementing the first norm. But Haque goes further, claiming that the use of imprecise weapons would be impermissible even when it does not involve the infliction of intentional, unnecessary, or disproportionate harm. Using a series of cases, Haque argues that our intuitive judgments support the thesis that "the probability of killing civilians makes an independent contribution to the moral status" of attacks. Haque then grounds this thesis on the more general principle that actions are justified only when they are supported by undefeated reasons and (epistemically) excused only when they are supported by undefeated reasons to believe that they are justified. Using this principle, he argues that the use of imprecise weapons can't be justified and is inexcusable when it will more likely than not strike civilians. Haque concludes by pointing out that the norm against using imprecise weapons clashes with rule-consequentialism, and particularly with expectabilism—the theory, roughly stated, that we ought to act in such a way as to produce the outcome with the highest expected value.

Another important aspect of *jus in bello* is the distinction between harming innocents intentionally and harming them only as a foreseen consequence of achieving a military objective. In the law of war, direct attacks on civilians are prohibited, while the destruction of military targets that foreseeably harms civilians can be justified if it satisfies requirements of necessity and proportionality. In

"Double Effect and the Laws of War," Kai Draper considers whether this legal distinction is *morally* grounded, and concludes that it is not. Instead, Draper argues, the justification for the legal distinction between direct and indirect attacks on civilians is purely pragmatic: the guiding thought is that the implementation of a rule prohibiting direct attacks while permitting some indirect attacks is more likely to reduce the costs of war (including human suffering) than would the implementation of some alternative rule.[5] Using a variety of counterexamples tied to hypothetical cases, Draper criticizes three deontological principles that have been thought to ground the direct/indirect distinction: the Principle of Double Effect (PDE), and two close cousins of that principle, namely, the Means Principle (MP) and the Restricted Claims Principle (RCP). According to PDE, it is more difficult to justify harm that is intended than it is to justify harm that is merely foreseen; according to MP, it is more difficult to justify harm that is the consequence of using a person to achieve one's ends than it is to justify harm that is not the consequence of such use; and according to RCP, it is more difficult to justify infringing a person's non-restricting claim than it is to justify infringing a person's restricting claim, where a claim against S is restricting if and only if, were S to respect that claim, S would be unable to achieve some good that S could achieve if the claimant were not present. Draper's argumentative strategy can be put in the form of a dilemma. Either these principles are strongly discriminating (in the sense that actions favored by the principle are much easier to justify than actions disfavored by the principle) or they are only weakly discriminating: if the former, then although they might serve as adequate grounds for the direct/indirect distinction, the principles are indefensible; if the latter, then although the principles might be defensible, they cannot serve as adequate grounds for the direct/indirect distinction.

Part IV—War's Beginning and Ending

Reductive individualism about war has implications for the conditions under which we can permissibly resort to war, as well as the conditions under which we are obligated to end wars. In addition, the focus on individuals—in combination with the US-led invasions of Afghanistan and Iraq—has also cast into glaring relief the trauma that soldiers suffer on their return from war. These are the issues on which the last three contributors focus.

---

5. Instead of conceptualizing the disagreement here as one between those who advocate a *moral* justification and those who advocate a *pragmatic* justification for a rule of war, one might conceptualize it as a disagreement, within the moral realm, between a *deontological* and a *rule-consequentialist* approach to justifying the rule.

Relatively few, perhaps no, societies in the world today came into existence as the product of a social compact. Rather, they exist as the outcome of conquest or usurpation, and are maintained in existence by institutional mechanisms that are not directly responsive to the will of the governed. When people chafe under unjust rule, it becomes important to determine whether, and if so, when, it is ever permissible for them to use (possibly lethal) violence in defense of their rights. In "Beyond the Paradigm of Self-Defense? On Revolutionary Violence," Mattias Iser explores whether the self-defense paradigm for justifying harm in war can provide insight into the necessary and sufficient conditions for the moral permissibility of revolutionary violence, and finds the model wanting. So, like May and Tanguay-Renaud (in this volume), Iser poses a challenge to the reductive individualist. Some have argued that the principles of self-defense against a culpable attacker do not sanction the use of lethal force as a means of protecting peripheral rights, including property rights and political rights. Extrapolation then yields the result that revolutionary violence designed to protect or establish political rights is justified only as a necessary and proportionate means of preventing such egregious wrongs as mass murder or enslavement. Iser argues that the self-defense paradigm ignores both the instrumental and expressive aspects of the public acknowledgment of rights: instrumentally, such acknowledgment secures important human goods for the right-holders; expressively, the same acknowledgment codifies the general understanding of what those with moral status can reasonably demand of others. In a severely unjust political system, Iser claims, both the instrumental and the expressive dimensions of public rights-acknowledgment are lacking. By contrast, an attack that violates a person's rights within a largely just political order does not have such instrumental or expressive features: the victim (should she survive an attack) retains her rights and has not been deprived of moral status. Ultimately, Iser argues, revolutionary violence is "permissible as a last resort in one's struggle against *institutions* which are guilty of an unnecessary and *grave* denial of persons' equal status." At the same time, Iser is mindful of the inherent dangers of violence, no matter the end that it is used to promote. For violence fed by indignation can lead to the demonization of opponents; indignation itself conduces to a sense of moral and epistemological superiority, which can lead to arbitrary and hence unjust decisions; and the use of violence itself has a hedonistic dimension that can perpetuate a "culture of violence." And all of these natural outgrowths of indignation-fed violence have a tendency to thwart post-revolutionary efforts at peace and reconciliation.

The end of all war is some sort of stable peace. In "War's Endings and the Structure of Just War Theory," Seth Lazar claims that too much of Just War theory has been focused on articulating principles governing resort to war (*jus ad bellum*) and the prosecution of war (*jus in bello*). Attuned to this concern, some theorists have sought to develop principles governing the transition from war to peace (*jus ex bello*) and war's aftermath (*jus post bellum*). However, Lazar argues, these Latinate categories should serve as no more than heuristic devices for policy-making: from the theoretical point of view, their use in carving up the moral territory relevant to the assessment of war and its constituent activities conduces to conceptual confusion rather than to analytical clarity. As a replacement for categorizing moral principles governing war in terms of the stages from peace to war and from war to peace, Lazar offers us two principles of categorization: (1) a distinction between ethical principles that apply to different levels of analysis, those for decisions governing the war as a whole (*Command Ethics*) and those for decisions governing the actions and operations that constitute war (*Combatant Ethics*); and (2) a distinction between positive reasons for action and negative constraints on action. Importantly, Lazar argues that neither Command Ethics nor the ethics of positive reasons for action reduces to the principles of *jus ad bellum*, and that neither Combatant Ethics nor the ethics of negative constraints on action reduces to the principles of *jus in bello*. And when we realize that the use of Latinate categories has been hampering the conceptual elucidation of the moral laws of war, we also come to realize that traditional Just War theory has given short shrift to the principles governing negotiation at every stage of war. These principles (namely, that all negotiation should be entered into in good faith, that negotiators should not be harmed, that negotiation should not issue in the establishment of new rights, and that negotiated settlements should be complied with), argues Lazar, are founded on trust, vulnerability, and the natural law principle that right cannot arise out of injustice. Lazar's hope, in the end, is that Just War theory will turn away from its roots in heuristic categories and toward new, heuristically unconstrained moral principles at various levels of analysis governing all war-related decisions.

When wars end and peace breaks out, normal life becomes possible, at least for those who have not been traumatized or who have not experienced the kind of suffering that unspeakable violence causes. But when soldiers come home, often, at least in volunteer armies, after multiple tours of duty, they face the mental and physical aftereffects of extreme stress. Although they may have been the agents of harm, they too have suffered, and need to heal. In "Moral Recovery After War: The Role of Hope," Nancy Sherman explores the role of hope in moral and psychological repair after war has ended. Following Adrienne Martin, Sherman distinguishes between two kinds of hope: normative and non-normative. Non-normative hope is hope for a good outcome, while normative hope is a kind of "aspiring attitude with regard to worthwhile ends we set for ourselves or others." As Sherman explains, non-normative hope, as in the case of a wounded veteran who has been told by medical personnel that it is unlikely that he will ever walk again, can be a galvanizing form of cognitive resolve or agential investment. Normative hope in others, the hope of a veteran in those who support her, and the hope of her support group in her, can play an important role in successful re-integration. And finally, normative hope in oneself, grounded in facts about one's own abilities and character traits, can help heal the wounds of survivor guilt and feelings of failure and inadequacy that stem from costly battlefield errors. In hope lies the possibility of happiness.

THE ETHICS OF WAR

PROPORTIONALITY IN WAR

1

LIABILITY, PROPORTIONALITY, AND THE NUMBER OF AGGRESSORS

Jeff McMahan

I. Liability Justifications and Numbers

Proportionality can be a demanding constraint on the use of force. It can prohibit an innocent person from engaging in necessary defensive action. Suppose that the only means by which a person can prevent herself from being killed by a culpable attacker would unavoidably kill five innocent bystanders as a side effect. This would be disproportionate, so the victim must submit to being wrongly killed. Defensive action may also be disproportionate because of its effect on the threatener. If the only way one can prevent oneself from being wrongly and painfully pinched is to kill the pincher, one must submit to being pinched.

The form of proportionality that weighs an act's good effects against the harms it causes to victims who are not liable to those harms is *wide* proportionality. Everyone agrees that wide proportionality is relevant to the morality of war, so that an act of war can be impermissible because the harm it would inflict on civilian bystanders would be excessive in relation to the act's good effects. Few people, however, accept that a war or act of war could be disproportionate just because of the harm it would cause to unjust aggressors. Yet, given that outside the context of war there can be disproportionality in harms caused to threateners, such as the culpable pincher, who are potentially liable to *some* degree of harm, there is no reason why the same cannot be true in war. Proportionality in harms to those who are liable to some degree of harm is *narrow* proportionality. (As I will indicate in section V, it can be permissible to inflict harm that is disproportionate in the narrow sense—that is, in excess of the harm to which the victim is liable—if that harm is nonetheless proportionate in the wide sense.)

In practice, disproportionality in war is usually a matter of the *number* of people harmed or killed. If an act of war would be disproportionate in the wide sense, that is generally because it would kill or injure too many civilian bystanders. And one might similarly suppose that a war or act of war could be disproportionate in the narrow sense because it would kill too many combatants (or, rather, too many combatants on the unjust side, on the assumption that combatants on the just side are seldom liable to attack at all). One might think, for example, that the Falklands War either was narrowly disproportionate or would have been if it had been necessary to kill a much larger number of Argentine combatants to preserve British sovereignty over the islands, as there must be some limit to the number of such people it could have been permissible to kill in pursuit of that arguably not very significant goal.

Although I have been attracted to this understanding of narrow proportionality, I now think it is mistaken. Narrow proportionality is a constraint on individual liability. It sets the limit to the amount of harm it can be permissible to inflict on an individual on grounds of liability. It has no application to numbers of individuals, unless a collection of individuals itself constitutes an individual that can be liable—an idea that I reject but cannot discuss here. Narrow proportionality in war is thus not sensitive to the number of combatants killed.

Yet, as the example of a hypothetical Falklands War in which it would be necessary to kill a vast number of Argentine combatants suggests, there must, at least in many cases, be some limit to the number even of unjust combatants that it can be permissible to kill in pursuit of a just cause. I will argue in the final section that to accommodate this fact we must recognize a further distinct form of proportionality, in addition to the wide and narrow forms.

(Some might object that if there were a proportionality limit to the killing of combatants, an unjust aggressor could then assemble sufficiently many conscripts, perhaps including child soldiers, to make defensive resistance disproportionate, thereby inducing moral paralysis in a scrupulous adversary. I think, however, that this is not an objection but a fact that we must accept, just as we must accept that an aggressor can make defensive action disproportionate in the wide sense by using a sufficient number of innocent shields.)

It will be helpful to examine four simplified examples rather than continuing to discuss the killing of combatants in war. This may prevent us from being distracted by intuitions specifically concerned with war that may reflect common but mistaken views about the ethics of war.

Suppose that a morally innocent and unthreatening person will be unjustifiably killed by a fully culpable aggressor unless the aggressor is killed. It seems permissible for the victim or a third party to kill the culpable aggressor, if this is the only way to prevent him from killing the victim, and if there would be no bad side effects that would outweigh the saving of the victim's life.

The justification for the defensive killing of the culpable aggressor is not that he deserves to die, or that killing him would have better consequences, or that killing him would be the lesser evil, in that the only alternative would involve substantially more harm to others. It is not that he has consented to be killed, or that the victim is permitted to give priority to her own life over his. Nor is it simply that he is the aggressor. It is instead that, by being the responsible, *unjustified* aggressor, he has made himself *morally liable* to be killed. For the victim or a third party, it is unavoidable that either the victim or the aggressor will be killed. The aggressor is responsible for this fact while the victim is not; it is, therefore, a matter of justice that the aggressor should incur the costs of his own voluntary, unjustified action. Provided there is no other compelling reason why the unavoidable harm should go to the victim instead, the victim or a third party is justified in killing the aggressor, who has forfeited his right not to be killed in the circumstances.

Next imagine that a thousand such culpable killers will attempt to kill the same innocent victim, each appearing one after the other, in rapid succession. Suppose the victim knows that if she kills the first one, she will immediately be killed by the second unless she kills him as well, and so on. Suppose further that there would be no interval of life worth living between the killings. Killing one killer would enable her to have only a second or two of terror before the next arrived. Only if she kills all thousand will she have any further life worth living. Finally, suppose that none of the culpable killers is specially related to anyone who would be harmed as a side effect of his being killed, and that none of them would again pose a threat to others.

I suspect that most people would accept that it is permissible for the victim to kill all thousand culpable potential killers (hereafter "culpable killers"). It may seem that an innocent and unthreatening person is never morally required to submit to being wrongly killed just to spare one or more people who would otherwise culpably kill her. In each such case, the culpable killer seems to make himself liable to be killed.

Liability justifications appear to work by "pairwise comparisons" – that is, by considering each choice between harmings on its own and determining on which of the parties the unavoidable harm ought, as a matter of justice, to be imposed. (This is part of the explanation of why narrow proportionality does not take account of numbers.) In each choice, it seems that the culpable killer is liable to be killed whereas the victim is not.

Next imagine a case like the first except that the aggressor is not culpable. Although he is responsible for the threat he poses, he is only minimally responsible, by which I mean "merely responsible," or responsible though not culpable. He might, for example, have chosen to engage in a permissible type of action, such as driving a car, that involves a very tiny risk of inflicting great harm on one or more innocent people. Through sheer bad luck, he now threatens the life of an innocent bystander.

The potential killer in this third example is a "minimally responsible killer" (hereafter, for brevity, "responsible killer"). Assume that he and the potential victim would suffer a roughly equal loss in being killed. Many people believe that it is morally permissible for the potential victim or a third party to kill the responsible killer if that is necessary to prevent him from killing the victim. This is because the responsible killer is liable to be killed in the circumstances. He has voluntarily chosen to engage in a morally optional activity that involves a reasonably foreseeable risk of causing great harm to others. If through bad luck his choice results in a threat to another's life, the fact that he, but not the victim, bears some responsibility for the fact that one of them must die provides a reason of justice for imposing the harm on him. Assuming that the harm they would suffer in being killed is much the same, and that any side effects would also be roughly equal, there is a liability justification for killing the responsible killer.[1]

The fourth and final example is like the second except that each of the thousand killers is only minimally responsible rather than culpable. Assume that each potential killer would suffer the same loss in dying as the victim and that the killers do not act in coordination but independently. If there is a liability justification for killing a single responsible killer, and if there is a liability justification for killing each of the thousand culpable killers, then by parity of reasoning there should also be a liability justification for killing each of the thousand responsible killers. Yet I find this intuitively implausible, and it would remain implausible even if the number of responsible killers was significantly lower—for example, a hundred. I have chosen the higher figure of a thousand precisely to try to elicit the intuition that killing that many responsible killers would be impermissible.

Even more troublingly, if there is a liability justification in each pairwise comparison that is unaffected by the number of killers, there is then *no* limit to the number of killers it would be permissible to kill in defense of a single victim. Many people may find this acceptable in the case of culpable killers, but it is implausible in the case of responsible killers, as the relevant difference between each responsible killer and the innocent victim is small—so small that some philosophers believe that even a single responsible killer on his own is not liable to be killed.

If one thinks that there is a limit to the number of responsible killers it can be permissible to kill in defense of a single victim, but no limit, or at least a higher limit, to the number of culpable killers it can be permissible to kill, one must explain how this can be so, particularly if the justification for killing potential killers of each type is the same – namely, a liability justification. More generally, if one

---

1. Jeff McMahan, *Killing in War* (Oxford: Clarendon Press, 2009), 166.

accepts that there is a liability justification for killing a single culpable killer and for killing a single responsible killer, and if both justifications work via pairwise comparisons, one must explain how there could be a limit to the number of responsible killers it can be permissible to kill. For if liability justifications work via individual pairwise comparisons, it seems that the justification for killing one aggressor should in general be independent of the justification for killing another, so that the number of aggressors ought not to matter to whether there is a liability justification for killing each. It may seem that whether one potential killer is liable to be killed depends only on facts about his own action and not on what other people might do independently. Furthermore, if a person's being liable to be killed is a defeasible justification for killing him, and if each responsible killer is liable to be killed, it should be permissible to kill all thousand, in the absence of countervailing considerations.

One might, of course, simply accept that there is no limit to the number of responsible killers that it can be permissible to kill in defense of a single innocent victim. One might argue that rights and liabilities are moral facts about relations between individuals, so that if one individual threatens to violate another's rights, he becomes morally liable to necessary and proportionate defensive force irrespective of how many others may threaten the same rights of the same victim.[2] If, moreover, the right that is threatened is the right not to be killed, killing the threatener should be proportionate.

Several prominent philosophers seem to accept this view. Frances Kamm writes that

> a response to multiple wrongdoers can satisfy narrow proportionality so long as the response of each is proportional to his wrongdoing. This is very clear in a domestic case, for if each of many people is trying to paralyze you…, it could be a proportionate response to kill all the wrongdoers to prevent the paralysis of one person. On the basis of this sort of case, one might describe the determination of a proportional response to wrongdoing as involving "pairwise comparison"…: One compares the wrong to be avoided with what would have to be done to each wrongdoer one at a time, and if there is no violation of proportionality in any individual comparison then there is no violation tout court.[3]

---

2. David Rodin, *War and Self-Defense* (Oxford: Clarendon Press, 2002).

3. F.M. Kamm, *Ethics for Enemies: Terror, Torture, and War* (Oxford: Oxford University Press, 2011), 133–34.

By stipulating that the many people are *trying* to cause the paralysis, Kamm presumably intends to suggest that they are all culpable. But her point about pairwise comparisons applies equally to merely responsible killers, as does her assumption that proportionality is not a relation between harms caused and harm prevented but between harms caused and the *wrong* "to be avoided."[4] So the implication still seems to be that if killing each responsible killer is proportionate, so that each is liable to be killed independently of what the others may do, there is no limit to the number it can be proportionate and permissible to kill in defense of the single victim.

II. Effectiveness as a Condition of Liability to Harm

If we assume, as I think we should, that proportionality weighs the harm an act will cause against the act's good effects, particularly the harms it will prevent, rather than against the strength of the rights the act might protect, then there is a simple way to avoid the conclusion that there is no limit to the number of responsible killers it can be permissible to kill. I have stipulated that the tiny interval of life the victim would secure by killing any one responsible killer before either killing or being killed by the next would not be worth living. Her killing any one responsible killer would thus be defensively ineffective. On its own it would do no good. As I understand liability, it is unlike desert because it is essentially *instrumental*, in that a person cannot be liable to be harmed if harming him will be neither a means nor a side effect of achieving some good effect. Effectiveness is thus a necessary condition of liability and if killing a responsible killer would be wholly ineffective, he is not liable to be killed.

There are ways in which killing a responsible killer might be effective other than as physical defense. Killing him might be an effective assertion of the victim's moral status, or it might preserve deterrence. Or we could suppose that each killing would afford the victim some short interval of life worth living. But even if one or all of these conditions obtained, the killing would still be narrowly disproportionate. This is in part because the killer's minimal responsibility diminishes the offense against the victim's moral status implied by his action and in part because efforts to preserve deterrence are less effective the less responsible potential threateners are. But if killing the responsible killer would be narrowly disproportionate, that too means that the killer is not liable to be killed; for, as I understand liability, it is a necessary truth that one cannot be liable to a harm that is

---

4. For a challenge to this latter claim, see Jeff McMahan, "The Limits of Self-Defense," in *The Ethics of Self-Defense*, ed. Christian Coons and Michael Weber (New York: Oxford University Press, 2016), 208–10.

disproportionate in the narrow sense—that is, a harm that exceeds that to which one is liable. Narrow proportionality, like effectiveness and necessity, is thus internal to liability.[5] (There are, of course, conceptions of liability according to which effectiveness, necessity, and narrow proportionality are not internal but are constraints on the permissibility of acting on a liability justification. In section III.3, I will indicate one implication of this view.) Effectiveness, necessity, and narrow proportionality are what may be called the "circumstantial conditions" of liability, in contrast with the "agential conditions," which for present purposes we may take to be causal and moral responsibility for a threat of wrongful harm.

It may seem that it cannot be right that none of the responsible killers is liable to be killed. For the same logic applies to killing the thousand culpable killers. If killing a single responsible killer would be ineffective, so would killing a single culpable killer. And I suspect that most people believe that a single culpable killer would not be wronged by being killed, even if the victim would then be immediately killed by a different culpable killer. I believe, by contrast, that even a culpable killer has a right not to be killed gratuitously, without producing any good effect, as would be the case if he alone were killed in a case involving overdetermination, such as the second case I introduced in section I. But I will not defend that claim here.[6]

I have thus far been assuming that each responsible killer, other than the last, is not liable to be killed because killing him would be defensively ineffective, given that the victim's loss of further good life is overdetermined. This, however, leaves open the possibility that killing any individual responsible killer *would* be effective on condition that the other 999 killers are killed as well. But this is a problematic condition for the liability of each; for, assuming compliance with morality, all the others *will* be killed only if it is *permissible* to kill them. Yet whether it is permissible to kill them seems to depend on whether each is liable to be killed. This is because a liability justification is the only possible form of justification for killing a thousand people as a means of saving only one. There is certainly no lesser-evil justification; neither do the responsible killers consent to be killed; nor does the victim have an agent-relative permission to give her life priority over those of a thousand people who are only minimally responsible for the threats they pose; and so on. If this is right, it can be permissible to kill all thousand only if each is morally liable to be killed; yet whether each is liable depends on whether it is permissible to kill them all. This seems viciously circular. I will return to this problem in section VI.

---

5. Ibid.

6. I have defended it in ibid., 206–10.

III. Beneficence Overrides Liability?

David Rodin has offered an appealing explanation of how there can be a limit to the number of responsible killers it can be permissible to kill. He suggests that, even though each killer is morally liable to be killed, the many individual liability justifications are overridden by a reason of beneficence (or, perhaps more precisely, non-maleficence) not to cause so much harm as would be involved in killing all thousand responsible killers. He begins by endorsing the view that liability justifications work via pairwise comparisons, which seem unaffected by how many such justifications there may be.

> Liability is a localized comparison between persons in a situation of conflict; it concerns their interacting rights and duties and so values outside that relationship are irrelevant.... Within a liability justification, harms inflicted on multiple [aggressors] are not aggregated, but considered separately. This is why inflicting defensive harm on *any* number of persons who are individually liable to that harm can be proportionate on a liability account.[7]

Rodin does not discuss the problem of overdetermination but goes on to contrast liability justifications with a different form of justification—a "lesser-evil justification," which

> aggregates the defensive harms inflicted on all affected persons. It discounts the evil attributed to harm inflicted on the liable, but unless the harm is discounted to zero, it is still possible that defensive harm inflicted on multiple liable persons will not be the lesser evil.[8]

I interpret this to mean that, even though all of the responsible killers are liable to be killed, and even if their interests are accordingly discounted for their responsibility, killing all of them would be so much the greater evil that it would not be permissible. There is thus a lesser evil justification for allowing the victim to be killed rather than causing the vast harm involved in killing all thousand responsible killers. While normally lesser evil justifications override the constraint against actively harming or killing an innocent person, here there is a lesser evil justification for *allowing* a nonliable person to be killed when the alternative is *killing* a

---

7. David Rodin, "Justifying Harm," *Ethics* 122 (2011): 74–110, at 99.
8. Ibid.

large number of people who are *liable* to be killed. The liability justifications are, as I have put it, overridden by a "greater-evil constraint."[9]

In an earlier draft of this paper, I presented three objections to Rodin's view. In his contribution to this book, Rodin has replied to these objections. I have therefore left the objections largely as they were in the draft to which Rodin has responded. I have also included some brief comments on his replies. I have, however, subsequently come to believe that his view and the view I will defend in section VI are quite similar. Our main differences concern, first, whether each responsible killer is liable on his own and thus whether there is a liability justification for killing each that must be overridden, and, second, whether the explanation of the impermissibility of killing them all also applies to the killing of all the culpable killers. I will consider the second in the following subsection and return to the first at the end.

III.1 Lesser Evil

One reason for skepticism about Rodin's view is that it seems to apply equally to the killing of the culpable killers. The problem is not that, unless harms to the culpable killers are discounted to zero, there must be some limit to the number of killers it can be permissible to kill. That may well be true. The problem is instead that on Rodin's view the responsibility (or culpability) of the killers has already been taken into account in the liability justifications. What is now supposed to weigh against those justifications is the combined harm that will be suffered by the many killers if all are killed. That is, considerations of well-being, or beneficence, now weigh against considerations of liability. But when the concern is with well-being rather than the bases of liability, the well-being of the culpable killers matters or counts in the same way as that of the responsible killers. While the culpability or responsibility of the killers is relevant to the determination of their liability in the establishment of a liability justification, it is not relevant to how much weight their well-being has in a lesser evil justification or greater evil constraint. Lesser evil justifications do not take account of responsibility or culpability precisely because they apply to harms to which the victims are not liable. It is for this reason that, if the individual liability justifications for killing the responsible killers are overridden by what Rodin now calls a "lesser evil obligation," the same must be true of the liability justifications for killing the culpable killers.

Rodin writes in response to this objection that in a passage he quotes (identified by his note 11), I myself acknowledged that, in his words, "harm inflicted on a person who is liable to that harm is not as bad from an impersonal perspective

---

9. For further discussion, see Jeff McMahan, "Duty, Obedience, Desert, and Proportionality in War: A Response," *Ethics* 122 (2011): 135–67, at 152–53.

as harm inflicted on a non-liable person." He then writes that "it therefore has less negative weight in lesser-evil reasoning."[10] This is not quite what I meant, though I concede that I did not express my meaning well. First, my reference to impersonal badness was unnecessary, as that was a side issue. In general, lesser evil justifications weigh harms against other harms. Thus, what seems to weigh against the killing of the responsible killers is primarily the harms they will suffer in being killed, not the impersonal badness of their absence from the world. There might, moreover, be impersonal considerations that favor killing them—for example, to paraphrase an old German legal maxim, that Right should not yield to Wrong.

Second, my claim in the passage he quotes is that a threatener's interests are discounted relative to those of his victim in the assessment of proportionality *in a liability justification*. What I meant is that it is often permissible to inflict harm on a threatener that is considerably greater than the harm that the threatener would otherwise have inflicted on his victim. It is thus in the determination of how much harm it can be justifiable to inflict on a person *on grounds of liability* that considerations of responsibility and culpability are relevant. A threatener's responsibility or culpability is one determinant of the degree of harm to which he is liable. It has then exhausted its power to justify the infliction of harm on the threatener. If we have determined the amount of harm to which a culpable threatener is liable but then come to believe that his culpability justifies harming him to an even greater degree, we should revise our judgment about the amount of harm to which he is liable.

III.2 The Justificatory Priority of Liability

A second ground of skepticism is that it is odd to suppose that it could be justifiable to inflict harms, or allow harms to be inflicted, on nonliable people as an alternative to inflicting harms on those who are liable to them. With two possible exceptions, a liability justification for the infliction of harm seems to exclude the permissibility of other distributions of the harm. This is because liability is a matter of justice in the distribution of unavoidable harm. Suppose that there are only two options for preventing a catastrophe. One is to kill some large number of people, all of whom are culpably responsible for the impending catastrophe and are thus liable to be killed as a means of preventing it. The other is to kill an innocent bystander as a means or side effect of preventing the action of those who are liable. It seems impermissible to sacrifice the one to spare the others from harms to which they have made themselves liable, even though this would be much the lesser evil.[11]

---

10. David Rodin, "The Lesser Evil Obligation," in this volume, page 38.

11. "The Limits of Self-Defense," Section 1.

The two exceptions to which I referred are these. First, in some cases it can be permissible (though not necessarily required) to harm a nonliable person rather than a liable person if the former freely consents to suffer the harm. Second, a liability justification for harming a person can be overridden when harming him would cause disproportionate harm to innocent bystanders as a side effect.

Rodin has two responses to this objection. The first appeals to the example of a pauper who recklessly damages a millionaire's car. Rodin says that, although the pauper is liable to compensate the millionaire, the latter has a lesser evil obligation to waive his claim because compensation would provide only a marginal benefit to him but would involve a "devastating loss" to the pauper. This, he says, shows that considerations of "distributive justice" can be overridden by a lesser evil obligation. I think, by contrast, that this is simply a case in which it would be narrowly disproportionate to coerce the pauper to pay full compensation, even taking the pauper's recklessness into account. If the harm to the pauper would be disproportionate in relation to the benefit to the millionaire, and if narrow proportionality is internal to liability, then the pauper is not morally liable to provide full compensation (though he may be legally liable to do so).

Rodin's second response is to present an example that challenges my claim that liability is a matter of justice in the distribution of unavoidable harm. In the example, X wrongly provokes Y but Y reacts disproportionately by trying to kill X. X can save his life only by breaking Y's wrist, which would be narrowly proportionate (in the harm it would inflict on Y), but would also prevent Y from performing a life-saving surgery on Z that only Y can perform. Rodin comments that "the incidental harm inflicted on Z is proportionate in the wide sense since a) the unjust harm inflicted on Z is not greater than the unjust harm averted from X, and b) the harm inflicted on Z is intended by X neither as a means nor as an end in itself."[12]

If the harm inflicted on Z were proportionate in the wide sense, that would not be for the reasons Rodin cites. Those reasons would also apply if X were to *kill* Z as a side effect of defending himself against Y, but that, I believe, would be disproportionate in the wide sense. Wide proportionality is arguably sensitive to the difference between killing an innocent bystander and preventing a bystander from being saved.[13]

It is not, however, widely proportionate to prevent Z from being saved as a side effect of saving X. It is arguable, though controversial, that it is widely disproportionate to prevent an innocent person from being saved as a side effect of saving

---

12. Rodin, "The Lesser Evil Obligation," in this volume, page 41.

13. Jeff McMahan, "Proportionate Defense," *Journal of Transnational Law and Policy* 23 (2013–14): 1–36, 34–35.

only one other innocent person, just as it is disproportionate to kill an innocent person as a side effect of saving only one innocent person. Wide proportionality is a constraint on a lesser evil justification for the infliction of harms to which the victims are not liable. When the deaths of two innocent people are equally harmful, neither seems to qualify as the lesser evil, no matter how it is brought about.

But what is decisive here is that X, but not Z, bears some responsibility for the fact that either he or Z must die, for he culpably provoked Y. Rodin in fact concedes that "if justice requires that unavoidable harm be borne by the party most responsible for the fact that the harm must be distributed, then as a matter of justice X rather than Z should bear the unavoidable harm."[14] Yet he thinks that this is incompatible with what my view implies about this case. He writes that if "liability is a matter of justice in the distribution of unavoidable harms, then it would not be the case that Y is liable to have his wrist broken" and "McMahan would appear to be committed to the conclusion that X is liable to be killed."[15]

But my view implies neither of these claims. Assuming that Y is more responsible for the threat he poses to X's life than X is on account of his provocation, my view implies that the breaking of Y's wrist is a narrowly proportionate defense against a wrongful killing and thus that Y is liable to have his wrist broken. Yet, while this is so, X may not act on that liability justification because doing so would be disproportionate in the wide sense because it would prevent Z from being saved. Furthermore, X is not liable to be killed by Y or anyone else. But because X bears some responsibility for the fact that either he or Z must die while Z bears none, he *is* liable to be *allowed to be wrongly killed*, either by himself or by third parties, when the only options are saving him, thereby preventing Z from being saved, and allowing Z to be saved.

III.3 Liability as a Robust Justification

A third ground of skepticism about Rodin's proposal is the most serious. As I noted, liability justifications can be overridden. They are only pro tanto justifications. They justify only the harm inflicted on the liable person. But they do unconditionally justify *that*. The person who is liable to be harmed has forfeited his right not to be harmed and there is a reason of justice to harm him, which is that if he is not harmed, harm will unavoidably befall someone else who bears no responsibility, or less responsibility, for the fact that someone must be harmed. Rodin's claim, however, is that the harms to the many aggressors that have been justified on the ground that those aggressors are liable to them somehow also override those same

14. Rodin, page 41.

15. Ibid., 41.

justifications. That is, the same harms for which there are liability justifications somehow defeat their own justifications. This seems incoherent.

Rodin's response to this is that "a justification is simply a consideration that defeats a moral objection." A liability justification, in particular, defeats the objection that a person has a right not to be harmed. Liability is the loss of such a right.

This seems right if effectiveness, necessity, and narrow proportionality are external constraints on a liability justification rather than circumstantial conditions of liability itself. That Rodin accepts this externalist understanding of what I take to be the circumstantial conditions of liability is suggested by his assumption that each responsible killer and each culpable killer is liable to be killed despite the overdetermination, which means that killing any one of them or any number fewer than all would be ineffective.

According to this understanding of liability, when a person becomes liable to be harmed, he has forfeited his right not to be harmed *in any way* or *to any degree*, even if harming him will have no good effects. Lacking a right, he cannot be wronged by the infliction of a harm that is narrowly disproportionate—even vastly disproportionate—and therefore wrong. For narrow proportionality is on this view an external constraint on the permissibility of acting on a liability justification. Nor can he be wronged by being harmed wholly gratuitously, for effectiveness is also only an external constraint.

For this and other reasons I have stated elsewhere, I think effectiveness, necessity, and narrow proportionality are internal to liability.[16] According to this conception of liability, a liability justification is, as I claimed above, more than merely the elimination of one barrier to permissibility. For acting on such a justification is necessary, when some harm is unavoidable within a set of individuals, for the harm to go to the only individual or individuals who will not be wronged by being harmed. For this reason, an act for which there is a liability justification is generally morally required, unless it is widely disproportionate or excessively costly to the agent. And a moral requirement to do some act involves more than merely the defeat of a moral objection to that act.

IV. The Harm of Making People Liable to Be Harmed

An alternative and highly ingenious explanation of why it is impermissible to kill all thousand responsible killers has been defended by Kerah Gordon-Solmon.[17] Gordon-Solmon accepts that, because of overdetermination, none of the killers is

---

16. "The Limits of Self-Defense."

17. Kerah Gordon-Solmon, "Self-Defense Against Multiple Threats," *Journal of Moral Philosophy* (published online 2015, awaiting publication).

liable to be killed in advance of defensive action. (Whether they are liable is, she says, indeterminate.) She concedes, however, that killing all of them would secure the conditions of their individual liability, as the killing of each would, as I have indicated, be effective, necessary, and narrowly proportionate *if* the other 999 were killed as well.

She then claims that it would be bad for the responsible killers to have "the liability justifications on the basis of which they're killed secured."[18] Yet there is no right not to be made liable to be killed and the responsible killers cannot forfeit a right that they cannot have; hence they cannot be liable to the harm of being made liable to be killed. That harm therefore counts in the assessment of whether killing them all is proportionate in the *wide* sense, as it is a harm to which they are not liable. Her claim is then that the aggregate badness of making a thousand people liable to be killed outweighs the wrongful killing of one innocent victim. Killing all thousand is thus disproportionate in the wide sense and cannot be permissible.

In section VI I will deny that killing all would make each liable to be killed. For the moment I will grant her assumption but note that not all harms to which the victims are not liable count in the determination of whether the act that causes them is proportionate in the wide sense. For example, a harm that the victim freely consents to suffer cannot make the act that causes it impermissible by making it widely disproportionate. In the case of the responsible killers, what seems to exclude the costs they incur in being made liable to be killed from the assessment of wide proportionality is that their being made liable consists solely in the withdrawal of a moral shield from liability to which they have no entitlement. The removal of an impediment to the circumstantial conditions of liability is not a relevant cost when the person shielded already satisfies the agential conditions.

Suppose that only one responsible killer is present and that he is about to kill the innocent victim. Another 999 responsible killers are on the way and will arrive in just a few moments. Their imminent arrival overdetermines the killing of the victim, thereby shielding the one responsible killer from liability to be killed by blocking the satisfaction of the circumstantial conditions. But suppose that a third party could prevent the 999 from arriving in a way that would be harmless to them. That action would secure the circumstantial conditions for the single responsible killer's liability to be killed. This would be bad for him. It would not, of course, make it impermissible to prevent the arrival of the others, for there is only this one harm to weigh against the potential harm to the innocent victim,

---

18. Ibid.

whereas in the original case there are a thousand such harms. Yet the fact that the removal of the one responsible killer's moral shield against liability would be worse for him does not seem to count *at all* against preventing the others from arriving. It is not a cost that weighs against the threatened harm to the innocent victim in the assessment of wide proportionality. Rather, it seems that the third party has a duty to prevent the one responsible killer from being morally shielded from liability and that the fact that the fulfillment of that duty would be worse for the responsible killer is irrelevant.

There seems, indeed, to be no morally significant difference between the harmless removal of the moral shield in this kind of case and the harmless removal of an innocent shield in the more familiar kind of case. Suppose that a single responsible killer is about to kill an innocent victim and that the only way the victim can save herself is to kill the killer. Her only means of doing this, however, would also kill two innocent bystanders as a side effect. (I think it makes no difference whether they have been placed there by the culpable action of others.) The responsible killer is liable to be killed but is shielded morally by the presence of the two bystanders, the killing of whom would be widely disproportionate. If, however, the victim could harmlessly remove the bystanders, thereby making the killing of the responsible killer widely proportionate, the fact that this would be worse for the responsible killer seems not to count at all against the permissibility of removing them. The only difference is that in this case the removal of the innocent shields secures the permissibility of acting on a preexisting liability justification, whereas in the original overdetermination case the removal of the 999 additional responsible killers secures the liability justification for killing the one by establishing the circumstantial conditions of his liability.

That this difference is not significant is suggested by the fact that the overdetermination case would be relevantly like the bystanders case if we were to assume, as many (such as Rodin) do, that effectiveness, necessity, and narrow proportionality are not internal to liability but are instead external constraints on the permissibility of acting on a liability justification. With that assumption, the responsible killer is in both cases liable to be killed and the harmless removal of the moral shields—again in both cases—simply eliminates an external impediment to the permissibility of acting on the liability justification.

One further objection to Gordon-Solmon's argument that I will mention only in passing is that it seems to imply that it is also impermissible to kill the culpable killers. If, as she says, there is no right not to be made liable to be killed, the culpable killers cannot be liable to the harm of being made liable to be killed. A thousand aggregated instances of this harm should thus outweigh the wrongful killing of the innocent victim, so that killing them would be disproportionate in the wide sense. Gordon-Solmon is aware of this problem but says only that the harms to the culpable killers in being made liable "either aren't impersonally bad at all, or aren't bad enough to clear the threshold of additivity" (a reference to a notion I introduced in earlier work). (8) This, however, does not seem correct, as the relevant harms are ones to which they are not liable and it seems arbitrary to suppose that they do not count just because those who would suffer them are culpable rather than minimally responsible. As I argued in the discussion of Rodin, culpability is relevant to narrow proportionality but not to wide proportionality.

V. Combined Justification

Some philosophers claim that even when there is only a single responsible killer, he is not liable to be killed. If that is right, and if it is also right that a single culpable killer *is* liable to be killed, it is then obvious why it is impermissible to kill a thousand responsible killers and also, perhaps, why it is permissible to kill a thousand culpable killers.

There are at least two reasons why one might deny that responsible killers are morally liable to be killed. One is that, while the explanation I gave of the liability of a responsible killer implicitly appeals to a comparative account of liability, many philosophers assume that the best account of liability is noncomparative, or at least that there is a noncomparative limit to the amount of harm to which a person can be liable. According to a comparative account of liability, when it is unavoidable that someone must be harmed and the only possible options each involve only one of the possible victims suffering a harm of a fixed magnitude, the one who is most responsible for the fact that harm is unavoidable is liable to suffer the harm.[19] According to a noncomparative account, by contrast, there is a limit to the degree of defensive harm to which a person can be liable that is set by the agential conditions of liability—that is, by the magnitude of the harm for which he would be responsible and the degree of his responsibility for the threat of that harm.

One might think that a person who is only minimally responsible for a threatened harm cannot be liable to a defensive harm that is as great as the harm he would otherwise cause. Saba Bazargan-Forward, for example, proposes the following formula for determining how much harm a threatener can be liable to suffer in defense of his victim. First, identify the amount of harm the threatener will otherwise cause and multiply it by the threatener's "percentage responsibility" for the

---

19. Jeff McMahan, "Who Is Morally Liable to Be Killed in War," *Analysis* 71 (2011), 552.

threat he poses. That yields the amount of harm he would be liable *for* (not *to*) were he fully culpable. Suppose that a responsible killer is 5 percent responsible for a threat of death, which has a numerical value of −100. He is, on Bazargan-Forward's view, liable to the same amount of harm as a threatener who is fully culpable for a threatened harm of −5. A fully culpable threatener is liable to defensive harm substantially greater than that which he would otherwise cause – for example, ten times greater. On this assumption, the responsible killer who will otherwise inflict a harm of −100 is liable to be harmed up to −50 in defense of his victim.[20]

The other reason why one might deny that responsible killers are liable to be killed is that liability is sensitive to matters of agency. When a responsible killer threatens an innocent victim, the choice that the victim or a third party faces is between *intentionally killing* one person as a means and *foreseeably allowing* another person to be killed. If in general the reason not to kill a person is stronger than the reason not to allow a person to die, and if the reason not to harm a person as a means is stronger than the reason not to harm a person as a foreseeable side effect, then there is a moral presumption against killing a person in self-defense. Only if there is a sufficiently significant moral difference between the threatener and the victim can that presumption be overridden.[21] In most instances, there is such a difference. But one might think that the difference between the responsible killer and the victim—the difference between minimal responsibility and no responsibility—is too slight to overcome the presumption against intentional killing.

These two reasons are not mutually exclusive but may reinforce each other. Suppose, then, that when there is only one responsible killer, he is not liable to be killed. It does not follow that it is impermissible to kill him. It might be permissible to kill him if he were liable to some significant proportion of the harm of being killed and there were a different justification for the infliction of the remainder of that harm. There might, for example, be a lesser evil justification—that is, a justification for the infliction of harm to which the victim is not liable when the only alternative would involve much greater harm to which the victim or victims would

---

20. Saba Bazargan, "Killing Minimally Responsible Threats," *Ethics* 125 (2014): 114–36. Bazargan writes on p. 121 that "the degree of harm to which an individual is liable is the harm that she threatens to cause multiplied by the percentage degree of her moral responsibility." But the subsequent text indicates that this is not in fact his view. In this sentence he seems to mean "for which" rather than "to which." I am grateful to Matthew Oliver for helpful discussion of Bazargan's text.

21. Jeff McMahan, "Self-Defense and the Problem of the Innocent Attacker," *Ethics* 104 (1994): 252–90, section 1.

also not be liable. I have elsewhere referred to this as a "combined justification."[22] That there can be a combined justification is implicit in the idea that it can be permissible to inflict harm that is disproportionate in the narrow sense provided that the harm to the victim beyond that to which she is liable is proportionate in the wide sense.

Suppose there can be a combined justification for killing a single responsible killer. There is a simple explanation of why that justification is not endlessly repeatable. Imagine a series of cases, in each of which there is one more responsible killer than in the case preceding it. Assume that each responsible killer is liable to the same degree of harm. With each additional responsible killer, there is more harm that has to be justified as the lesser evil. But as the harm that has to be justified increases, the harm to be averted—the death of the victim—remains constant. At some point, the combined harm to the responsible killers beyond that to which they are liable will no longer be the lesser evil in relation to the death of the victim. At that point, the lesser evil element of the combined justification ceases to apply. On the reasonable assumption that there is no other justification for killing further responsible killers, the limit of justification has been reached and the killing of any further responsible killers would be unjustified. This explains why there is a limit to the number of responsible killers it can be permissible to kill in defense of a single victim. If it were known at the outset that the number of responsible killers exceeds the number that could permissibly be killed on the basis of a combined justification, it would be impermissible to kill even one, as that would be ineffective, assuming the agent would respect the limits of the combined justification.

The appeal either to a noncomparative account of the limit of liability or to a strong moral asymmetry between intentional harming and foreseeably allowing harm to occur, together with an appeal to a combined justification, thus seems to offer a good explanation of common intuitions about the killing of responsible killers. Although I have been tempted by this explanation, I now think it is unsatisfactory. While there may be a combined justification for killing one or more responsible killers in certain cases, in most cases there is unlikely to be a combined justification for killing even a single responsible killer.

Suppose that both killer and victim would suffer the same harm in being killed: −100. And suppose that, in accordance with the assumption that a minimally

22. Jeff McMahan, "What Rights May Be Defended by Means of War?" in *The Morality of Defensive War*, ed. Cécile Fabre and Seth Lazar (Oxford: Oxford University Press, 2014), 133–35. For an earlier discussion, see Jeff McMahan, "Targeted Killing: Murder, Combat, or Law Enforcement?" in *Targeted Killings: Law and Morality in an Asymmetrical World*, ed. Andrew Altman, Claire Finkelstein, and Jens David Ohlin (New York: Oxford University Press, 2012), 138.

responsible threatener cannot be liable to a harm as great as that which he would cause, a responsible killer is liable to a harm of no more than −90 (an assumption significantly more favorable to a combined justification than Bazargan-Forward's). For it to be permissible to kill the responsible killer, there must be a lesser evil justification for inflicting on the responsible killer the remaining harm of −10, which is a harm to which he is not liable. That harm must be widely proportionate in relation to allowing the victim to suffer a harm of −100, to which she is also not liable.

One concern about this reasoning is that it may involve an objectionable form of double counting.[23] The first claim in the combined justification is that the responsible killer is liable to a harm of −90 as a means of preventing the victim from suffering a harm of −100. The second is that inflicting −10 (which together with the −90 constitutes the harm of death) is the lesser evil in relation to allowing the victim to suffer a harm of −100. The prevention of the full harm of −100 to the victim is thus serving twice—once to justify part of the total harm to the victim and then again to justify the other part. But the killing of the victim is not being prevented twice. If the prevention of the killing justifies inflicting a harm of only −90 on grounds of liability, that exhausts its power to justify the harming of the killer. If defense of the victim could justify inflicting greater harm on the threatener, he would be liable to greater harm.

There may be a plausible response to this objection.[24] Suppose that to defend herself from a responsible killer, a potential victim must harm the killer as a means and harm an innocent bystander as a side effect. She could incapacitate the killer by inflicting a harm of −90 on him but her act would unavoidably inflict a harm of −10 on an innocent bystander as a side effect. Call this the "three−person case." Suppose that the responsible killer is liable to a harm of −90 as a means of preventing the death of the victim (a harm of −100) and that there is a lesser evil justification for the infliction of a harm of −10 on a bystander as a side effect of preventing the harm to the victim. The defensive act is thus proportionate in both the narrow and wide senses. The harm to the victim is averted only once but it seems to have counted twice – yet this seems legitimate. And it seems that the same can be said of the application of a combined justification to the original case involving only the responsible killer and the victim (the "two−person case").

In the two−person case, to determine whether killing the responsible killer is proportionate in the narrow sense, one must compare the harm of −90 that the victim would inflict on the responsible killer with the harm of −100 to herself that

---

23. I am grateful to Stephen Bero and Victor Tadros, who both independently pressed this objection.

24. I am indebted to Patrick Tomlin for this response.

she would avert. To determine whether inflicting harm on the killer beyond that to which he is liable is proportionate in the wide sense, one must compare inflicting the further harm of -10 with the harm of -100 that would be averted. As in the three-person case, the prevention of the full harm of -100 is counted twice, once in the assessment of narrow proportionality and again in the assessment of wide proportionality. The main difference is that in the original two-person case, the harm that must be assessed for narrow proportionality and that which must be assessed for wide proportionality are harms to the same person rather than harms to different people.

I will not attempt to determine whether this comparison is sufficient to rebut the double-counting objection. For it helps us to see what I think is a more serious objection to the application of a combined justification to the original two-person case. There are two significant differences between the two cases.

First, in the three-person case the harm to the responsible killer is completely effective on its own. Together with the assumption that this harm is narrowly proportionate because it is less than the harm it averts, this ensures that the killer is liable to suffer it. In the two-person case, by contrast, the maximum harm to which the responsible killer is potentially liable is -90. But only death (-100) can be effective; hence the infliction of -90 on its own is wholly ineffective.

Second, in the three-person case, the bystander is harmed as a side effect, whereas in the two-person case, the additional harm of -10 that must be justified as the lesser evil is inflicted as a means. Killing the responsible killer is the means of saving the victim and all portions of the harm of death are included within that means.

Both these facts about the two-person case are problematic for the combined justification. That the infliction of -90 on the responsible killer would be wholly ineffective might suggest that he cannot be liable to it, if effectiveness is internal to liability. One can claim, however, that the single defensive act is overall effective, even if the percentage of the defensive harm to which the responsible killer is liable (ninety percent) would be ineffective if it could somehow be inflicted on its own. Yet if we assume compliance with morality, so that the defensive act will be done only if it is permissible, then the infliction of the -90 can be part of an overall effective act only if the infliction of the other -10 can be justified as the lesser evil. If the infliction of the additional -10 beyond the responsible killer's liability cannot be justified as the lesser evil, the act may not be done and the infliction of -90 in any other way will be ineffective, so that the killer cannot be liable to it.

The harm of -10 cannot, however, be justified as the lesser evil. For there to be a lesser evil justification for the infliction of harm on a person who is not liable to that harm, the harm caused must be sufficiently small, or that prevented sufficiently great, to justify overriding the constraint against harming. A harm of −10 is ten percent of the harm of death. Suppose that in both the two-person and three-person cases, both the victim and the responsible killer would lose fifty years of good life in being killed. On that assumption, ten percent of the harm of death is equivalent to the loss of five years of good life. In the three-person case, it would not be justifiable as the lesser evil to cause an innocent bystander a loss equivalent to the loss of five years of good life as a side effect of preventing the innocent victim from losing fifty years of good life. That would be disproportionate in the wide sense.

In the two-person case, effective defense requires that the same harm be inflicted not as a side effect but as an intended means. Most discussions of wide proportionality presuppose that it is sensitive to the distinction between means and side effect. They presuppose, that is, that to offset an intended harm to which the victim is not liable, it is necessary to prevent a harm greater than that which would be necessary to offset an equivalent unintended harm.[25] If this familiar assumption is correct, then the harm beyond that to which he is liable that it might be widely proportionate to inflict on the responsible killer must be *less* than that which it would be widely proportionate to inflict on the innocent bystander in the three-person case.

In the three-person case, it seems plausible to suppose that the harm it might be widely proportionate to inflict on an innocent bystander as a side effect of saving the innocent victim must be less than −1—that is, less than one percent of the harm of death. If death involves the loss of fifty years of good life, one percent of that is a harm equivalent to the loss of a half a year of good life. If harms inflicted as a means are harder to justify than equivalent harms inflicted as a side effect, the harm it might be widely proportionate to inflict on the responsible killer in the two-person case beyond that to which he is liable must be significantly less than −1.

One might argue that because the harm that must be justified as the lesser evil in the two-person case would be inflicted on a person who is already liable to a substantial harm, it can be greater, other things being equal, than the maximum that could be justified if the victim were not liable to any harm at all, as is true of the innocent bystander in the three-person case. This would be analogous to the view that to inflict a certain amount of punishment on a guilty person beyond what he deserves is less objectionable than to inflict the same amount of punishment on an innocent person. I am skeptical of both these views but cannot discuss them here.

---

25. "Proportionate Defense," section VII.

Putting aside this last point, it seems reasonable to conclude that in the two-person case, the amount of harm that it can be justifiable to inflict on the responsible killer *as the lesser evil* is substantially less than −1. That means that for there to be a combined justification for killing the responsible killer, he must be liable to a harm greater than −99—that is, greater than ninety-nine percent of the harm of death. While this is formally compatible with the assumption that a responsible killer cannot be liable to as much harm as he would cause, in substance it trivializes that assumption. It seems, therefore, that there cannot be a combined justification for killing even a single responsible killer. Yet very few people accept that it is impermissible for an innocent victim to kill a responsible killer in self-defense. Those who deny that a responsible killer is liable to be killed have therefore been assuming that some form of combined justification can provide the required justification. But the foregoing discussion shows, I think, that this is mistake.

VI. Proportionality in the Aggregate

The problems I have been discussing—how, if there is a liability justification for killing one, there can also be a limit to the number it can be permissible to kill, and why the number of killers seems more obviously constraining when they are culpable than when they are minimally responsible—have thus far proved intractable. In earlier work, I proposed a solution about which I now have doubts.[26] I will not review that suggestion here but will instead pursue a new and different line of thought that seems more promising.

Assume that if there is only one responsible killer, he is morally liable to be killed, provided that the circumstantial conditions are satisfied. Now suppose that there are 999 others. The killing of the innocent victim is now overdetermined, which means that killing the original responsible killer, or any one of the others, has become either ineffective (if life during the interval before the next killer would act would not be worth living) or narrowly disproportionate (if that interval would be worth living, though short). If effectiveness and narrow proportionality are circumstantial conditions of liability rather than external conditions of permissibility, none of the thousand responsible killers is liable to be killed. Each has a moral shield against liability provided by the presence of the others. But, as I noted earlier, none has a right to this shield. If there were only one responsible killer and a third party could prevent the other 999 from being present without harming them, she would have a duty to do that. Similarly, if there were a thousand responsible killers and the third party could remove 999

---

26. McMahan, "Who Is Morally Liable," 554–55; and McMahan, "Duty, Obedience, Desert," 155–57.

without harming them, she would have a duty to do that. But suppose that the only way that anyone can remove them is to kill them. Only if all are killed can the victim survive. Yet if all are killed, each killing is effective in preventing the victim from losing a significant amount of good life. For in that case each killing occurs in a context in which no one of the other 999 responsible killers will kill the victim. The killing of each responsible killer is morally as it would be if he were the only one present. In short, killing all the responsible killers establishes the circumstantial conditions for the liability of each. Yet, assuming compliance with morality, all will be killed only if it is permissible to kill them.

This again raises the question whether the permissibility or impermissibility of killing all can be determined independently of determining whether each is individually liable to be killed. I suggest that, when we consider the harm that would be involved in killing a thousand responsible killers, taking into account that each is only minimally responsible for the threat he poses, and compare that harm to the threatened harm to the victim, taking into account that she bears no responsibility for the fact that killing is unavoidable in the circumstances, we can judge intuitively that killing all thousand would be disproportionate. We can see this without first determining whether each of the thousand responsible killers is liable to be killed. This is a judgment of proportionality that, like narrow proportionality but unlike wide proportionality, takes account of the moral responsibility of those who would be harmed. But, like wide proportionality and unlike narrow proportionality, it also takes account of the number who would be harmed. We can refer to this form of proportionality as *proportionality in the aggregate*.

I believe that we can infer that killing all thousand responsible killers is disproportionate in the aggregate just from facts about the harms that would be caused and prevented, the varying degrees of responsibility of the different possible victims, and the number of people who would be killed in each option. If this is right, it resolves the circularity problem mentioned in section II. That was that it seemed that whether it is permissible to kill all thousand responsible killers depends on whether each is liable, which depends on whether killing each would be effective, which in turn depends on whether the others will be killed, which depends, assuming compliance with morality, on whether it is permissible to kill them all. But whether it is permissible to kill all thousand does *not* depend on whether each is liable. We can know that it is *impermissible*, because disproportionate in the aggregate, without knowing whether each is liable.

When they consider the culpable killers, many people—perhaps most—think it is permissible to kill all thousand. If so, they implicitly judge that killing all is proportionate in the aggregate. If that is so, and if the victim has the ability to kill all the culpable killers sequentially, it is then permissible for her to kill each in turn. Because in killing each she knows that it will be permissible for her to kill the others, she is justified in regarding each killing as effective and narrowly proportionate. Each killing is narrowly proportionate because it affords her the opportunity to kill the remaining culpable killers in the sequence, thereby enabling herself to have many further years of good life.

My claims about the responsible killers may seem to have a rather paradoxical implication. I claim that it is impermissible to kill all the responsible killers because killing them all would be disproportionate in the aggregate. Yet if the victim does kill them all, she thereby creates the circumstantial conditions of the liability of each. It seems, in other words, that in killing them all, she establishes the conditions of a liability justification for killing each, thereby establishing the permissibility of killing each, thus establishing the permissibility of killing all. (This is the reasoning that Gordon-Solmon seeks to block with her claim that making all thousand liable is widely disproportionate.)

Suppose that the thousand responsible killers are queued up at a distance and will be appearing one by one, in rapid succession. In this version of the example, however, the victim does not have the means to kill them one at a time. But she has a large artillery weapon that can kill all of them at once. If she fires this weapon, it may seem that her act creates the conditions of its own permissibility; for by simultaneously killing them all, it ensures the satisfaction of the circumstantial conditions of liability of each person killed, thereby establishing a liability justification for each killing.

I think, however, that we should not accept that the act guarantees its own permissibility. The act of killing all is impermissible because it is disproportionate in the aggregate. If the victim fails to comply with morality and kills all thousand, she will have done what was disproportionate in the aggregate and her act will still be objectionable on that ground. It is true that she will also have created the circumstantial conditions of the liability of each victim. But those conditions did not obtain when she acted. The thousand responsible killers were not liable to be killed when she acted, and it was impermissible for her to create the conditions of their liability by killing them. She could not, therefore, act in the expectation of permissibly creating the conditions of individual liability, as she *could* if the killers were culpable.

We should accept, however, that if she does kill them all, she makes it the case that none of them has been *wronged* by being killed. This should not be surprising, for in killing all she has ensured that each killing was both effective and narrowly proportionate. Suppose the victim had had a gun and 999 bullets and had killed the first 999 responsible killers, only to be killed by the last one. In that case, each of the 999 killed *would* have been wronged, for he would have been killed wholly gratuitously. But if she kills all thousand, none of them can complain of having been killed gratuitously, for killing him was, in the circumstances, necessary and effective in securing her survival.

But, again, that in killing them all she makes it the case that none was wronged does not entail that she acted permissibly, on the basis of a set of liability justifications. The reason her act was impermissible—that it was disproportionate in the aggregate—is a matter of the numbers, which is independent of whether any individual is wronged.

Earlier I conceded that the view I would defend is similar to Rodin's view. I will close by explaining how my appeal to the notion of proportionality in the aggregate differs from his view that there is a lesser evil obligation not to act on the liability justifications for killing the responsible killers. The main difference is that he believes that all the responsible killers are liable to be killed because they all satisfy the agential conditions of liability, which are, in his view, the only conditions of liability. Even when there are a thousand responsible killers, there is a liability justification for killing each. (This implies—implausibly, in my view—that if the victim kills only one of the thousand, she does not wrong him, for he has forfeited his right not to be killed, even gratuitously.) If it is impermissible to act on those justifications, it seems that they must be overridden by countervailing considerations. He claims that what overrides the justifications are the harms that the killers would suffer in being killed. I claimed that this implies that the justifications are overridden by the same harms that they justify.

My view, by contrast, denies that there are liability justifications for killing any of the thousand responsible killers. Even though killing them all would secure the circumstantial conditions of their liability, killing them all is impermissible because it would be disproportionate in the aggregate. And even if the victim or a third party were to kill them all, that would not justify their having been killed by retroactively supplying a liability justification for each killing. It would merely make it the case that none of those who had been wrongly killed had been wronged in being killed. The wrongness of killing them was not in any wrong done to each but was instead a matter of the numbers.[27]

27. I am very grateful to the Institute of Advanced Study at the University of Birmingham for generous support during the writing of this essay. I have greatly benefited from comments on earlier versions by Ben Bronner, Tony Coady, Roger Crisp, Adam Gastineau, Kerah Gordon-Solmon, Richard Holton, Andrew Lister, Victor Tadros, Larry Temkin, Jesse Tomalty, Patrick Tomlin, Stephen Woodside, and, especially, Derek Parfit.

2 THE LESSER EVIL OBLIGATION

David Rodin

Introduction

The lesser evil justification is a familiar feature of applied moral reasoning and jurisprudence. Yet it is seldom noted that the lesser evil justification is merely one component of a broader normative mechanism in which a moral right is outweighed by competing considerations that are independent of the possession conditions of that right. In particular the lesser evil justification has a counterpart that I will call "the lesser evil obligation." Lesser evil justifications arise when competing and independent moral considerations make it the case that an agent is all things considered justified in transgressing some person's rights. A lesser evil obligation arises when competing and independent moral considerations make it the case that a right bearer has an all-things-considered obligation not to exercise his own rights.

Reflecting on the lesser evil obligation can help to solve a puzzle that has recently vexed theorists of war and self-defense: why it may be impermissible to defensively kill a large number of persons each of whom is liable to be killed. This fact is puzzling because proportionality assessments for liability to harm (what Jeff McMahan has called "narrow proportionality"[1]) do not aggregate harm across multiple aggressors, but rather consider separately the proportionality of harm inflicted on each individual aggressor. Yet it seems clear that the number of aggressors who must be harmed to achieve a defensive goal can make a difference to the permissibility of defensive action in certain circumstances. This is particularly true when the aggressors are only minimally responsible for the unjust harm they pose but, as I will suggest below, the problem also arises for fully

---

1. Jeff McMahan, *Killing in War* (Oxford: Oxford University Press, 2009), 20–21.

culpable aggressors. The lesser evil obligation can explain this phenomenon. A putative defender has the right (liberty) to kill all of a large number of liable aggressors, but it is a right he morally ought not to act on because of a requirement to realize competing goods or values.

We can approach the idea of a lesser evil obligation by reflecting on the more familiar case of the lesser evil justification. Standard examples of lesser evil justification include a farmer who justifiably destroys his neighbor's field to stop a wildfire from engulfing a town, a fireman who breaks down a door to rescue a child from toxic fumes, the mandatory quarantining of a person suspected of carrying a highly infectious disease, and standard cases of justified side effect harm or "collateral damage" in war.

These are all cases in which an agent justifiably transgresses certain person's rights in order to further the rights, interests, or welfare of third parties.[2] But it is clear that lesser evil justifications can also be grounded in the rights, interests, or welfare of the rights-transgressing agent himself, or indeed of the person whose right is transgressed. The later phenomenon occurs in cases of justified paternalism in which an agent infringes the rights of some person in order to protect that person from a far greater harm to their interests.

Lesser evil justifications have a number of familiar features that contrast sharply with situations in which a person has forfeited a right, and is therefore liable to certain harm or treatment. Lesser evil considerations and considerations of liability are both forms of justification (that is to say, they both function to explain why something that is presumptively impermissible is in fact permissible in the circumstances). But the way that the two considerations justify action is very different. It is instructive to consider these differences and to reflect on how they might be explained.

With a lesser evil justification, we explain how it can be permissible to treat a person in a certain way *despite* facts about their rights—in particular despite the fact that the person has rights against such treatment. With a liability justification, we explain how it can be permissible to do something to a person *because* of facts about their rights—in particular because a person who possessed rights against such treatment in the past no longer possesses such rights. The first form of justification is synchronous (it involves the comparison of competing values at a particular point in time), whereas the second is diachronic (what was contrary to an agent's rights at a previous point in time is not contrary to them now).

---

2. A right is "transgressed" when some agent performs an action inconsistent with the content of that right. A right that is justifiably transgressed is "infringed." A right that is transgressed without justification is "violated."

Unlike liability justifications, a lesser evil justification leaves underlying rights undisturbed. A person who possesses a lesser evil justification for harming nonetheless transgresses the harmed person's rights, that is to say, treats him in a way he has a right not to be treated. We signify this by saying that such a person has justifiably *infringed* (but not violated) the person's rights. The fact that the right remains extant, even if it is outweighed by other considerations, has normative consequences. Most obviously someone who justifiably infringes a right thereby assumes a residual obligation to make good the harm—and the wrong—inflicted on the beneficiary.[3] The infringer might do this by restoring the interest protected by the right, compensating for the loss, apologizing, or in some other way. This contrasts with a liability justification, in which a person who is liable to be harmed has no right against the harm and is owed no subsequent compensation or apology.

There are also significant differences in the way that goods and harms contribute toward proportionality judgments within the two justifications. Many goods and harms that are relevant to proportionality for the purposes of a lesser evil justification are not relevant to proportionality for the purposes of a liability justification. For example, if one is assessing whether there is a lesser evil justification for harming a number of persons in order to avert some further harm, then the aggregated harm inflicted on all these persons is relevant to the proportionality of the action. However, if one is considering whether a number of persons is liable to be harmed in order to avert a further harm for which they are together responsible, then one does not aggregate the harm to be inflicted on the potentially liable persons, but rather compares the harm for which each is responsible with the harm that would be inflicted on him. There are also differences in the way that the benefits produced as a result of harm-inflicting acts offset those harms for the purposes of proportionality in liability and lesser evil justification. Many resulting benefits do not offset harms for the purposes of proportionality judgment in a liability justification. For example, if the killing of an aggressor would save the life of a man waiting for an organ transplant, this fact does not contribute to the proportionality assessment for the purposes of determining his liability to be killed in defense. But resulting benefits do typically offset harms for the purposes of lesser evil justifications.[4]

These distinctive features of the two forms of justifications stem from the fact that they involve the operation of two very different kinds of moral consideration. Liability justifications involve moral considerations that affect the underlying

---

3. The wrong and the harm may be independent: for example, paternalistic acts may benefit a right holder, even as they infringe his rights. The right holder may still be owed compensation or apology though he is a net beneficiary of the rights-infringing action.

4. I analyze these phenomena in more detail in "Justifying Harm," *Ethics* 122 (2011): 74–110.

grounds for the possession of the right. When one becomes liable to treatment against which one in the past possessed a right, this is necessarily because the underlying grounds for the possession of the right are no longer operative. Lesser evil justifications, in contrast, involve considerations that do not affect the underlying grounds of the right in this way. In a lesser evil justification a right is "overridden" or "outweighed" by considerations that are independent of the underlying grounds for the possession of the right. They provide a moral justification for transgressing the right, without undermining the moral grounds that support the existence of the right.

This characterization captures the way that lesser evil and liability justifications present in moral and legal reasoning. To explain these features, however, requires some account of the possession conditions of rights, and therefore of what it means for a moral consideration to be "independent" of those conditions. I have recently attempted such an explanation by arguing that rights against harm are grounded in reciprocity relations between moral agents. Rights against harm emerge from the reciprocal compliance of agents with mutual moral obligations. Thus I have the right that you not kill me because and to the extent that I comply with your right that I not kill you. Similarly, you have the right that I not kill you because and to the extent that you comply with my right that you not kill me.[5]

This reciprocity account has a number of advantages. In particular it can explain, better than rival accounts, the conditions for the possession and forfeiture of rights. If your possession of the right not to be harmed is rooted in your reciprocal compliance with the rights of others, then this explains why you can become liable to be harmed by responsibly threatening to infringe the rights of others. The account also captures and explains the intrinsically interpersonal nature of many rights. Rights are interpersonal in the sense that they specify relations between pairs of moral agents as described by W. N. Hohfeld.[6] Moreover, the conditions for the possession and forfeiture of rights concern facts about the normative relationship between those agents, often to the exclusion of broader impersonal values. Whether or not one accepts the reciprocity account of rights, making sense of the differences between lesser evil and liability justifications that we have reviewed will require some comparable account of the interpersonal nature of rights against harm, and of the impersonal nature of the lesser evil reasons that can sometimes override them.

---

5. "The Reciprocity Theory of Rights," *Law and Philosophy* 33 (2014): 281–308.

6. W. N. Hohfeld, *Fundamental Legal Conceptions as Applied in Judicial Reasoning*, edited by W. W. Cook (New Haven: Yale University Press, 1919).

Now that we have a basic characterization of the lesser evil justification, let us contrast it with a related but distinct case. Imagine that you are subject to an unjustified assault that would likely leave you with a painful, but impermanent, injury. Suppose you could avert this injury by breaking the assailant's arm, and that this treatment would be narrowly proportionate in the circumstances (it would not be excessive in relation to the assailant's liability to be harmed). However, the assailant is a manual laborer whose large family is entirely dependent on him. If he breaks his arm he will lose his income and the family will be destitute, moreover there is no evidence that breaking his arm will prevent the assailant or any other person from committing assault in the future. It is plausible that you would have an all things considered obligation not to engage in self-defense in these circumstances—despite the fact that you clearly have the right of self-defense with respect to the assailant (you would not wrong him or infringe *his* rights by breaking his arm).

In this case your right (liberty) of self-defense with respect to the assailant is outweighed by moral considerations stemming from the rights and interests of third parties. As with the lesser evil justification, the same phenomenon can also occur without the involvement of third parties. For example, suppose that a poor person recklessly drives into the car of a millionaire causing it damage. The recklessness of the action generates a claim right to compensation on the part of the millionaire against the poor man. But suppose the compensation would make a marginal contribution to the millionaire's welfare and would constitute a devastating loss to the pauper. Arguably the millionaire, all things considered, ought to waive his claim right to compensation in such a situation.[7]

These cases are similar to the lesser evil justifications considered above in that they also involve a situation in which a right is outweighed—but not expunged—by considerations that are independent of the ground of the right. (The right to break the laborer's arm is grounded in his liability for the unjust threat he poses; the right to compensation is grounded in the reckless damage caused by the poor man.)

But unlike lesser evil justifications, these cases involve a situation in which the right holder, himself, has an all things considered reason not to exercise his own rights. These cases do not involve the justification of a presumptively impermissible act, but rather an obligation to refrain from a presumptively permissible act.

Let us specify the contrast more precisely. In a lesser evil justification, a person is all things considered justified in treating the right bearer in a way that is inconsistent with his rights. In the current cases the right bearer is all things considered

---

7. As in the previous example, I put to one side any potential deterrence effects of the compensation.

obligated to behave in a certain way toward a person despite the fact that they have the right with respect to that party to behave otherwise (this right may be a claim, liberty, power, or immunity). I will call this phenomenon "the lesser evil obligation" to distinguish it from the more familiar lesser evil justification.[8]

Just as lesser evil justifications leave underlying rights undisturbed, so too do lesser evil obligations. Thus, although you have an all things considered obligation not to break the assailant's arm, it is clear that you still possess the liberty with respect to the assailant to break his arm (you would not violate or infringe any of *his* rights if you did so and you would owe him no compensation or apology). Similarly, although the millionaire morally ought to waive his right of compensation from the pauper, it is clear that he possesses the right to compensation (otherwise he could not waive it).

We require a terminological counterpart in the case of lesser evil obligations to the notion of infringing a right in the case of lesser evil justifications. If a person has an all things considered obligation to behave in a certain way toward a party despite the fact that they have the right with respect to that party to behave otherwise, I will say that their right has been *subsumed*. A right that has been subsumed has a comparable status to a right that has been infringed. Thus, a justifiably infringed right is an extant right that generates a subsequent duty on the infringing party to apologize and compensate the right holder. A subsumed right is an extant right that generates a duty of gratitude on the party that has received a benefit that he does not have a right to receive. This duty may be fulfilled by

8. In fact, the description of both forms of considerations as forms of "lesser evil" reasoning is potentially misleading. First, there is no fundamental reason to refer to a requirement to avoid a "lesser evil," rather than a requirement to achieve a "greater good." Although one locution or the other may be more natural in certain cases, it is possible to rephrase all "lesser evil" considerations as "greater good" considerations and vice versa. Second, both the "lesser evil" and "greater good" language suggest a form of utilitarian reasoning, but this is also misleading. Utilitarianism is maximizing, but lesser evil reasoning involves the surpassing of a threshold that is considerably more demanding than simple maximization. The justifications and obligations in question only arise when independent considerations substantially outweigh the rights in question. However, the language of "lesser evil" is well entrenched for justifications, and so long as we are mindful of its potential pitfalls we should not be led astray by applying it also to obligations. I first introduced the notion of this form of obligation in "Justifying Harm" (*Ethics* 122 [2011], 74–110, at 99). Jeff McMahan rightly objected that my terminology in that paper was less than clear. McMahan's own proposed terminology is to refer to such cases as involving a "greater evil constraint" (Jeff McMahan, "Duty, Obedience, Desert, and Proportionality in War: A Response," *Ethics* 122 [2011], 135–67, at 153). However, this terminology would appear too narrow. There is no fundamental difference between cases in which an agent is obligated to refrain from exercising a right with respect to a particular person (which is captured by the term "constraint") and cases in which an agent is obligated to act in a way that benefits a person who has no claim right to the benefit. The broader term "lesser evil obligation" is intended to capture both forms of case.

adopting an appropriate attitude of gratitude or by rendering a comparable benefit in a similar context.

For example, in the case above, your defensive right against the laborer has
been subsumed by a lesser evil obligation stemming from the rights and interests
of the laborer's family. Because the laborer has received a benefit (your refraining
from breaking his arm) to which he has no claim right, he has a duty of gratitude
toward you. This duty is distinct from the duty to compensate for the unjust
harm he inflicts on you. Even if full compensation for the injury has been made,
the aggressor would have a duty of gratitude above and beyond this, resulting
from the fact that his victim had rendered him a benefit or consideration (not
breaking his arm) that he had no claim right to receive.

The notion of a lesser evil obligation is important because it can help to
explain many normative phenomena. For example, it helps to make explicit the
logic implicit in a standard collateral damage case. A pilot plans to bomb a valuable military target in a just war, knowing that it will incidentally kill a number of
innocent civilians. If the attack is proportionate in the wide sense (the value of
the target outweighs the rights and interests of the civilians) then he possesses a
lesser evil justification for acting and the rights of the civilians have been justifiably infringed. So far, so familiar. But what is often not explicitly recognized is that
if the attack is disproportionate in the wide sense (the rights and interests of the
civilians outweigh the value of the target), then there is a lesser evil obligation not
to kill the unjust combatants and the right to kill the liable unjust combatants has
been subsumed. It is not that the unjust combatants cease to be liable to attack; it
is rather that the pilot has a lesser evil obligation not to act on the liberty that is
correlative to their liability. Just as the noncombatants subject to the proportionate harm are owed compensation, so the liable combatants whom the pilots abstain from attacking owe him a debt of gratitude.

I. The Number of Aggressors

We will now investigate how the idea of the lesser evil obligation can help to resolve a puzzle concerning the numbers of aggressors in defense situations. It can
often be permissible to defensively kill a large number of aggressors to save the life
of a single victim. This striking fact is one of the clearest demonstrations that utilitarianism does not provide a complete description of morality. The explanation
for this permission lies in the fact that the justification for defensive killing is
principally grounded in the liability of those killed, and as we have already seen,
liability is a fact about interpersonal rights. In cases involving multiple aggressors,
we examine whether the harm inflicted on each aggressor, individually, is proportionate to the harm they responsibly threaten to impose. We do not aggregate the

defensive harm inflicted across multiple aggressors. If each of a large number of aggressors is individually liable to be killed as a result of culpably threatening the life of a single victim, then this explains why it can be permissible to kill many to save just one.

This reasoning seems plausible when the number of aggressors is relatively small, but it becomes implausible as the number of aggressors rises. This is particularly clear when the aggressors have impaired responsibility for the threat they pose. Suppose that two men make an unjustified attack on an innocent child that will cause her to lose a limb. The men have been coerced by mobsters who have threatened to torture and kill their own children. Intuitively it seems that it would be permissible to defensively kill the assailants if necessary, despite their minimal responsibility arising from the excuse of duress. But what if there were one thousand such coerced assailants? It is not clear that it would be permissible to kill one thousand such minimally responsible assailants. When the number of unjust assailants becomes sufficiently large, it is implausible to disregard the aggregated harm inflicted on them entirely from the all things considered permissibility of engaging in defensive action.

Many commentators take the numbers problem to exclusively concern minimally responsible aggressors. They correspondingly believe that there is no limit to the number of fully culpable liable persons one may kill to prevent the unjust harm that is the basis of their liability. This is also the view of traditional Just War theory, which has historically denied that the killing of liable combatants can ever itself be disproportionate. However, the problem arises also with fully culpable aggressors when the numbers become sufficiently large. Suppose a pernicious sect has dedicated itself to the destruction of an innocent child's limb, and the only possible way to defend her is by killing each and every member. The sect has one million members. Would it be permissible to kill one million culpable aggressors to defend the limb of one child? My intuition is that it would not. When the number of aggressors is sufficiently large, the number of even fully culpable aggressors who must be killed can be relevant to the all things considered permissibility of defensive action.[9]

The problem is to explain why the number of aggressors seems irrelevant to the all things considered permissibility of defensive action at lower numbers but becomes relevant as the numbers increase to very high levels. Furthermore, why does the number of combined aggressors become relevant to the all things

---

9. If you do not share my intuition that there is some extremely large number of culpable aggressors beyond which it would be impermissible to kill all of them in defense, then I would ask you to suspend judgment, as I will provide argumentation to support this conclusion below.

considered permissibility of defensive action at lower levels than when the aggressors are minimally responsible compared with when they are fully culpable?

The simplest and best solution to the number of aggressors problem is to observe that it involves a form of lesser evil obligation. Consider again the case of the pernicious sect. Why might it be impermissible to kill one million culpable assailants in order to defend a threatened limb, when each assailant is individually liable to be killed? To begin, consider that each assailant likely has a family, a job, and friends. Killing them would inflict considerable harm on the very large number of persons who love and depend on them. When this incidental harm is sufficiently great, it plausibly outweighs the liberty right of a putative defender to kill all the aggressors. If he may not kill all of the aggressors, then he may not kill any of them, since this would inflict harm with no countervailing moral benefit. The right to kill the culpable assailants has not been expunged (the assailants are still liable to be killed) but it has been *subsumed* because there are sufficient independent moral considerations to outweigh it, all things considered. This is a typical lesser evil obligation.

The same reasoning would apply if it were the putative defender's own arm that was threatened with destruction. Lesser evil considerations can generate a duty to sacrifice a good that one has a right to possess, by requiring an agent to abstain from self-defensive acts he has a liberty to perform. As was noted before, an agent who acted on this lesser evil obligation would be owed a duty of gratitude on the part of the person who has received a benefit that he had no right to receive.

This explanation turns on the unintended harmful effects of a defensive action on third parties who are not themselves liable to harm. McMahan calls this the "wide proportionality" constraint.[10] But wide proportionality alone seems an insufficient explanation of the numbers problem. Defensive acts that harm large numbers of aggressors will not always inflict harm on non-liable third parties. Yet even in these cases it seems that there is some number of aggressors that it would be impermissible to kill in defense. How can we explain how sufficiently large numbers of aggressors can be relevant to the permissibility of defensive action in such cases? Moreover, to explain why the numbers problem is more acute with minimally responsible aggressors compared with culpable aggressors, it would seem that the harm inflicted on the liable persons themselves, as well as non-liable third parties, must be playing a role. How can we explain this?

We can do so by noting that harm inflicted on a liable person is still an evil from an impersonal point of view. McMahan explains this point eloquently in his

---

10. Jeff McMahan, *Killing in War* (Oxford: Oxford University Press, 2009), 21.

account of the distinction between liability and desert. It is worth quoting the passage at length:

> If a person deserves to be harmed, there is a moral reason for harming him that is independent of the further consequences of harming him. Giving him what he deserves is an end in itself. Although a deserved harm is bad for the person who suffers it, it is, from an impersonal point of view, intrinsically *good*. By contrast, a person is liable to be harmed only if harming him will serve some further purpose—for example, if it will prevent him from unjustly harming someone, deter him (or perhaps others) from further wrongdoing, or compensate a victim of his prior wrongdoing.... Moreover, in further contrast with deserved harms, harms to which people are liable are bad not only for those who suffer them but also from an impersonal point of view. Although their weight is discounted in proportionality calculations, they are never of merely neutral or positive impersonal value, unless of course they are harms that the victim also *deserves* to suffer.[11]

If justified defensive harm is merely something to which an aggressor is liable, rather than something he deserves, then it is bad from an impersonal point of view. If this harm is bad from an impersonal point of view, then it plays a role in lesser evil reasoning. Thus the death of even a culpable aggressor, who is fully liable to be killed, is still a moral evil for the purposes of lesser evil reasoning. Of course one might believe that a culpable aggressor is both liable to, and deserving of, harm in a self-defense situation, so that the justification for harm is overdetermined. If that were true, then it would not be the case that the death of a culpable aggressor is a moral evil for the purposes of lesser evil proportionality. Although I cannot argue the case here, I believe that it is not the case that aggressors deserve to be harmed in self-defense: the notion of deserving harm is suspect even in the domain of punishment, and it has no role to play in a theory of self-defense.

As we have seen, impersonal harms are aggregated for the purposes of proportionality in lesser evil reasoning. Therefore, if the number of liable aggressors that must be killed to avert an unjust threatened harm increases while the threatened harm remains the same, then at some point the aggregated impersonal harm inflicted on the aggressors must exceed the prospective good by such a margin that the right to kill them becomes subsumed. This is the case, even though it remains true that each aggressor is individually liable to be killed, since the harm inflicted on that aggressor remains narrowly proportionate to his responsibility for the unjust threatened harm.

---

11. Ibid., 8.

However, the number required to generate a lesser evil obligation to abstain from defensive action against liable parties will be very high indeed. The aggregated impersonal value of the aggressors' lives would need to exceed the impersonal value of the putative defender's life by a very significant margin in order to generate a lesser evil obligation not to kill them.[12] For this reason, the lesser evil obligation is irrelevant to the permissibility of defensive action in almost all normal cases (and particularly when culpable aggressors are concerned) and its effects can in normal circumstances be safely ignored.

But here we may have a concern. We have already seen that the number of aggressors becomes relevant to the permissibility of defense at lower numbers when the aggressors are minimally responsible aggressors compared with cases in which the aggressors are culpable. How can this be if the constraint on killing large numbers of aggressors derives from a lesser evil obligation? McMahan presses this criticism: "the well-being of the culpable killers matters or counts in the same way as that of the [minimally] responsible killers. While the culpability or responsibility of the killers is relevant to the determination of their liability in the establishment of a liability justification, it is not relevant to how much weight their well-being has in a lesser evil justification."[13] If that were true, then a lesser evil obligation would be generated at the same level for culpable as for minimally responsible aggressors.

However, McMahan is here mistaken. It is not the case that well-being or benefits always count in the same way for the purposes of lesser evil reasoning. One way to see this is to note that responsibility and culpability are determinants of liability. As McMahan correctly observes in the passage quoted above, harm inflicted on a person who is liable to that harm is not as bad from an impersonal perspective as harm inflicted on a non-liable person. It therefore has less negative weight in lesser evil reasoning. Those who believe that it is possible to deserve harm are committed to the stronger claim that deserved harm has an impersonal moral value that is positive and therefore has a positive weight in lesser evil reasoning. Lesser evil reasoning is therefore not a form of utilitarianism that aggregates and compares simple states of well-being. It is rather a form of moral reasoning that compares the impersonal moral value of different states of affairs. Whether a harm or benefit is one that the recipient deserves or is liable to will materially affect its impersonal moral value in this form of reasoning.

---

12. To get a sense of how significant this margin is, we may reflect on the number of innocent lives one would need to be able to save in order to generate a lesser evil justification for killing a non-liable person. This is not a strictly analogous case, since one involves the moral permission of an act of killing while the other involves a moral restraint on necessary defensive acts, but the two are roughly comparable.

13. Jeff McMahan, "Liability, Proportionality, and the Number of Aggressors," in this volume, 10.

But it might seem that the problem simply recurs in a different form. After all, a minimally responsible aggressor would still appear to be liable to be killed. If liability to harm makes a difference to the impersonal assessment of the harm, then why should the impersonal harm of the minimally responsible aggressor's death not be discounted to the same degree as the death of a culpable aggressor?

There would seem to be two potential responses to this challenge. The first is to deny that minimally responsible aggressors are in fact (fully) liable. Both McMahan and Saba Bazargan-Forward have proposed accounts of the defensive killing of minimally responsible lethal aggressors that claim that such persons are liable to *some* defensive harm, but are not liable to be killed. It is nonetheless permissible to kill such persons because the harm to which they are not liable may be justified by a lesser evil justification (McMahan calls this "the combined justification," Bazargan-Forward calls this "the hybrid approach"[14]). If this account were correct, then it would explain why lesser evil obligations become relevant at lower numbers when the aggressors are minimally responsible. Because they are not fully liable, the impersonal badness of their deaths is not discounted as steeply compared with fully liable culpable aggressors, enabling it to play a more significant role in generating a lesser evil obligation. Moreover the aggregate value of the harm inflicted on large numbers of such aggressors (particularly the harm for which they were not liable) would undermine the lesser evil justification for killing them.

The second potential response is to insist that liability is not the only consideration relevant to the weighting of harm for the purposes of lesser evil reasoning. The responsibility or culpability of an agent for an unjust harm may play a role in determining the impersonal badness of harming that agent that is independent of the role it plays in determining the agent's liability to be harmed. Thus liability to be harmed and the impersonal badness of harming may come apart. There is indeed strong precedent for considerations of responsibility playing an independent role in the determination of different moral facts. For example, an aggressor who is minimally responsible because he acts under duress may be liable to be killed in self-defense, but not liable to be punished for his aggression. In this case, diminished responsibility mitigates liability to punishment, but not liability to defensive harm. There would seem to be a strong analogy with the role played by responsibility with respect to impersonal badness and liability to defensive harm: diminished responsibility may mitigate impersonal badness, without necessarily eliminating liability to defensive harm. On this view, harm inflicted on minimally responsible liable persons is less bad from an impersonal perspective

---

14. Saba Bazargan, "Killing Minimally Responsible Threats," *Ethics* 125 (2014): 114–36.

than harm inflicted on a non-liable person, but worse than harm inflicted on a fully culpable liable person, exactly as our pre-theoretical intuitions predict.

Let me now consider two further objections raised by McMahan against the lesser evil obligation solution to the numbers problem. The first objection is that it could not be permissible to allow or require harm to be inflicted on an innocent or non-liable person in preference to a large number of liable persons because such a distribution of harm would necessarily contradict the requirements of justice: "a liability justification for the infliction of harm seems to exclude the permissibility of other distributions of the harm. This is because liability is a matter of justice in the distribution of unavoidable harm."[15]

This claim is, however, mistaken in two respects. First, if it is possible for rights to be overridden or subsumed by lesser evil considerations, then it must be possible for the requirements of distributive justice to be overridden or subsumed in precisely the same way. We can clearly see this in cases where the allocation of rights and the demands of distributive justice coincide. For example, in the case of the pauper and the millionaire considered above, it is also a matter of distributive justice that the pauper bear the costs of repair to the damaged car (since he is responsible for those costs). Yet as we have seen there is a strong lesser evil reason not to require the pauper to compensate the millionaire.

Second, I believe that McMahan is mistaken to view liability as fundamentally a matter of justice in the distribution of harm. The requirements of distributive justice and liability to harm do indeed often coincide. But this is because it is (generally) a requirement of justice to distribute unavoidable harm to those who are morally liable to it in preference to those who are not liable. It is not the case that liability to harm is morally grounded in, and explained by, a prior requirement of justice regarding the distribution of unavoidable harm.

This is a deep disagreement concerning the moral foundation of liability to harm that cannot be conclusively settled here. However, I will introduce a case that shows how considerations of distributive justice can sometimes be inconsistent with liability to harm, and secondly reiterate how a reciprocity account of rights can explain liability to harm without any problematic recourse to considerations of distributive justice.

Suppose X engages in some mild, but unjustified provocation of Y (he says unkind and untrue things about Y's wife). Y flies into a homicidal rage and attempts to kill X. X can save his own life only by using force that would leave Y with a broken wrist. Unfortunately, Y is the only person capable of performing a

---

15. Jeff McMahan, "Liability, Proportionality, and the Number of Aggressors," in this volume, 10.

life-saving operation on Z. With a broken wrist he will be unable to perform the operation, and Z will die.

In these circumstances it is clear that Y is liable to have his wrist broken by X. This follows from the following facts: Y is responsible for an unjust attack on X; the broken wrist that X will inflict on Y is narrowly proportionate to the unjust harm Y threatens to inflict on X; the incidental harm inflicted on Z is proportionate in the wide sense since a) the unjust harm inflicted on Z is no greater than the unjust harm averted from X, and b) the harm inflicted on Z is intended by X neither as a means nor as an end itself.

Yet considerations of justice in the distribution of harm lead to a very different conclusion. In this case there is one unavoidable harm (death, which must be borne by either X or Z) and one avoidable harm (a broken wrist that may, but need not, be borne by Y). Z is in no way responsible for the fact that the harm of death must be unavoidably distributed, but X is partially responsible for this fact. If justice requires that unavoidable harm be borne by the party most responsible for the fact that the harm must be distributed, then as a matter of justice X rather than Z should bear the unavoidable harm (remember that Y is not a possible recipient of the unavoidable harm). In addition the avoidable harm (Y's broken wrist) is in fact avoided in this scenario.

If it were true, as McMahan believes, that liability is a matter of justice in the distribution of unavoidable harms, then it would not be the case that Y is liable to have his wrist broken in defense by X in this situation. Moreover, since distributive justice requires that X bear the unavoidable harm of death, McMahan would appear to be committed to the conclusion that X is liable to be killed.

In contrast, the reciprocity theory of rights referenced above can explain liability to harm in a way that involves no such counterintuitive results. On this view, Y's liability to harm by X is a result of the fact that the possession conditions of Y's right against being harmed by X no longer obtain. Prior to the fracas, Y possessed the right against being harmed by X, because and to the extent that he complied with X's right not to be harmed by Y. By engaging in an unjust attack on X, Y makes it the case that the possession conditions for his right against harm no longer obtain; which is to say he makes himself liable to the defensive harm. Considerations of distributive justice, though relevant to an all things considered assessment of the case, are entirely tangential to the moral grounds of his liability to harm. For these, and related reasons, I believe that the reciprocity theory provides a superior explanation of liability to harm to the distributive justice theory.

McMahan's final criticism of my position, and the one he considers "most serious," is that it "seems incoherent."[16] He writes: "Liability justifications are... only

---

16. Ibid.

pro tanto justifications. They justify only the harm inflicted on the liable person. But they do unconditionally justify *that*…Rodin's claim, however, is that the harms to the many aggressors that have been justified on the grounds that those aggressors are liable to suffer them somehow also override those same justifications. That is, the same harms for which there are liability justifications somehow defeat their own justifications."[17]

However, this criticism once again rests on a misunderstanding of the nature of liability justification. A justification is simply a consideration that defeats a moral objection—which would ordinarily be decisive—to undertaking some action. In the case of harming another person, X, there are many such potentially decisive moral objections. One objection would be that X has a right against being so harmed. Another is that a third party has a right that X not be harmed. Another is that harming X would be inconsistent with the requirements of distributive justice. Yet another is that there are lesser evil reasons for not harming him (harming this person would constitute [or contribute to] an unacceptable impersonal moral disvalue).

To say that there is a liability justification for harming X is to say no more and no less than that X does not (any longer) possess a right against being so harmed. Thus when McMahan writes that liability justifications "do unconditionally justify [inflicting harm on the liable persons]," this is at best half true. Liability justifications unconditionally justify inflicting harm on the liable person in the sense that they defeat one potentially decisive moral objection to inflicting such harm—the supposition that he has a right against the harm. But this is entirely consistent with the same harm playing a decisive role in other moral objections against inflicting it: perhaps X is liable to be harmed, but you promised his brother not to harm him.

A lesser evil obligation is simply one additional way in which harm can figure in a decisive moral reason against action. If we accept that even harm inflicted on the liable is an impersonal moral disvalue, and if such harm can be aggregated for the purposes of lesser evil reasoning, then it must be possible for this aggregated impersonal harm to generate a decisive reason against the harm-producing action. This is entirely compatible with the supposition that the person harmed lacks a right against being so harmed (i.e., is liable to it). This is not a case of a justified harm somehow defeating its own justification. As we saw above, lesser evil justifications and obligations leave underlying rights undisturbed. A lesser evil obligation subsumes the liability to harm, but it does not "defeat" it. That is why, as I argued above, a liable person who is spared harm because some other agent acted out of a lesser evil obligation owes that party a debt of gratitude.

---

17. Ibid., 11 (italics in the original).

II. Alternative Solutions

There are a number of alternative solutions to the number of aggressors problem. Unfortunately, they suffer from significant problems. Jeff McMahan has in previous work suggested that the problem can be explained by what he calls the "variable contribution explanation."[18] Consider a large number of aggressors engaged in a coordinated unjust attack against a victim. If each makes an equal or comparable contribution, then the proportion of the total harm that is attributable to each decreases as the number of collaborators increases. At some point, the harm attributable to each aggressor will drop below the level at which killing is narrowly proportionate. At this point none of the multiple aggressors is liable to be killed and the defensive act is therefore impermissible.

But in addition to a number of weaknesses noted by McMahan himself, the variable contribution account gets many standard cases wrong. Suppose that the threshold of unjust harm required to make killing in defense narrowly proportionate is the loss of a limb (an aggressor who threatens to inflict a harm below this level would not be liable to be killed). Suppose now that two culpable assailants make a concurrent and coordinated attack on the limb of a victim. If the variable contribution account were correct, then the unjust harm attributable to each assailant is half the threshold level required to make defensive killing proportionate, and therefore killing them would be impermissible. Yet it seems clearly permissible to kill two assailants who will together inflict a threshold unjust harm for defensive killing. As we have already seen above, this seems true even if two (or more) assailants are minimally responsible for the infliction of the threshold harm.

The variable contribution account gets cases like this wrong, because it presupposes an untenable view of moral attribution of harm. It treats the attribution of harm like the sharing of a pie, such that if one party has more, then some other party necessarily has less. But the moral attribution of harm is in fact elastic and variable, so that it is possible for a given harm to be fully attributable in a moral sense to multiple agents simultaneously. This is particularly true when each of a number of agents intends the unjust harm that they collectively inflict. This elastic view of the moral attribution of harm is required, not only to make sense of cases where multiple aggressors can be liable to be killed for the infliction of a threshold unjust harm, but also to make sense of the law and morality of complicity and conspiracy offenses.

---

18. Jeff McMahan, "What Rights May Be Defended by Means of War?" in *The Morality of Defensive War*, ed. Cecile Fabre and Seth Lazar (Oxford: Oxford University Press, 2014), 115–59, 37–138.

In this volume McMahan introduces a tentative alternative solution to the numbers problem. He suggests that in addition to the "agential conditions of liability" (responsibility for an unjust harm) and the "circumstantial conditions of liability" (necessity and wide and narrow proportionality) there is also a condition of "proportionality in the aggregate" for justified defensive action.[19] Suppose that it would be necessary to kill one thousand minimally responsible aggressors in order to save one innocent victim, and we can determine intuitively that this would be disproportionate in the aggregate. If we assume compliance with the demands of morality, then all one thousand minimally responsible aggressors will not in fact be killed. But, in that case, killing any lesser number of aggressors would be ineffective, and hence disproportionate in the narrow sense. Therefore none of the one thousand minimally responsible aggressors is liable to be killed.

One difficulty is that what wants explaining is why it can be impermissible to kill a large numbers of aggressors when each aggressor would be clearly liable were the numbers smaller. But in this argument the explanandum is the first premise of the explanans.

Moreover, how are we to understand this concept of "proportionality in the aggregate," and why is it a constraint on permissible defensive action? McMahan tells us that we can assess the condition intuitively "just from facts about the harm that would be caused and prevented, the varying degrees of responsibility of the different possible victims, and the number of people who would be killed in each option."[20] Like wide proportionality it aggregates harm across multiple agents, and like narrow proportionality it takes into account the responsibility of those who would be harmed.

Described like this, the condition sounds very much like the concept of a lesser evil obligation, only dislocated from its theoretical and explanatory context in the tradition of lesser evil reasoning. As I argued above, once we understand how lesser evil reasoning can create an obligation to abstain from harmful acts that we have a liberty right to perform, we have a full solution to the numbers problem without the requirement to demonstrate a lack of liability on the part of aggressors. This solution is considerably simpler than McMahan's "proportionality in the aggregate" proposal, and accords better with our pre-theoretical intuitions that the liability of individuals to harm ought not to be affected by the number of aggressors.

---

19. Jeff McMahan, "Liability, Proportionality, and the Number of Aggressors," in this volume, 15–16.

20. Ibid., 16.

To be fair, McMahan makes clear that this is a tentative proposal that requires further work and elaboration. It is possible that the notion of proportionality in the aggregate can be given a firm theoretical foundation and be shown to perform important work that the notion of a lesser evil obligation cannot perform. However, in its present form it does not.

Conclusion

Practical ethics has been very substantially enhanced in recent years by our increasingly sophisticated understanding of the relationship between rights and lesser evil justifications. It seems likely that comparable rewards will result from further investigation of the counterpart to the lesser evil justification: the lesser evil obligation. Lesser evil justifications justify an agent in transgressing some person's rights. Lesser evil obligations obligate a right bearer not to exercise his own rights. A right that is transgressed with a lesser evil justification has been infringed and generates a residual obligation to compensate. A right that is not exercised because of a lesser evil obligation has been subsumed and generates a residual obligation of gratitude. One immediate dividend of the theory of lesser evil obligation is to provide a simple and intuitive solution to the number of aggressors problem. I am confident that further work and development will reveal many more.

3 HUMAN RIGHTS, PROPORTIONALITY, AND THE LIVES OF SOLDIERS

Larry May

Introduction

In this essay I will explore the recent legal and moral controversy about a new paradigm in both *jus in bello* and *jus ad bellum* that argues that the laws and rules of war should change to be more in line with a human rights perspective. According to some theorists and courts, necessity and proportionality considerations dictate that soldiers not be treated as cannon fodder, contrary to a long history of thinking about war and armed conflict. On the human rights model, those initiating war, and those prosecuting a war, must take account of the casualties of combatants as well as civilians, because both of these people have rights. Soldiers as well as civilians have human rights and hence proportionality should reflect this fact. In particular, the right to life is non-derogable (inviolable and not subject to change by treaty) and the pinnacle of the human rights domain.

In this essay I will explain what proportionality and necessity assessments in war or armed conflict would look like if the human rights perspective were taken more seriously than it has been in the past. In the first section, I explain how human rights law is challenging international humanitarian law today. In the second section, I discuss how taking human rights more seriously would affect current debates in Just War theory. In the third section, I discuss two of the most prominent ways that theorists are pushing back against the human rights approach, the idea that soldiers forfeit their human rights and the idea that humanitarian law should override human rights law, but only in special circumstances (*lex specialis*). In the fourth section I discuss the relationship between necessity and proportionality from the human rights perspective.

I. Humanitarian Law and Human Rights Law

In international humanitarian law, soldiers can be killed and hence do not retain the same rights they had when they were noncombatants, but there are many rights that soldiers retain even on the battlefield. Soldiers retain the right not to be subjected to excessive or superfluous suffering in all circumstances. Soldiers retain the right not to be killed treacherously or perfidiously. If captured, soldiers have many rights as "prisoners of war." Similarly, if they are wounded or otherwise disabled and in the custody of the enemy, soldiers also have many rights insofar as they are "*hors de combat*." The principle that soldiers cannot be treated inhumanely is a crosscutting norm that applies in all types of conflicts to all participants in armed conflicts. One might well ask, then, why have soldiers forfeited their rights to life, but retained their rights not to suffer? This is one of several puzzles that motivates this essay.

Additionally in international humanitarian law soldiers, whose activities have not crossed the armed conflict threshold, retain even the full protection of their right to life. Imagine a group of soldiers who engage in sporadic violence aimed at pressuring their government to give them higher wages and greater health benefits, or even aimed at toppling the government. The government does not have the right to kill these soldiers except perhaps in a situation of emergency where the self-defense of the State is jeopardized. Yet once the soldiers constitute an insurgency that crosses the armed conflict threshold they can be legitimately killed by the security forces of the State. One might here ask how it is that being a soldier, and yet still a human being, has changed when armed conflict is afoot—where the supposedly inviolable right to life is no longer the preeminent norm that they enjoyed just a short while earlier. This is another piece of the landscape of interconnected law and morality I will try to portray and comment upon in this essay.

In international human rights law, in contrast to international humanitarian law, people generally do not forfeit such essential rights as the right to life. Indeed, human rights law stands as a fairly strong contrast to humanitarian law in this respect. The Universal Declaration of Human Rights (UDHR), in Article 2, says that "everyone has the right to life, liberty and security of person." The International Covenant on Civil and Political Rights (ICCPR) seeking to enforce the UDHR's rights, in Article 6.1 says, "Every human being has the inherent right to life. This right shall be protected by law. No one shall be arbitrarily deprived of his life." From the human rights perspective, war is not generally regarded as a situation where non-arbitrary deprivations of the right to life occur. In times of emergency that "threaten the life of the nation," where the very essence of the State is jeopardized, there can be derogation of some of the rights guaranteed by the Convention, although not the right to life.[1]

The key is to delimit the domain of what counts as arbitrary deprivation of the right to life, or rather to understand what counts as the non-arbitrary deprivation of the right to life. This is especially important in determining how international criminal law will treat the killing of soldiers in various situations that are likely to arise increasingly in the new forms of asymmetric warfare that are emerging in the world today. In what follows in this section I will discuss the recent trend to incorporate human rights considerations more and more into areas, such as armed conflict, that used to be the exclusive purview of international humanitarian law.

Let us start by considering a recent case from the Grand Chamber of the European Court of Human Rights (ECHR). In the *Case of Al-Skeini and Others v. The United Kingdom*,[2] decided on July 7, 2011, the ECHR held that Article 2 of the Human Rights Act applied to States whose agents were acting outside the territorial boundaries of that State. In particular, the court held that the United Kingdom could be held liable for the arbitrary killing by its soldiers of civilians in Iraq. Armed conflict has historically been governed by humanitarian law, which also recognizes prohibitions on arbitrary killing of civilians. What is noteworthy is that in *Al-Skeini*, the application was made in terms of violations of human rights law applicable during the period of occupation following the Iraq War, and the Court allowed such an application, ultimately deciding in favor of the victims' families.[3]

In *Al-Skeini*, the ECHR relied in substantial part on the International Court of Justice (ICJ) Advisory Opinion, *Legal Consequences of the Construction of a Wall in the Occupied Palestinian Territory* (July 9, 2004), where it was held that both international humanitarian law and human rights law applied in cases of armed conflict. In that case, the ICJ rejected Israel's claim that "humanitarian law is the protection granted to conflict situations such as the one in the West Bank and Gaza Strip, whereas human rights treaties were intended for the protection of citizens from their own government in times of peace" (par. 90). Human rights treaties do allow for derogation "in times of public emergency which threaten the life of the nation and the existence of which is officially proclaimed." But, as

---

1. See Emily Crawford, *The Treatment of Combatants and Insurgents Under the Law of Armed Conflict* (Oxford: Oxford University Press, 2010), 132–33.

2. Case of *Al-Skeini and Others v United Kingdom*, ECHR (Grand Chamber), Application no. 55721/07, July 7, 2011.

3. Occupations are normally the subject of international humanitarian law, not human rights law.

noted above, such derogation is only allowed "to the extent strictly required by the exigencies of the situation" (par. 90).

International humanitarian law, in contrast to human rights law, has largely followed the Just War tradition in regarding some wars as just even though war involves the intentional killing of humans. As long as the cause is just (normally these days understood as self-defense and, controversially, some cases of defense of innocent others) and the war is a last resort as well as proportional, then war is recognized as a legally just war. So even though war often involves a massive killing of combatants and arguably the infringement of their rights to life, according to international humanitarian law, some wars are seen as justifiable today. And *jus in bello* proportionality is not seen as concerned with the lives of enemy soldiers in armed conflict, but only with the incidental killing of civilians.

Judith Gardam captures the current state of international humanitarian law on combatants when she says:

> Combatants are legitimate targets in armed conflict, whereas civilians are not. For this reason, the level of combatant casualties never became an issue in IHL [International Humanitarian Law] and remains a matter for the probability equation in the *jus ad bellum*. In IHL, it is the prohibition of means and methods of warfare that are of a nature to cause superfluous injury or unnecessary suffering that today purports to limit the impact of armed conflict on combatants.[4]

To put the point somewhat differently, international humanitarian law today does not count the loss of lives of soldiers in *jus in bello* proportionality calculations. Instead, *jus in bello* proportionality only concerns whether the soldiers are treated cruelly in the sense that they experience unnecessary or superfluous suffering. International humanitarian law generally starts from the position that some wars can be justified even though there is lots of killing of combatants, but that it is important to diminish the level of suffering of soldiers and to curtail attacks on civilians. International human rights law starts from a very different assumption, namely that all people have the inviolable right to life.

In an important book, *The Humanization of International Law*, Theodor Meron summarized and defended the myriad ways that human rights law has intruded into international law generally. Meron recognizes the primary problem I want to highlight in this essay when he notes:

---

4. Judith Gardam, *Necessity, Proportionality and the Use of Force by States* (Cambridge: Cambridge University Press, 2004), 14.

To speak of the humanization of humanitarian law or the law of war is thus in many ways a contradiction in terms. Consider, for example, the law of war term "unnecessary suffering." To genuinely humanize humanitarian law, it would be necessary to put an end to all kinds of armed conflict. But wars have been part of the human condition since the struggle between Cain and Abel, and regrettably they are likely to remain so.[5]

Notice here that Meron forthrightly recognizes the radical potential of human rights law to change the very nature of the laws of war. Concerning proportionality, Meron sees the need for radical change if human rights are taken seriously, since "classical international law allowed a State which had a just cause for war to apply the maximum degree of force and destruction to bring about a speedy victory."[6] This understanding comports with the deepest desires of the men and women who must carry on the conflict because it is they who bear its costs most directly and they who most earnestly desire a return to a sustainable peace.

Meron nonetheless states that "human rights norms have infiltrated the law of war to a considerable extent."[7] He traces this influence back to the natural law tradition, but its clearest modern influence is in the Martens Clause of the Hague Conventions. Meron says that the Martens Clause epitomizes the humanizing aspect of the law of war.[8] The Martens Clause appeared in the Preamble to the 1899 Hague Regulations and would be substantially replicated in other treaties. The Martens Clause states:

> Until a more complete code of the laws of war is issued, the High Contracting Parties think it right to declare that in cases not included in the Regulations adopted by them, populations and belligerents remain under the protection and empire of the principles of international law, as they result from the usages established between civilized nations, from the laws of humanity and the requirements of the public conscience.

The Martens Clause is often cited today by legal theorists who support the intrusion of human rights norms into international humanitarian law.

---

5. Theodor Meron, *The Humanization of International Law* (Leiden: Martinus Nijhoff, 2006), 9.

6. Ibid., 61.

7. Ibid., 6.

8. Ibid., 5.

In particular, the reference to "the laws of humanity and the requirements of public conscience" are seen as principles of general international law that, in the words of a member of the International Court of Justice, may change as "the outlook and tolerance level of the international community" change.[9] It does seem today as if the tolerance for war is changing in international legal discussions, where the ascendency of human rights will mean that fewer and fewer wars are considered to be legally justified. But Meron ends this discussion by saying that while the Martens Clause has had far-reaching effect he is "far less confident, however, that the Martens Clause has had any influence on the battlefield."[10]

In the 1970 Report of the Secretary-General on Respect for Human Rights in Armed Conflict, there was a very strong statement about the intended effect of having the General Assembly examine armed conflicts in human rights terms: "It is an endeavor to provide a greater degree of protection for the integrity, welfare and dignity of those who are directly affected by military operations pending the earliest possible resolution of such conflicts."[11] Yet the United Nations' examination on the effects of human rights in battlefield situations was mainly restricted to the protection of civilian lives, even though the lives of soldiers are certainly those that are most directly affected by military operations. Forty years after the Secretary-General's report, things seem to be changing in international law. Let us next examine similar changes in Just War theory.

II. Just War Theory and Human Rights

Contemporary Just War theory of the version that Michael Walzer has elaborated is supposed to be premised in a deep concern for human rights. Walzer begins his book, *Just and Unjust Wars*, by proclaiming that "the morality we shall expound is in its philosophical form a doctrine of human rights."[12] Walzer maintains this view contrary to what he regards as the dominant strain of realism in international relations theory. In this sense, Walzer seeks to humanize the discussion of war in a similar way to the way scholars such as Theodor Meron have recently tried to humanize discussion of war in international law. Yet when he comes to

---

9. Ibid., 20, quoting the ICJ's Advisory Opinion on Nuclear Weapons, dissenting opinion of Shahabuddeen.

10. Ibid., 28.

11. Respect for Human Rights in Armed Conflict. Report of the Secretary-General, A/8052, par. 13 (1970).

12. Michael Walzer, *Just and Unjust Wars* (New York: Basic Books, 1977), xxii.

discussions of the lives of soldiers, Walzer defends the "central principle that soldiers have an equal right to kill."[13]

Walzer defends what he calls the moral equality of soldiers: combatants have an equal right to kill and are themselves subject to be rightfully killed as well. The rationale offered by Walzer seems to be mainly a prudential one, although he calls it moral, namely that without the recognition of such an equality of soldiers "war as a rule-governed activity would disappear."[14] For suffering to be minimized during war we must recognize the legitimacy of war itself, most especially the killing of one soldier by another. Walzer's argument explicitly parallels the argument concerning traditional *jus in bello* legal reasoning in international humanitarian law, not what one might have expected, namely the analysis provided in international human rights law.

In Walzer's view, war can be defended in terms of the collective rights of people not to be forcibly subjugated. States have a right to go to war in order to defend sovereignty, just as individual people have an inherent right to engage in self-defensive killing. What Walzer calls the analogical argument explains why States have a right to engage in war. Such a right is significant for thinking that soldiers may be killed in wars. And the main reason why soldiers can be legitimately killed is that they have forfeited their rights:

> The theoretical problem is not to describe how immunity is gained but how it is lost. We are all immune to start with, our right not to be attacked is a feature of normal human relationships. This right is lost by those who bear arms "effectively" because they pose a danger to other people. It is retained by those who do not bear arms at all.[15]

All people start with the human right not to be attacked or killed, but then what they choose to do can restrict or forfeit those rights in this view.

Walzer's view is premised in the idea that all soldiers have made themselves into the kind of dangerous people that can be killed without major worry about proportionality.

> He can be personally attacked only because he is already a fighter. He has been made into a dangerous man, and though his options may have been few, it is nevertheless accurate to say that he has allowed himself to be made

---

13. Ibid., 41.

14. Ibid.

15. Ibid., 145 note.

into a dangerous man. For that reason he finds himself endangered...the risks can be raised to their highest pitch without violating his rights.[16]

In Walzer's view, soldiers forfeit their rights because of their "warlike activities."[17]

Walzer has said that proportionality will hardly ever come into effect because of the problem of incommensurability and because the threshold is so high that most military acts would satisfy it in any event.[18] Proportionality considerations are so hard to figure out that they come into play only in the most extreme and most clear-cut cases. Such considerations do not ever concern the calculation of the lives or rights of soldiers since those soldiers, in Walzer's view, have forfeited their human rights.

Another, more recent, revisionist version of Just War theory, supported by Jeff McMahan,[19] criticizes Walzer for failing to recognize that *only* those who fight in an unjust war have forfeited their rights and are hence liable to be attacked and killed. Those who fight in a just war retain their rights and cannot be killed except in extreme circumstances. In this respect, as we will see, this contemporary school of Just War theory makes a radical departure from Walzer in that some soldiers retain the full range of their human rights, but only those who fight on one side, the just side, of a war.

McMahan claims to be driven by a concern for human rights even though he has also argued that so-called aggressive, or unjust, soldiers are liable to be killed in large numbers.[20] Here is how McMahan characterizes his view:

> For a person to cease to be innocent in war, all that is necessary is the for-feiture of the right not to be attacked *for certain reasons*, by certain per-sons, in certain conditions. There is no loss of rights in general, nor even any loss of the right against attack, understood as the right that holds

---

16. Ibid., 145.

17. Ibid.

18. Ibid., 129.

19. Jeff McMahan, *Killing in War* (Oxford: Oxford University Press, 2009).

20. In his most recent writing on this topic, "Liability, Proportionality, and the Number of Aggressors," in this volume, McMahan seems to distance himself from the view that any number of liable combatants can be killed. He distinguishes the combatant who is fully respon-sible from the combatant who is minimally responsible for a threatened harm. McMahan now seems to think that the latter group of soldiers cannot be killed in large numbers in most cases. Yet he still thinks that large numbers of the former group (fully responsible combatants) can be killed in large numbers. In my view, McMahan thus still fails to take the human rights of com-batants as seriously as he should.

against all agents at all times. The right against attack is instead forfeited only in relation to certain persons acting for certain reasons in a particular context.[21]

This restricted view of rights forfeiture is meant to apply to those who fight in an unjust war, and is an objective determination—either it is true that one has forfeited one's rights by fighting in a war that is objectively unjust, or not. Since human rights are also supposed to be matters of objective morality, those who fight in an unjust war have objectively forfeited their rights whether they realize it or not. Human rights obtain objectively, and, in McMahan's view, they can be objectively forfeited, although in a restrictive way, as well.

Concerning proportionality, McMahan has argued that there are two types, narrow and wide, but that neither places a serious limitation on what just combatants are entitled to do to unjust combatants during war. For McMahan "proportionality is a constraint on action that causes harm. In most cases, for an act that causes harm to be justified, it must be instrumental to the achievement of some valuable goal against which the harm can be weighed and assessed."[22]

Narrow proportionality involves harms inflicted "on those who were potentially liable to lesser harms." Wide proportionality involves harms inflicted "on those who were not liable to any harm at all."[23] Harms inflicted in the narrow sense are normally intentional, whereas harms inflicted in the wide sense are normally unintentional. McMahan claims that only wide proportionality is relevant to wartime situations. In this McMahan partially follows the traditional international humanitarian law model of focusing proportionality only on collateral killings of civilians, not on the loss of lives of soldiers, at least if we are thinking of the lives of those who fight on the unjust side of a war.

McMahan puts his finger on one of the main reasons for the traditional restriction of *jus in bello* proportionality to wide, that is, unintentional, harm to those who are not at all liable to be harmed, that is, to innocent civilians:

Harms inflicted on those who are liable to suffer them have traditionally been assumed to have no role in determining proportionality. Otherwise the resort to war might be ruled out if, for example, the number of expected killings of enemy combatants would exceed the number of people

---

21. McMahan, *Killing in War*, 10.

22. Ibid., 19.

23. Ibid., 21.

on one's own side whose lives the war could be expected to save—an implication that to my knowledge no just war theorist has been willing to embrace.[24]

He puts the point simply and clearly when he says: "Acts of war by unjust combatants are in practice very unlikely ever to be proportionate in the wide sense."[25] So, at least in this sense, McMahan seems to go quite a ways toward taking the human rights of soldiers seriously. But again, notice that this is only true of the human rights of what he calls "just combatants," not of "unjust combatants." Unjust combatants have forfeited their rights, even if on his view this is not a general but a highly contextualized and conditional forfeiture.

In my view, Just War theory today does not take the individual rights of all soldiers seriously, at least in part because these views continue to think of soldiers as a class rather than as individuals. Walzer is quite explicit about this when he says that war is an enterprise of a "class" not of an individual.[26] McMahan, as in all such things, is much more subtle. Indeed, McMahan has rather harsh things to say about collectivist approaches to the morality of war.[27] Yet his view seems to treat soldiers in terms of whether they are just or unjust combatants, thereby treating them primarily based on what their States have done. Seemingly in a similar vein, Brian Orend has said that if the enemy State lacks a just cause then everything the enemy soldier does is tainted and seemingly disproportionate.[28] Let us now examine how legal and moral theorists have sought to limit the reach of human rights norms in wartime situations.

III. *Lex Specialis* and Rights Forfeitures

There are various responses that have been given by theorists who want to keep human rights law and morality from encroaching too far into traditional humanitarian law and Just War domains. Legal theorists argue that the domain of humanitarian law is *lex specialis*. Moral and political theorists argue that when one person unjustly threatens the life of another person the first person has forfeited

---

24. Ibid., 19.

25. Ibid., 27.

26. Walzer, *Just and Unjust Wars*, 144.

27. See McMahan, *Killing in War*, 209.

28. Brian Orend, "Jus Post Bellum: A Just War Theory Perspective," in *Jus Post Bellum: Towards a Law of Transition from Conflict to Peace*, ed. Carsten Stahn and Jenn Kleffner (The Hague: T. M. C. Asher Press, 2008), 38.

his or her rights and can be attacked or killed without violating human rights. I will take up these arguments in more detail now.

The *lex specialis* argument has been restated in several recent decisions of the ICJ. In the *Nuclear Weapons* Advisory Opinion, the ICJ said:

> In principle, the right not arbitrarily to be deprived of one's life applies also in hostilities. The test of what is an arbitrary deprivation of life, however, then falls to be determined by the applicable *lex specialis*, namely the law applicable in armed conflict which is designed to regulate the conduct of hostilities. Thus whether a particular loss of life, through the use of a certain weapon in warfare, is to be considered an arbitrary deprivation of life contrary to Article 6 of the Covenant [International Covenant on Civil and Political Rights], can only be decided by reference to the law applicable in armed conflict and not deduced from the terms of the Covenant itself.[29]

Here, then, is the expression of the *lex specialis* doctrine thought to save humanitarian law from being completely swamped by human rights law.

The idea is that human rights law creates a kind of prima facie case for thinking that certain behavior, especially deprivation of the right to life, is to be proscribed. But the all things considered case is determined only after looking at the legal requirements that may be applicable to the specific kind of case in question. If the case falls directly under a specific provision of humanitarian law, then even though human rights may be infringed, this can be justified by reference to the laws of war.

One recent commentary on this decision and the general doctrine of *lex specialis*, by Marko Milanovic, has raised a skeptical question:

> If human rights accrue to human beings solely by virtue of their humanity, why should these rights evaporate merely because two states, or a state and a non-state actor, have engaged in armed conflict? More limited these rights may be, but they cannot be completely extinguished or displaced if their basic universality premise, that they are immanent in the human dignity of every individual, is accepted.[30]

---

29. International Court of Justice, *Legality of the Threat or Use of Nuclear Weapons*, Advisory Opinion of July 8, 1996, ICJ Reports (1996): 226, par. 25.

30. Marko Milanovic, "Norm Conflicts, International Humanitarian Law, and Human Rights," in *International Humanitarian Law and International Human Rights Law*, ed. Orna Ban-Naftali (Oxford: Oxford University Press, 2011), 95–125, at 101.

Notice, though, that Milanovic allows that human rights can be limited or restricted during war, but not that they can be extinguished, which is the position I support as well.

The *lex specialis* doctrine cannot carve out an area of human rights law that makes these rights never applicable to armed conflict and still allow human rights to have universal scope. So the main question then becomes how human rights can legitimately be restricted in certain situations in war or emergencies. If the entirety of human rights law is suspendable on *lex specialis* grounds then there is a danger of undermining all human rights. So some kind of restriction on humanitarian law considerations needs to be drawn so that the entirety of the doctrine of human rights, or what is of central importance to it, is still operable for some wartime situations and other emergencies where clearly the individuals who are involved are still human.

At the moment, international law is definitely unsettled about how precisely the doctrine of *lex specialis* is to limit human rights law in armed conflict situations. On most views, human rights remain fully in force during armed conflict, but the source of protections is seen as being embedded in the prevailing *jus in bello* framework. This view is largely satisfactory, but cannot account for the recurring collision between the core rights to life and liberty.

The conservative view is that human rights law only comes into effect when there are no rules of humanitarian law that could be applicable to a given situation. The emerging more liberal view is that only when a rule of humanitarian law is clearly and unequivocally applicable are human rights considerations completely inapplicable in battlefield situations. The newer, more liberal, view is the one that seems to me to be gaining ground and provides a serious challenge to the old regime where soldiers are simply "free targets."

I now turn to the forfeiture argument advanced by most Just War theorists to try to blunt the effects of human rights on *jus in bello* considerations. The revisionist Just War theorists maintain that when a State is an aggressor its soldiers have forfeited their right not to be killed. It is also often said that when a State or a soldier is acting in self-defense many more action-options are justifiable than otherwise. And such a position on self-defense calls into question the concern for the lives of enemy soldiers that I argued needs to be part of the proportionality assessment in human rights terms. In the remainder of this section I will address the way self-defense is often understood in philosophical debates about killing in war.

Let us start by making an assumption drawn from criminal law and human rights law, namely that if a person is attacked that person is not justified in using whatever force he or she chooses. Self-defense does not automatically grant the one attacked the right to kill. Instead, the one attacked only has the right to do what is necessary to stop the attack. Rather than discuss this in terms of the right to kill, human rights law seems to call for a change in orientation that would instead posit the right to *disable* the attacker, rather than the right to kill the attacker. The attacker has made himself or herself liable to be disabled, not to be killed. It may turn out that the only way to disable the attacker before the attacker kills is to kill the attacker. But it is misleading to discuss this case by saying that the attacker has made himself or herself liable to be killed since this is only one of several ways that the attacker can be disabled.

The one who is the attacker should be granted fewer options than the one attacked, and in this sense there is a prima facie preference for the one attacked vis-à-vis the one doing the attacking. But, from a human rights approach, it is a mistake to think that the attacker has forfeited his or her right to life, or right not to be killed, even temporarily. It would be unnecessary and disproportionate for the one attacked to use lethal force when non-lethal force will fend off the attack. But beyond this clear line other choices are often not clear-cut.

Joel Feinberg was right to argue that certain basic rights are mandatory in the sense that they cannot be alienated by waiver. And his position on forfeiture of rights also seems to have at least initial appeal, namely, that even the most basic rights can be forfeited at least temporarily due to one's wrongful or negligent behavior. Rejecting the idea that one cannot waive the right not to be killed does not mean that one must also reject the idea that one cannot forfeit this right.[31] What is most important here is over what period of time one forfeits one's right to life. If it is forfeited henceforth, then it is hard not to infer that it is also true that henceforth the person who has forfeited the right to life is also not truly a human any more.

The most defensible version of the rights-forfeiture view in Just War theory is that basic rights, such as the right not to be killed, can be forfeited only for a certain period of time, not permanently, as McMahan has contended. In McMahan's view the unjust combatant forfeits his or her right not to be killed for as long as he or she participates in an unjust war. And the forfeiture is only to those who fight in the just war. But why is the forfeiture to everyone else on the other side of the war? It seems to me that forfeiture should only occur to those whom one is wronging at the moment. The wrong of participating in an unjust war is not exactly parallel to participating in an attack on another person. Not everyone on the other side has their lives threatened in the same way as in the two-person case of someone who must defend herself in a dark alley against an unknown assailant.

In the two-person case, the one who attacks with lethal force forfeits certain rights by her or his wrongdoing. But from a restrained view provided by human

---

31. See Joel Feinberg, "Voluntary Euthanasia and the Inalienable Right to Life," *The Tanner Lectures on Human Values* (1977): 223–56.

rights considerations, even in this case there is no automatic forfeiture of the right to life of the attacker. Vis-à-vis the one who is attacked, the attacker loses whatever rights would have otherwise prevented the one attacked from successfully and rightfully thwarting the attack. Things get even more difficult in the case of a soldier who participates in an unjust war. Here that soldier forfeits, if he or she forfeits at all, whatever rights would normally stand in the way of the soldiers on the just side of the war from preserving their lives and protecting their fellow citizens.

Soldiers fighting in an unjust war are jeopardizing the self-defense of enemy soldiers in quite variable ways over the course of participating in war. They are creating risks for their enemies, but, as in the two-person case, in many situations what is needed to nullify the risk does not necessarily involve lethal action. Yet if soldiers can only be killed when they are highly dangerous or when killing them is necessary for defense of others, those who attack them take a risk in that the soldiers attacked may not at any given moment have forfeited their rights not to be killed.[32] In any event, the key is the principle of necessity, along with related issues concerning the principle of proportionality, a topic to which I turn in detail in the next section.

In general, the terminology of forfeiture of rights seems inapt. There is a great risk that such talk will make us think that the so-called unjust combatant is deprived of his or her most basic rights. Yet this is not true since the loss of rights only in certain limited contexts and only vis-à-vis a very restricted set of people is not the sort of deprivation of rights that opens up a class of people to anything like a general liability to be killed or harmed. From a human rights perspective, we should start from the position that all lives are to be treated the same. And I definitely do not think that the fact of very limited forfeiture of rights means that the human rights of enemy soldiers can be dismissed or severely devalued in proportionality assessments. I next look at the relation between proportionality and necessity against this human rights background.

IV. Necessity's Relation to Proportionality

Necessity seen through the prism of human rights sets a limit for all proportionality assessments.[33] Lethal force can only be justified to begin with if it is the required strategy (and in this sense necessary) to achieve a goal that is a significant one. In my view, if this necessity threshold is not crossed, then it makes no sense

---

32. In some views, the goals of the State and the goals of the soldiers of that State are to be treated as the same. I reject this view. See my *Contingent Pacifism: Revisiting Just War Theory* (Cambridge: Cambridge University Press, 2015).

33. See Jens Ohlin and Larry May, *Necessity in International Law* (New York: Oxford University Press, 2016).

to discuss whether the response is proportionate or not.[34] There is a double meaning for "necessity": the strategy must be needed to accomplish a specific military objective, and this objective must itself be needed for some larger goal, normally winning the war. If human rights law is applicable, that larger goal will presumably be drawn in terms of the preservation of human rights. It might be thought that lethal force can be used when it is the least costly way to achieve a militarily necessary goal. But from a human rights perspective, it is not possible to justify lethal force merely by showing that it is least costly compared to all alternatives.

It is sometimes thought that as long as killing soldiers is militarily necessary then it can be justified; after all, that is what war involves. But, again from a human rights perspective, war is not about killing soldiers; rather war is about achieving reasonable objectives through the least objectionable (again, in terms of human rights) use of force. Wars should be aimed at incapacitating enemy soldiers, but there is a range of tactics that can incapacitate, including in many cases the capture rather than the killing of enemy soldiers. When incapacitation of the enemy is seen as the key to legitimate military objectives, the use of lethal force even against other enemy soldiers must itself be justified as necessary. Full implementation of a human rights–based model during armed conflict would necessitate a shifting of burdens onto the war-fighter beyond those already found in the laws and customs of war. And proportionality assessments would therefore also be drawn in terms that take account of possible loss of soldiers' lives, even when those soldiers are enemies who are on the unjust side of a war.

In Part IX of its Interpretive Guidance on the Notion of Direct Participation in Hostilities under International Humanitarian Law, The International Committee of the Red Cross (ICRC) inserted an entire section addressing restraints on the lawful use of lethal force during armed conflicts. This section postulated that the "kind and degree of force which is permissible against persons not entitled to protection against direct attack must not exceed what is actually necessary to accomplish a legitimate military purpose in the prevailing circumstances."[35] This is the narrowest reading of "necessity," that is, "necessity" is a literal term drawn in the narrowest tactical terms.

The ICRC Interpretive Guidance relied on its assertion of moral authority (*lex ferenda*) and indirect application of the protections that are universally accepted as applying to persons who are not clearly combatants, in particular employing an expansive notion of the principle of necessity in the way I have just indicated:

---

34. See Michael Newton and Larry May, *Proportionality in International Law* (New York: Oxford University Press, 2014), chapter 5.

35. ICRC, *Interpretive Guidance on the Notion of Direct Participation in Hostilities under International Humanitarian Law*, 77.

It would defy basic notions of humanity to kill an adversary or to refrain from giving him or her an opportunity to surrender where there manifestly is no necessity for the use of lethal force. In such a situation, the principles of military necessity and of humanity play an important role in determining the kind and degree of permissible force against legitimate military targets.[36]

The ICRC also cited Jean Pictet for the idea that "if we can put a soldier out of action by capturing him we should not wound him, if we can obtain the same result by wounding him, we must not kill him, if there are two means to achieve the same military advantage we must choose the one which causes the lesser evil."[37]

To see why some proponents would maintain that even so-called unjust combatants should not be killed if it is possible to capture them instead with little cost, consider the example of so-called Stand-Your-Ground laws that are currently the focus of intense public debate in the United States. Even if an aggressor is wrongful, considering the aggressor as a person with rights rather than as someone primarily defined by his or her status (as an "aggressor") makes a huge difference. That one does not want to retreat, and that one has in some sense the right not to retreat, is not dispositive of the issue. One does not respect the person who is the aggressor as a bearer of rights by allowing such considerations to trump the rights of even a person who is an aggressor. And when we move to considerations of war, there seems to be even less reason for saying that anything other than necessity can override the rights of enemy soldiers, even those on the unjust side of a war.

War or armed conflict cannot be initiated or conducted unless it satisfies the necessity condition. It is relatively uncontroversial that the initiation of war (*jus ad bellum*) can only be justified if it is a last resort, that is, where all other strategies have been attempted or are patently unlikely to succeed at accomplishing a justified aim. According to many theorists the only aim that is justified if war or armed conflict is to be employed is self-defense. Today, as well as historically, some have argued that defense of innocent others is also a "just cause" to initiate war.[38] Suffice it here to say that even in cases of self-defense the strategy of using lethal force can only be justified if it is the last resort when the human rights domain is dominant.

---

36. Ibid., 82.

37. Ibid.

38. See Augustine, *The City of God*, trans. Henry Bettenson (New York: Penguin Books), (c. 420), chapter 14, 874; Ferdinand Teson, *Humanitarian Intervention*, 3rd rev. ed. (Leiden: Martinus Nijhoff, 2005). Also see Larry May, *Aggression and Crimes Against Peace* (Cambridge: Cambridge University Press, 2008) for a different view.

The *jus in bello* condition of necessity has a strong affinity with this last resort principle in *jus ad bellum* considerations. Necessity establishes a threshold that must be crossed first in order for the use of lethal force to be justified. Only then does proportionality enter the picture. Last resort and self-defense play important roles in how to understand necessity in a *jus in bello* context, just as is true in *jus ad bellum*. We can think of military necessity at both the initiation of a war and also at the stage where war is conducted and intermediate military goals are set. For these intermediate goals, such as clearing an area of enemy soldiers, necessity in its strictest sense requires that all other non-lethal avenues be exhausted, or shown to be clearly ineffective. From a human rights perspective, it is not sufficient that the soldiers to be attacked are enemies, or even unjust combatants. To be justified in attacking these soldiers with lethal force requires that the necessity threshold be crossed, that is, the action is "forced" upon the participant (to echo the verb used in Italian domestic law). This means that the dual aspects of necessity must be met: that the goal cannot be achieved by any other means, and that the goal itself is necessary for achieving the wider goal of winning the war.

However, when we think of these goals in human rights terms it becomes easier to see whether proportionality is met. In the *jus ad bellum* context, self-defense of a population against an aggressor can be understood rather straightforwardly. But what of the *jus in bello*? Here the military goals all have something to do with facilitating the larger goals of the war. Some of these goals are intermediate in that they are stages in the overall *jus ad bellum* plan, that is, necessary to eliminate the ongoing threat posed by the enemy. And some of the military goals are merely ones that turn out to be necessary for achieving the *jus ad bellum* plan, such as not losing too many soldiers so that there are still enough to launch a successful offensive, for instance. Here the lives of one's own soldiers are weighed against the lives of enemy soldiers, but there is also put into the balance a portion of the value of the larger war's goal seen in human rights terms.

Winning a war, as well as achieving an intermediate military objective, can often be accomplished by taking enemy soldiers prisoner rather than killing them during battle. So it is often difficult to show that the necessity condition has been met for *jus in bello* killing in a narrow tactical sense based on the ICRC approach. And when we add considerations of proportionality, it is not clear that the use of lethal force to accomplish an intermediate military objective can easily be justified since the force must not only be a last resort but must also be such that, among other things, the loss of life of enemy soldiers that is risked is less than the value of the goal to be accomplished. In human rights terms, then, it may be that what is necessary is still not justified because of its being disproportionate. Achieving a military objective, even one that is necessary for winning a war, may not be proportionate because even as necessary for winning the war, the overall goal of the war may not be significant enough to justify the killing that it will take to accomplish it. So just because achieving a military objective requires lethal use of force, such use of force may still be disproportionate and hence unjustified.

Satisfying a threshold consideration is not sufficient for an all things considered justification, only for prima facie justification. Proportionality is an independent concept from necessity, each is a condition in its own right, and each has a different threshold level. But these concepts are linked in my view in the sense that while proportionality is not exhausted by necessity considerations, proportionality does not even apply to a given situation until the necessity condition has been satisfied.[39] Similarly, once proportionality's threshold is crossed, still other conditions may come into play before all things considered justification can be achieved. What this means in human rights terms is that the lives of everyone affected are assessed at two distinct levels: to see whether all the lives lost were necessary for a given objective, and to see whether the lives lost were proportionate, in the sense of having less value than the value of achieving the military objective.

Lastly, consider *jus ad bellum* justification. Assume for a moment that a just cause to go to war has been established by showing that the war will be one of self-defense. As indicated above, one must then show that the necessity condition has been satisfied, namely that the war (which can involve lethal or non-lethal tactics) is the only way the State can indeed prevent itself from being conquered or destroyed. Many people would think that the justification is now firmly established. But there are proportionality considerations here as well even in cases of self-defense. Only proportionate strategies can be used to defend sovereign interests. Just as in the two-person case, where one is not permitted to kill an opponent if merely wounding him stops his attack, so in war or armed conflict in most cases one should not obliterate one's enemy when merely capturing some of its troops will accomplish the military mission. Indeed, this is the conceptual basis for the historically inarguable war crime of "declaring that no quarter will be given" (i.e., no prisoners taken alive).[40] At a minimum, one cannot simply discount the value of human lives irrespective of their role in the conflict. And we should not shy away from admitting that such a view moves us close, perhaps dangerously close, to what some of us have recently called contingent pacifism.[41] This in my view is how human rights concerns should affect both *jus ad bellum* and *jus in bello* considerations.[42]

---

39. See my unpublished essay, "Humanity, Necessity, and the Rights of Soldiers," winner of the 2015 Frank Chapman Sharp Prize of the American Philosophical Association.

40. Rome Statute Article 8(2)(b)(xii).

41. See Larry May, *Contingent Pacifism: Revisiting Just War Theory* (Cambridge: Cambridge University Press, 2015).

42. This essay, in a somewhat different version, is taken from parts of Michael Newton and Larry May, *Proportionality and International Law* (New York: Oxford University Press, 2014).

RESPONSIBILITY IN WAR

4 RESOLVING THE RESPONSIBILITY DILEMMA

Richard Arneson

Introduction

Recent work on the morality of war has unsettled the accepted version of Just Warfare theory for this domain. This accepted doctrine is a synthesis of traditional Just War theory and twentieth-century international human rights views on wars of aggression and humanitarian intervention.[1] Its key thesis is that independently of the moral merits of the cause for which one fights, a combatant who fights for her country in a declared war is morally entitled to aim fire at enemy combatants, forbidden to aim fire at noncombatants, and required to refrain from military activity that would impose disproportionate unintended side effect damage on noncombatants.

The unsettling move denies that combatants fighting an unjust war have any right to kill enemy combatants opposing their efforts. In just the same way, individuals engaged in armed robbery have no moral right to fight back against others who oppose the robbers' efforts with lethal force (provided that this is necessary to stop the robbers).

The standard-bearer for this revisionary Just War theory is Jeff McMahan.[2] In a nutshell, McMahan's view is that each individual has a moral right not to be killed, but one can partly forfeit this right and render oneself liable to justifiable attack. Someone who is a mere bystander to a conflict is not liable to be killed even if his death would serve our purposes in the conflict. One becomes liable to justifiable lethal attack by being responsible for an injustice or unjust threat that is sufficiently bad that

---

1. The canonical statement of the accepted view is Michael Walzer, *Just and Unjust Wars*, 4th ed. (New York: Basic Books, 2006).

2. Jeff McMahan, "The Ethics of Killing in War," *Ethics* 114 (2004): 693–732; also McMahan, *Killing in War* (Oxford: Oxford University Press, 2009).

killing, if necessary to block the threat or eliminate the injustice, is warranted. To be responsible here does not require being morally culpable or blameworthy. The responsibility that triggers liability obtains when an individual voluntarily does an act that foreseeably causally contributes significantly to the posing of the threat or maintenance of the injustice. Let us say that those who pass this test for liability to permissible attack are *agent responsible* for perpetrating injustice.

I.

The revisionary Just War theory has attracted many criticisms. One concern is that this doctrine has implications for conduct and policy that collide with some of our strongest convictions about morally permissible conduct in war. Seth Lazar has pressed this concern in the form of a dilemma.[3] We intuitively firmly believe that it is acceptable for combatants to shoot at combatants and morally forbidden for combatants to aim their fire at noncombatants. Revisionary Just War theory as presented by McMahan has trouble vindicating this firm conviction. On the one hand, it is not clear that combatants fighting for an unjust cause are plausibly regarded as forfeiting their normal human right not to be killed on McMahan's account. Soldiers in modern wars standardly can appeal to the excuses of duress and ignorance that block any imputation that they are culpable for fighting for an unjust cause if their cause is indeed unjust. If merely voluntarily making choices that foreseeably contribute to an unjust cause suffices to establish liability to be killed, then if this standard allows the killing of many combatants fighting an unjust war, it equally allows the killing of many noncombatants who in one way or another contribute to the same enterprise. On the other hand, if the standard that triggers liability to be killed is raised, so that noncombatants on the side of the country waging an unjust war are deemed morally ineligible targets of those fighting for the just cause, then by the same token that same standard will shelter unjust combatants from liability to morally permissible violence. Either way, revisionary Just War theory cannot deliver the verdict that is the centerpiece of modern moral sensibility regarding war—that it is permissible to aim fire at combatants (when various satisfiable conditions are met) but morally impermissible to aim fire at noncombatants. Lazar concludes that "McMahan must choose between two unpalatable options: either adopt a contingent form of pacifism, or concede that many more noncombatants may be killed than is currently thought defensible."[4]

---

3. Seth Lazar, "The Responsibility Dilemma for *Killing in War*: A Review Essay," *Philosophy and Public Affairs* 38 (2010): 180–213.

4. Ibid., 181.

In response: the two horns of the responsibility dilemma are not equally sharp. Acceptance of the idea that under modern conditions of war there will be no morally permissible means one can employ to carry out a successful just war effort threatens moral disaster. Under modern conditions there will continue to be massive unjust war campaigns, which if unopposed by effective military force will bring about catastrophic levels of human rights violations. In many such situations nonviolent endeavors will not be an effective substitute for military force. If as a contingent matter morality properly construed demands that we be pacifists in the face of thuggish threats, that would be deeply troubling.[5]

In contrast, the thought that morality does not forbid, or does not categorically and unconditionally forbid, the killing of noncombatants in war might be an implication that reasonable people should accept. The line between combatants and noncombatants does not obviously track deep and compelling moral distinctions, but is rather invented as part of a convention intended to reduce the morally bad consequences that waging war tends to generate. Some historical examples of deliberately aiming fire at noncombatants and civilians are arguably justifiable or at least suggest imaginary variant cases in which targeting noncombatants would be justifiable. Think of terror bombing directed at the inhabitants of German cities in the course of World War II. For an example that is similar in some ways though it does not occur in the context of declared war, think of John Brown's raid on slave-holding plantation owners and their families in the pre–Civil War United States. Perhaps sound moral argument could convince us to give up the idea that deliberately aiming fire at noncombatants in war is always and everywhere morally wrong.

The responsibility dilemma posed by Lazar raises the question, under what conditions is it morally permissible deliberately to aim to inflict violence on a person in the context of war. This essay proposes an answer to this question, or at least a framework for settling it. The proposal in short is that at the fundamental

---

5. For a view of these matters pretty much entirely opposed to the position this essay defends, see Larry May, "Human Rights, Proportionality, and the Lives of Soldiers," in this volume. However, the extent of our disagreements may be mitigated, to a degree, if we note that there are different levels of moral thinking, and his discussion is oriented, in part, to what current international law properly understood implies about what our practices should be. Besides the level of fundamental moral principles, which fix what we ought to do, there are derivative levels, including the intuitive level morality into which members of a particular society are trained, and also laws, and social norms. The derivative levels ought to be set with an eye to bringing it about that cognitively limited, selfish, and poorly informed beings like us conform as closely as possible to fundamental level norms. Following R. M. Hare, most accept that the idea of there being different levels of moral thinking makes good sense within a consequentialist moral framework, but I would contend that a plausible nonconsequentialism needs to accept it also. If we should be nonconsequentialists, we should be multilevel nonconsequentialists. See R. M. Hare, "The Archangel and the Prole," *Moral Thinking: Its Levels, Methods, and Point* (Oxford: Oxford University Press, 1982), 44–64.

level of moral principle, no version of the distinction between combatant and noncombatant plays a substantial role in determining who is a permissible object of violent attack. The suggestion then is that we should embrace the second horn of Lazar's dilemma and so deny there is really a dilemma here to be faced at all.

A preliminary clarification is in order. McMahan and Lazar and others discuss when a person is liable to be attacked. A person who is liable to attack has forfeited, to some extent, her deontological moral right not to be the object of deliberate attack. But without doing anything to forfeit one's rights and without triggering liability to attack, one might still become the object of permissible attack, according to the views under discussion. The moral right not to be harmed might not be regarded as absolute and exceptionless, but as overrideable when the consequences of refraining from doing what the right standardly forbids would be extremely bad. Some would say that up to the limit of disaster or catastrophe, we should honor each individual's important moral rights not to be targeted for attack. In other words, according to moderate deontological views, people are inviolable, up to a point.

This essay proposes abandoning this two-tier structure of liability and overrideability. For any moral right not to be treated in certain ways, the right gives way if the ratio of the badness to nonrightholders if the right is not acted against to the badness to rightholders if the right is acted against is sufficiently favorable. This sliding scale is affected by the moral praiseworthiness and blameworthiness of the persons our rights-respecting or rights-infringing action would affect, so that the more morally culpable an individual is with respect to the situation in question, the less tilted the balance of consequences needs to be in order that acting against her right be morally justified.

II.

In order to make progress in deciding whether a huge moral gulf separates the action of aiming fire at noncombatants and that of aiming fire at combatants, we need to look at the notion of a *noncombatant*. It's somewhat hazy. The term suggests that the line is between those actually engaged in combat and those who are not, but this distinction lacks moral significance. Scientists developing weapons for the war effort, political leaders responsible for bringing it about that the nation they lead goes to war, and top administrators coordinating the manufacture and delivery of material the troops need to fight would all qualify as noncombatants on this construal, but all three seem to be morally eligible targets.

G. E. M. Anscombe suggests that the morally relevant line is between soldiers and those who are supplying soldiers with the means of fighting—bullets and munitions—on the one side, and on the other side people who are not doing that, but instead are carrying on activities characteristic of peacetime. So by this test, farmers supplying soldiers with food are not combatants and are protected by the moral shield of noncombatant immunity. The farmers are not aiding the soldiers qua soldiers but just qua human beings.[6]

If we are seeking moral principles that should govern the conduct of war and also govern the use of violence and threat of violence in other contexts, Anscombe's suggestion should strike us as dubious. Suppose I am the owner of the only gas station for miles, and the famous bank robbers Bonnie and Clyde pull up and want to purchase gas. In the circumstances it is perfectly clear that they need the gas to use their car for a planned armed bank robbery. If I sell them the gas, they will be able to rob a bank and will do so; if I don't sell them gas, their plan will be foiled. Suppose I am operating the gas station from behind a bulletproof counter. I can say no to their request with impunity, but instead I sell them gas. Suppose I know for certain that they will go on a killing spree as they rob the bank, so innocent lives are at stake. I am not aiding the armed robbers qua armed robbers; I am aiding them qua travelers on the highway, just as if they were peacefully moving along. Nonetheless in this example I am, morally speaking, complicitous in a murderous armed robbery. Someone who knows all the facts of the story and can only prevent the murders of the innocents at the site of the developing bank robbery by shooting me to prevent me from selling gas to the robbers in these circumstances would be morally justified in doing so.

This argument suggests that we need to accept a wide rather than narrow account of combatant status. At least, those who knowingly act in ways that causally advance the perpetration of significant injustice to a significant degree should count as combatants.[7] But even if a reconfigured way of drawing the line between combatant and noncombatant does not agree with the common thought that combatants are soldiers and noncombatants are civilians, this does not gainsay the possibility that according to revisionary Just War theory, it is impermissible to target noncombatants for deliberate attack.

III.

In this section I present considerations that support the claim that people who qualify as noncombatants according to any sensible interpretation of the notion,

---

6. G. E. M. Anscombe, "War and Murder," reprinted in *Ethics, Religion, and Politics: Collected Philosophical Papers*, vol. 3 (Oxford: Wiley-Blackwell, 1991), 51–61. Anscombe's proposal regarding how to understand the distinction between combatant and noncombatant is supported by C. A. J. Coady, *Morality and Political Violence* (Cambridge: Cambridge University Press, 2008).

7. If classifying as combatants people who do not engage in combat is deemed to offend ordinary usage, we could instead say that the combatant/noncombatant distinction should be replaced by a distinction between those who knowingly causally contribute to a war effort and those who do not.

revisionary or not, may become permissible targets of attack by those conducting a just war campaign in virtue of their culpable conduct. Noncombatants in war can fail to fulfill moral duties that bear on them as noncombatants, lack sufficient excuse for their wrongdoing, and become morally culpable on this basis. They can also fail to set their will toward the right and the good, as they ought, with respect to their moral duties as noncombatants, and become morally culpable on this basis. These failures on their part can become the core of a compelling case for the claim that, depending on further circumstances, they can be morally permissible objects of attack.

To borrow an example introduced by Robert Nozick, suppose that you are working quietly in your office, minding your own business.[8] A suspected criminal in the act of escaping from a crime scene takes refuge in your office building and is being hunted by police with a view to apprehending him. Your presence in your office interferes with the police efforts to nab the suspected criminal. In this situation you have a moral duty to cooperate with legitimate law enforcement efforts by getting out of the way, and if you deliberately or recklessly or negligently fail to comply, you forfeit some of your rights to be treated by the police only in ways that do not threaten your safety. If the criminal matter involves a sufficient threat to public safety, it may be reasonable and permissible for police to remove you from the premises even if doing so harms you, or to shoot at the suspect to prevent him from being an immediate threat to others, even if their bullets may strike you, or (if the stakes are high enough) even deliberately to aim fire at you if that is the only way to prevent the criminal suspect from inflicting grave harm on others.

Exactly the same can be true in a just war context. I may forfeit some of my rights not to be harmed if without adequate excuse I fail to meet my duties as a noncombatant to cooperate with just war efforts or at a minimum not impede those efforts. My culpable acts or omissions as a noncombatant may render me liable to what would otherwise be impermissible infliction of collateral harm on me or even to being the intended target of attack. These points, generated by the logic of revisionary Just War theory, unsettle our views as to what those engaged in just war may permissibly do to civilian noncombatants who are failing to accommodate (as they ought) just war efforts being undertaken by others. The civilian noncombatants may have moral duties to remove themselves from the scene of conflict, not allow their presence and ordinary activities to be a hindrance to just war efforts, prevent themselves from being used as shields or hideaways by unjust warriors, and so on.

---

8. Robert Nozick, "War, Terrorism, Reprisals—Drawing Some Moral Lines," review of *Just and Unjust Wars*), by Michael Walzer, reprinted in Nozick, *Socratic Puzzles* (Cambridge, Mass.: Harvard University Press, 1997), 300–304.

These points get flipped around if the just warriors are being besieged by forces wrongly trying to defeat their cause and the besieged take refuge among noncombatants or seek help from them. Consider the example of a just guerrilla war, a just effort to resist an unjust occupation or a tyrannical government or some other set of gravely unjust arrangements. If you are part of an informal guerrilla force conducting a just war campaign, uninvolved civilians in your vicinity will likely have a moral duty to assist your efforts and to bear some risks and some expectable harm in order to do their part to bring this just war campaign to a successful end. In this situation, it may be morally permissible for guerrilla fighters to take shelter among civilians, even if this puts the civilians at grave risk of harm from becoming the intended or foreseen but unintended target of counter-guerrilla fire. For similar reasons, it may be permissible for informal fighters waging a just war campaign to coerce uninvolved civilians into contributing to the cause. The guerrillas may simply be enforcing duties that all members of the community have to resist tyranny or unjust occupation. The claim that one is an uninvolved bystander so one should be let alone rings hollow if those claiming bystander status are bound by duties of beneficence (or reciprocity or justice promotion) to join the fray. Guilty bystanders can forfeit their rights not to be put in harm's way.

IV.

Suppose one claims that soldiers fighting for an unjust cause are agent responsible for perpetrating injustice of sufficient magnitude to render them liable to be deliberately subject to lethal attack. One objection to this claim is that agent responsibility without culpability is too insubstantial to serve as a pivot point in an account of liability to be justly killed.[9] Consider this example: in the aftermath of a highway accident, someone volunteers for the dangerous mission of driving an

---

9. On this point, see Seth Lazar, "Responsibility, Risk, and Killing in Self-Defense," *Ethics* 119 (2009): 699–728. My view (not defended here) is that agent responsibility for perpetrating evil in the absence of culpability is not just insufficient to trigger liability to violence (provided the violence will mitigate or undo the evil), but is not even a significant moral factor weighing in favor of liability. Also, independently of that idea, I would hold that fault forfeits first: other things being equal, the morally preferred target for violence directed at undoing or preventing a serious evil or injustice is an agent who is seriously culpable with respect to that evil or injustice and more culpable than anyone else involved in the situation. See Arneson, "Just Warfare Theory and Noncombatant Immunity," *Cornell International Law Journal* 39 (2006): 663–88. The example in the text does not by itself support these claims even if one accepts it as a counterexample against the claim that agent responsibility for evil can be a sufficient condition for liability to violence (that will avert or undo the evil). In the example, the moral praiseworthiness of the agent responsible individual arguably outweighs the agent responsibility factor in this case. This leaves it wide open that agent responsibility might be a morally significant factor, whose significance emerges in other examples.

ambulance past bandit-infested territory to the accident site. The driver is behaving virtuously, even heroically, but driving any vehicle on roads imposes some risk on others on the road in the event of an accident, and failure to drive in a sufficiently competent manner renders one at fault in the event of an accident. Suppose the ambulance driver faultily but without culpability loses control of the vehicle and skids toward a pedestrian, who could save himself by killing the driver. Describe the case so it is clear that the driver is responsible for the imposition of what in the event turns out to be wrongful threat of death on the pedestrian. The claim that the driver has forfeited her right not to be killed here seems incredible. So, it is said, agent responsibility for perpetrating serious injustice is insufficient to render one liable to deliberate lethal attack. This line of thought presses us toward the contingent pacifist horn of the responsibility dilemma.

There is a further difficulty with McMahan's claim that soldiers serving in a military force waging an unjust war become liable to permissible attack by being agent responsible for causally contributing to significant harmful wrongdoing. Wars are waged by large bureaucratic organizations. Not all soldiers fighting for one side or the other in a war are plausibly regarded as making significant causal contributions to the war effort. So if the claim is that being agent responsible for making a significant causal contribution to posing wrongful grave harm or risk of that on morally innocent nonthreatening persons is the trigger that renders it morally permissible for others to subject one to violent attack that is necessary to avert or undo the grave wrongful harm, a problem arises: many soldiers standardly deemed combatants do not actually make significant causal contributions to wrongful grave harm imposition. Some soldiers march in parades or keep the barracks clean or provide entertainment to the troops or do other tasks that do not amount to significant causal contribution to imposition of harm. So in this way also the corners of the McMahan revisionary just war doctrine do not fit together coherently.

It is worthwhile to pause to consider the train of thought that might lead one to accept agent responsibility as a basis for forfeiture of one's serious rights not to be harmed. Consider the generic situation of uncertainty that shrouds an agent who is considering whether to undertake a certain course of action or refrain. The action will serve one's purposes, or likely do so, but there is some risk, large or small or even tiny, that the action taken will bring about harm to another person in such a way that, with uncertainty resolved, it becomes clear in retrospect that the action one has taken is wrong in the specific sense that had one known in advance the actual consequences of doing the act, one ought to have refrained from doing it. When one acts in these circumstances, if the risk of bringing about harm is sufficiently great, relative to the expectation of gain and the nature of the gain one hopes to generate by the action, choosing and doing this act in these circumstances is morally wrong, and blameworthy if one lacks a sufficient excuse. If the risk of harm is sufficiently small, relative to anticipated gain, one's action is morally permissible and not blameworthy at all, and if the expected gain far exceeds the expected harm and in addition the gains accrue to others and the agent is incurring cost and risk of harm to herself to secure these gains for others, the agent's action can be morally admirable and the agent morally praiseworthy. However, one can regard the agent in all of these cases as taking a gamble, and if the gamble turns out badly, and foreseeable harm to others actually comes about or threatens to come about, forfeiture of the agent's own moral rights occurs.

Some have responded that in these scenarios the situation is ex ante symmetrical as between agent and potential victim. When the agent drives a car knowing a crash might ensue (such that, had one known of the crash in advance, one should not have started driving), the pedestrian threatened with injury also faces a choice, whether to take a walk along this path, knowing one might be harmed in a car crash (such that, had one known in advance of the car crash, one should not have started walking along that very path). Both agent and victim are taking a gamble when acting, and if the gamble each takes is reasonable, why see forfeiture of rights on the part of agent not victim? I suppose the response is that had the victim known of the future sequence that will unfold, she would be imprudent to commence walking, whereas had the agent known of the future sequence that will unfold, she would be guilty of moral wrongdoing if she commenced walking. But had the victim clairvoyant foresight, she would foresee that she will be bringing about a situation in which she will have to kill a nonculpable agent to save her own life, and proceeding to walk along anyway in the face of this knowledge looks to be wrong. Even if the situation is asymmetrical with respect to risk imposition—suppose the driver imposes a greater risk on the potential victim than the victim imposes on the driver by way of possible infliction of defensive harm if an accident unfolds—the gain to self and others expected to accrue from action may also be asymmetrical, and favor the driver. The moral disagreement here boils down to disagreement as to whether there is any sliver of asymmetry here, and if so, whether it is enough of a plank on which to hang a claim of significant forfeiture of rights.[10]

---

10. Larry Alexander and Kimberly Kessler Ferzan, "Culpable Acts of Risk Creation," *Ohio State Journal of Criminal Law* 5 (2008): 375–405; also Kimberly Kessler Ferzan, "Culpable Aggression: The Basis for Moral Liability to Defensive Killing," *Ohio State Journal of Criminal Law* 9 (2012): 669–97. They also make another point: if one held that the driver forfeits her right not to be killed when she is agent responsible for skidding toward a pedestrian, then it would be morally wrong, not merely imprudent, for the pedestrian to have commenced walking along that path that will cross the path of the skidding car, had she known in advance of the sequence that would unfold.

Even if we have a case in which the factor of agent responsibility weighs in favor of one party in the interaction, one might hold that this factor absent any culpability is insufficient to justify self-defensive killing. One might hold that at most the person threatened in such a situation is entitled to act to equalize the chances that one or the other of the innocent risk imposer and risk sufferer will die (or be severely harmed) if death or severe harm must fall on someone in this situation.

V.

One could avoid being pressed to contingent pacifism if one could show that soldiers fighting for an unjust cause are (usually or nearly always) culpable (that is, blameworthy). If soldiers fighting for an unjust cause are nearly always seriously blameworthy for doing so, then the responsibility dilemma seemingly does not get off the ground. Showing that soldiers fighting for a just cause may deliberately attack unjust soldiers will then be as easy as downhill sledding. Culpable perpetrators of significant injustice may permissibly be killed if doing so is necessary to prevent or undo the injustice.

But the responsibility dilemma is not so easy to avoid. There are two lines that press against the idea that soldiers fighting for an unjust cause are mostly culpable so it is morally acceptable deliberately to kill them. First, on any plausible understanding of culpability, many soldiers will qualify as nonculpable. Many will sincerely believe they are doing the right thing after making reasonable efforts to discover what is right to do in the face of the call to arms. Many will have an excuse of duress or coercion, if the regime that initiates unjust war institutes draconian punishment against those who refuse conscription into military service and against soldiers who refuse to participate in an unjust war endeavor. Second, if the military force fighting for injustice contains a mix of culpable and nonculpable combatants, and culpability is necessary for liability to justified attack, then one will as a practical matter not know which of the combatants one faces are morally permissible targets. If one shoots at any and all enemy combatants in order to attack the culpable combatants, one is arguably aiming fire at morally innocent combatants, and injuring them is not merely a side effect of what one is doing. (One would be aiming at innocents either as a means to killing the culpable or in virtue of the fact that aiming at all combatants in the circumstances includes aiming at the innocents among them.) If so, one would be violating the constraint against targeting morally innocent persons.

The defender of the position that it is generally morally acceptable to aim fire at combatants who are prosecuting an unjust war has available some resources for pushing back against the lines of argument just described. Consider the excuse of nonculpable ignorance. In war, many are killed and maimed, many are displaced from their homes and become refugees, many people's important rights go unfulfilled, and so on. Joining a war effort, one is contributing to deliberate large-scale killing.

In ordinary life, there is a high moral bar against deliberately taking up arms and shooting at people. One must have very strong grounds for believing that the killing one is facilitating is justified. If evidence is scanty, one has a duty to investigate further, or refrain from fighting if the epistemic situation is completely and unavoidably cloudy.

The same high bar holds under the extraordinary circumstances of warfare. One cannot satisfy one's duty to make serious good-faith efforts to discover the reasons there are that bear on the justifiability of the war effort and thus the acceptability of one's joining it just by trusting the declarations of public officials. The historical record is rife with attempts by national leaders and elite intelligentsia to persuade the public that an unsavory, unjust war enterprise being undertaken is really just and fair and morally admirable. (For a comparison, note that even if my wife is generally a nice and trustworthy person, if she suddenly declares that I should kill the neighbors, I surely ought not to kill the neighbors just on her say-so.) In a democratic regime or one that promotes free expression and open debate, one has a duty to investigate thoroughly before deciding that joining the military and becoming committed to kill on command is justified. In a dictatorship or a regime that throttles free expression and debate, there should be a strong presumption that the declarations of public leaders are not to be trusted and that any war plans being contemplated by their rulers are very likely going to serve some unjust cause. The sheer fact that someone sincerely believes his nation's warmaking is in the service of a good cause is a very long way from sufficient to establish that his joining a war effort on this basis is nonculpable.

Regarding the excuses of coercion and duress, we should again notice that the use of war as an instrument of policy for all practical purposes automatically raises the moral stakes, given the destructiveness of war, so that if a war is unjust, the moral wrong being perpetrated is extremely large, even gigantic. Hence if political leaders threaten harsh punishment if one does not comply with an order to join the war effort or contribute to it, the level of harm threatened that suffices to excuse wrongful killing and wrongful infliction of mayhem in an unjust war endeavor is very large. Again a comparison to ordinary life situations is instructive. If the robber threatens to break my legs if I do not shoot and kill the bank guards that are impeding her robbery effort, it would be blameworthy of me not to accept broken legs rather than perpetrate murders. The same holds, I would say, if the robber credibly threatens to kill me unless I murder two bank guards. One extra murder is a very large consideration, to which my decision making should be responsive. Human nature being what it is, it is understandable that I might murder several to save my life and even murder several to save myself from suffering broken legs, but some understandable behaviors are still morally blameworthy. Now imagine that the bank robber issues a coercive threat that unless I make a necessary contribution to a robbery that will kill thousands of innocent non-threatening people, he will murder me along with my immediate family. Here my yielding to this threat would be both wrong and blameworthy, I would say. Even a strong excuse can dampen culpability without extinguishing it. In making this claim I allow that there are morally wrong actions that are not at all blameworthy (culpable).

There are further possibilities that might favor the claim that a soldier fighting for an unjust cause against enemy soldiers who have a just cause to fight might yet have an excuse, or even possibly a justification, arising from duress.[11] One consideration is that the unjust soldier might be being asked to do seemingly wrongful acts but in circumstances such that he or she can truly say, "It makes no difference whether or not I do it." The soldier will perpetrate no harm that would not have come about anyway whether he or she did it or refrained from doing it. Another consideration is that the unjust soldier might be thought to be under an especially stringent duty to family, friends, or fellow countrymen, to prevent their coming to harm if possible. Both considerations are in play in this example: suppose the evil dictator threatens the young peasants that unless they join his army and fight and kill for an unjust cause, he will kill their immediate family members. The dictator adds that if the peasants refrain from taking up arms to fight for an unjust cause, he will conscript other peasants who will do exactly the same unjust killing as the initially conscripted peasants would have done.

The special-ties excuse raises large issues this essay cannot address. Here I simply report the view I believe we should take: there are no special-tie duties that justify doing a wrong to avoid a similar wrong falling on a person to whom one has special ties. It is not permissible for me to commit a murder to avoid a similarly wrongful killing of my wife. So a threat to murder one hundred fellow villagers unless I murder one hundred strangers fighting against me in a just cause does not excuse, much less justify, my taking up arms in an unjust cause.

The assertion that "it makes no difference whether or not I do it" does not necessarily give me an excuse for doing it from the standpoint of a nonconsequentialist ethics. However, it is always and everywhere a consideration. Yet I doubt that it is standardly or even often available to one who is a participant in an unjust

---

11. On this issue see Victor Tadros, "Duress and Duty," in this volume.

war. First, the availability of the excuse depends on its actually motivating the participation in unjust war by the unjust combatant. If I am gung-ho for unjust battle, the orientation of my will is culpable even if I am making no difference in outcome terms. Same goes if my will is culpable by virtue of my negligence or recklessness in calculating whether I would be doing wrongful harm if I enter the fray. Second, if I decline to participate and further resources must be expended to induce another to do the exact wrongful harming I would have done, there are then extra resources in the hands of an evil dictator for prosecuting his unjust cause in other ways, so I will have made a difference in wrongdoing after all. Third, even if those who would take my place would do similar or even equivalent wrong, they are unlikely to be harming wrongfully just the persons in just the ways I would have done, and if so, "it makes no difference whether or not I do it" is just false. However, I acknowledge that there can be cases in which duress can excuse wrongdoing or even justify conduct that absent duress would qualify as wrongdoing.[12]

What about the concern that many soldiers serving an unjust cause, even if culpable, cannot be seriously culpable, because they engage in tasks that do not significantly advance the war effort? One response is that in an efficiently organized collective enterprise, tasks that work in the background to keep the enterprise functioning well do indirectly make a causal contribution. If entertaining the troops boosts morale and leads to more effective fighting, entertaining the troops causally contributes significantly to harmful wrongdoing. On the other hand, if some troops are really out of the causal loop altogether, they do acquire the status of bystanders (albeit culpable bystanders). If some soldiers serving a force that is waging unjust war are irreversibly assigned to guard paintings in museums from civilian vandalism, and are unavailable for any military purpose, they should count as bystanders for purposes of deciding the permissibility of attacking them.

In this discussion I have tried to put our judgments on decisions to contribute to war efforts into perspective by considering parallel cases from ordinary life. Anchoring judgments about choices regarding war to ordinary standards of wrong and blameworthy conduct is helpful, in that it counteracts a widespread tendency to consider the ethics of war as a special case in which individuals following the rules laid down get a free pass or something close to that and choices and actions that would seem abhorrent in the ordinary course of events are regarded much more leniently when the agents whose conduct is under review are wearing military uniforms and participating in wars declared by established governments.

---

12. See Tadros for a convincing argument on this point.

It is one of the singular achievements of revisionary Just War theory to insist that one set of moral standards governs choices about whether killing in war is permissible and whether killing one's neighbor or work mate is permissible.

Suppose that we could establish that in a particular conflict the overwhelming bulk, or at least the majority, of those we classify as combatants fighting for an unjust cause are to some degree culpable for their contributions to this wrongful endeavor. If we can gain no more fine-grained information about who is culpable and who is not, then combatants fighting for a just cause are entitled to suppose that any given enemy combatant they encounter is likely culpable to some degree for serious wrongdoing and hence is likely liable to be attacked if doing so advances the just cause and hence may permissibly be attacked. There is a worry that obtrudes at this point. Even if for any given enemy combatant, the odds are that she is at least to some degree culpable for her participation in this war effort, it must be the case that if there are many enemy combatants targeted for attack, the odds will be overwhelming that some of them, we know not which ones, are innocent in the sense of being morally blameless. In this situation, should this fact shield the enemy combatants from attack? (For a comparison, note that we do not believe that criminal punishment is unjustified even though it is certain that operating any criminal justice system will in fact find guilty and subject to punishment some innocent accused persons. We insist on rather high odds of guilt to warrant criminal conviction, but attacking someone in combat is not punishing the person and due process in combat situations is anyway out of the question.)

However, merely establishing that it is morally permissible (sometimes, usually, or always) for just combatants to attack unjust combatants does not by itself dissolve the responsibility dilemma. The dilemma as stated binds so long as there is symmetry in the liability to being a permissible object of attack in the situation of being a combatant or a noncombatant who happens to be on the unjust side. Just showing that combatants are liable to be attacked does not establish asymmetry. Maybe the strict account that holds unjust combatants liable to be permissibly killed also shows that unjust noncombatants are liable to be permissibly killed.

It might seem that once we have accepted a broad understanding of what constitutes a combatant, such that anyone who significantly causally contributes to an unjust war effort qualifies as a combatant, the problem just stated cannot arise. If the culpable are those who act wrongly and are blameworthy for their wrongdoing, then those who do no wrongdoing cannot be culpable, and if you do not causally contribute to the unjust war effort, it might be thought, you do not harm anyone, so a fortiori you do not wrongfully harm anyone, so the question whether you are culpable for wrongdoing does not arise.

This line of thought might appear to be sound but in fact harbors mistakes. Section III of this essay produced examples in which one can become culpable not by causally contributing to wrongdoing but by failing to fulfill a duty to help prevent wrongdoing. But further examples to be introduced in the next section entirely sever the link between causation, wrongdoing, and culpability. Without causally contributing to wrongdoing and without failing causally to contribute to prevention of wrongdoing a person can be morally at fault and morally culpable with respect to that wrongdoing.

VI.

This last claim might encounter resistance. How can those who do not causally contribute to wrongdoing be culpable for that wrongdoing? But not all culpability is *culpability for*.

Culpability is standardly understood as culpability for wrongful action or inaction that an agent has done or chosen. Culpability is nested within two prerequisite elements of responsibility. One is causal responsibility. If your action, or omission of action, does not cause harm or the threat of harm, and in addition does not fail to cause harm prevention you have a duty to bring about, you cannot be blameworthy. A second is agent responsibility. Agent responsibility enters the picture when what you are causally responsible for emerges from an exercise of your agency. Being agent-responsible for an action, the action and its outcome can properly be attributed to you, and you can be morally praiseworthy or blameworthy depending on their features.

There is nothing questionable about the idea of being culpable for some outcome, where this involves causal responsibility and agent-responsibility. But culpability or moral blameworthiness can also be freestanding, unanchored to causal responsibility or agent responsibility. Suppose in the Hitler era in Germany I vote for the Nazis and am an enthusiastic supporter of Nazi policies, and exult in their success. These acts might be causally impotent. They do not make any causal contribution, even a small one, to any wrongful harm or threat of wrongful harm that Nazis inflict on victims. So there is no wrong for which I am culpable, but I am culpable with respect to the Nazi crimes, in virtue of failing to make good faith efforts, within my capabilities, to orient my will toward the right and the good. Being seriously disposed toward significant evil in this way suffices to render me seriously morally culpable with respect to Nazi perpetration of injustice, such that I am an eligible target of just war violence directed at preventing or undoing Nazi injustice. Being eligible for this violence means that if harming or even killing me is useful for advancing the anti-Nazi cause, I have no moral right not to be killed for this reason, and no moral right to defend myself with lethal force against those who are advancing the anti-Nazi cause by attacking me.[13]

The upshot of this reflection is that we should acknowledge that culpability with respect to a war effort can attach to people who make no causal contribution to that war effort. So if we conceive of the combatant and noncombatant distinction as one between those who do and those who do not (significantly) knowingly causally contribute to a war effort, we should allow that noncombatants can be culpable with respect to the waging of a war and hence legitimate targets of attack if (sufficient) culpability renders one liable to be the permissible object of legitimate attack. Moreover, on the view advanced here, one can become culpable simply because, as it were, one's heart is in the wrong place, independently of failure on one's part actually to choose and act as one ought.

A slight complication here is that someone might contribute unknowingly but negligently to a war effort, and qualify as a noncombatant according to the proposed stipulation. Contributing unknowingly but negligently to the production of a large evil can surely qualify as acting wrongly and if one lacks an excuse for this faulty conduct, one can be blameworthy for it. This can happen. However, we should accept a more unsettling possibility, as illustrated by the example of the Nazi supporter whose supportive activities are causally inert and do no harm: one can be morally at fault and blameworthy with respect to a situation without wrongfully harming anyone. In fact we should go further: even if I engage in no activities at all, I can become culpable with respect to a situation by setting my will toward evil even if that orientation of my will never issues in action at all, much less wrongful harming of anyone. It matters morally not just what we do and deliberately refrain from doing. It also matters morally whether we make ourselves disposed positively toward the right and the good and negatively toward moral wrong and evil.

So far the position on culpability affirmed here is just advanced by assertion. Why accept the assertion? The reason is that insulating judgments of culpability from judgments about causation is required by the plausible idea that "people cannot be morally assessed for what is not their fault, or for what is due to factors

---

13. Freestanding culpability as just characterized may perhaps involve causation in a hypothetical fashion. If my will is turned to Nazi evil, then I am disposed to act under some range of circumstances I might encounter to advance the Nazi cause. If that is not so, we might wonder whether my will is sufficiently evil to render me liable to be harmed in order to block Nazi advances. Perhaps merely being disposed passively to wish for Nazi victory, without any disposition to act so as to promote Nazi aims, cannot render one sufficiently culpable to be legitimately subject to violence. But even if that is right, it remains the case that there can be serious culpability without culpability for.

beyond their control."[14] At least some types of moral assessment are not subject to this kind of luck.

Since we should accept that so far as is possible our moral judgments of the moral blameworthiness and praiseworthiness of an individual should not be affected by moral luck (contingencies beyond the individual's power to control), we should hold as equally blameworthy an individual who hates Jews and would murder them if he could but through sheer luck fails to encounter any and another individual who has the same murderous disposition, encounters Jews, and murders them. If the only difference between the two individuals is that one happens to encounter Jews and the other does not, this difference is not a proper basis for differential moral assessment of the two individuals.

Objection: two individuals might be equally disposed toward evil, but when they encounter opportunities to act on their murderous impulses, one resists the temptation and does not do evil and the other does not resist and does actually do evil. So assessing individuals simply by their standing dispositions or traits of character (so far as they bear some responsibility for their formation) would be mistaken.

Reply: insofar as individuals facing decision problems make choices, for which they are responsible, in ways that do not simply reflect their dispositions at the time of choice, then choices independently contribute to an individual's moral praiseworthiness or blameworthiness. This leaves standing the point that if two people are equally disposed to an act, and one has an opportunity to do it, and one does not, and both would have done the act if given the opportunity, the two should be deemed equally praiseworthy or blameworthy so far as this combination of disposition and choice is concerned.

The general claim being invoked at this juncture is that whether one has the opportunity or the causal capacity to do harm lies beyond one's power to control. If what we are morally responsible for at most is what lies within our power to control, we are morally responsible at most for the orientation of our will, not whether the will encounters opportunities to do good and evil, and not whether one is causally efficacious if one does encounter such opportunities.

This general claim could be disputed. Suppose we accept it. This is a claim about what triggers moral praiseworthiness and blameworthiness. Of course it does not follow from claims about what triggers moral blameworthiness (culpability) that culpability alone triggers forfeiture of rights in a way that renders one

14. Thomas Nagel, "Moral Luck," reprinted in his collection *Mortal Questions* (Cambridge: Cambridge University Press, 1979), 24–38, at 25. Nagel characterizes the no-moral-luck position but rejects it. In this connection one should note Robert Adams's forthright acceptance of moral luck in his "Involuntary Sins," *Philosophical Review* 94 (1985): 3–31.

liable to permissible attack. Above I argued that agent responsibility for bringing about unjustified harm is an insufficient basis for such liability. But there are intermediate possibilities. One is that when one acts in a way that violates another person's moral rights, doing what at the time of action there was sufficient evidence available to the agent to establish as morally wrong, even if the agent is entirely blameless for the doing of it, the agent thereby forfeits some of her moral rights, the nature and extent of this forfeiture being determined by the character of the moral rights the agent has violated.[15] Let's say the agent is fully agent responsible for rights violation in these circumstances.

This is a possibility, but we should be unmoved by it. An agent's entirely morally nonculpable behavior does not trigger forfeiture of rights. Suppose two persons do the best they can, but one has reasoning talents the other lacks, so equally admirable efforts to figure out what is morally required in this situation result in the talented individual getting the right answer and acting on it and the less talented individual getting the wrong answer and acting on it. Sheer lack of talent does not render one less morally considerable, degrade one's moral status, or lower whatever moral bar prevents others from harming one. Perhaps the less talented individual should have made good faith efforts to avoid the situation in which his lack of reasoning and decision-making talent would cause harm to others. If that is so, there is moral culpability in the background, which might distinguish the agents, and provide grounds for the claim that the culpable has to some degree forfeited her moral rights. But when that is not so, the agent's moral innocence despite doing wrong is untarnished.

Being agent responsible and being fully agent responsible for serious rights violations often accompany another factor that I would contend is a significant determinant of the moral permissibility of acting against some agent's right. Attacking an agent who is (maybe fully) agent responsible for some wrongful threat of an unjust condition is often a very effective means to avert the threat or to eliminate or reduce the bad condition. Often attacking an individual who is agent responsible for a threat is pulling on a very effective causal lever for improving the situation. My suggestion is that we tend to be misled by the confluence of possible factors and tend to ascribe to agent responsibility, including full agent responsibility, a determining moral power it lacks. Even when attacking an individual who is fully agent responsible for some rights violation will not help to boost rights-fulfillment here and now, doing good to the particular threatened individual, we might expect that attacking the agent responsible agent will boost

---

15. Jonathan Quong mentions this position but does not affirm it in his "Liability to Defensive Harm," *Philosophy and Public Affairs* 40 (2012): 45–77.

rights-fulfillment in the future by deterring others from similar action that similarly threatens individual rights.

One step to downgrading the claimed role of agent responsibility (causing harm) in bringing about forfeiture of rights is to recognize that fault forfeits first.[16] This means that if someone must be made to suffer harm to protect people's moral rights, the preferred person who should be made to suffer harm is the person who is most culpable with respect to that situation, provided she is significantly culpable. So suppose Amy's moral rights are threatened with violation, Ben is agent responsible for the threat but entirely morally blameless, and Clare is a bystander who is morally culpable with respect to this situation. Fault forfeits first says that if one can prevent Amy's rights from being violated by harming either Ben or Clare, Clare should be the one who is harmed. Fault forfeits first is plausible, I submit. But its acceptance would not amount to eliminating entirely the factor of causation of harm as a partial determinant of one's moral status as possessing or forfeiting one's moral rights. One could accept fault forfeits first but also maintain that when there is no appropriate culpable individual imposing harm on whom would serve to avert or undo a moral rights violation of some person, an individual who is agent responsible (or on another view, fully agent responsible) is the next-in-line eligible target for violence or harm imposition aimed at maintenance and restoration of people's moral rights, provided the moral gain of rights-fulfillment expectable from such action is sufficiently great.

However, one might discern a kind of ripple effect from the insulation of an individual from moral culpability by moral luck considerations. Not all moral judgments are subject to moral luck constraints. The judgment that my practical reasoning efforts on some occasion have been deficient is not deflected by the claim that my failures were beyond my power to control. Another example: the judgment that I lack virtue, for example, that I am cowardly rather than courageous, is not undermined by the fact that my failure to possess traits necessary for achieving virtues is beyond my power to control. But if judgments of culpability are blanketed by the fact that the conduct for which one is subject to blame is beyond one's power to control, there is a case for holding also that downgrading of a person's moral status by deeming her to have forfeited some of her moral rights is also defeated by a showing that the act or choice that is supposed to trigger forfeiture was beyond the individual's power to control. The judgment that one is liable to harm in virtue of one's faulty conduct or omission is not a judgment that one merits punishment, but it arguably shares with that judgment the

---

16. See the Arneson essay cited in footnote 9. See also Arneson, "Desert and Equality," in *Egalitarianism: New Essays on the Nature and Value of Equality*, ed. Nils Holtug and Kasper Lippert-Rasmussen (Oxford: Oxford University Press, 2007), 262–93.

feature that its appropriateness requires blameworthiness on the part of the person singled out for negative judgment. In contrast, the judgment that it is permissible to harm a person simply in virtue of the fact that harming her will prevent large bad consequences or bring about large good consequences does not contain any negative judgment at all on the character or conduct of the person judged, so this judgment can surely be appropriate in the absence of any showing of culpability on the part of the person being judged a permissible object of attack.

VII.

Perhaps the crucial reason why it is morally permissible to attack and kill enemy soldiers when they are prosecuting an unjust war and one is fighting for a just cause in opposing them is that killing enemy soldiers in these circumstances makes a contribution to winning the just war, and in the case at hand, the moral stakes in this conflict are very high. The crucial point is not that the enemy soldiers have made themselves liable to be killed but that their right not to be killed is overridden by the bad consequences of respecting their right.

Any non-absolutist deontology will allow for such overriding by catastrophe. Judith Thomson long ago noted that the morality of self-defense might differ from the morality of war in just this respect: in war, the stakes of a single battle may be high, and the battle may be linked to an ongoing campaign with gigantic stakes.[17]

However, the view I am tentatively proposing will strike some as carrying counterintuitive implications. Suppose a just cause of great moral importance can be advanced equally well by killing completely nonculpable soldiers fighting for the unjust cause or by killing an equal number of totally uninvolved bystanders. Just suppose. The view that denies that sheer causing of wrongful harm or sheer perpetration of wrongful harm opens the door to liability to be killed will say that it is in itself a matter of indifference whether we advance the just cause in this situation by killing soldiers or bystanders. Notice that accepting a deontological constraint against harming innocent bystanders even to bring about greater good does not settle the stringency of the constraint. Better to allow two murders than to perpetrate one morally exactly comparable murder oneself, perhaps, but still better to murder one than to allow (say) three murders. I am tentatively suggesting, if those one must harm to prevent a greater harm are really entirely morally innocent in the sense of blameless, and if the harm one would avert justifies the

---

17. Judith Jarvis Thomson, "Self-Defense," *Philosophy and Public Affairs* 20 (1991): 283–310. The suggestion is made in passing.

harm one perpetrates, one should prefer to inflict the least harm on the morally innocent no matter what their further relations are to the harming one is averting. Fault forfeits first says that to advance the just cause, harming the culpable is morally preferred to harming the nonculpable, even if the nonculpable are causally responsible or agent responsible for the injustice one's harming will avert. But fault forfeits first taken by itself is silent on the further question, when choosing among nonculpable targets, whether bystanders are morally less eligible for harm than those causally or agent responsible or fully agent responsible.

From a deontological perspective, the fact that the consequences of one's action may be very large does not wash away all further deontological considerations as irrelevant. Perhaps the various factors interact. The greater the ratio of the costs to non-rightholders overall if a particular right is respected to the costs to rightholders if their particular right is not respected, the greater the case for not respecting the right in this case. The case is amplified if the person whose right will be violated has partly forfeited the right in question by her moral culpability with respect to this situation. Contrary to what I have urged in this essay, but do not claim to have conclusively defended, the case might sometimes also be amplified by considerations of agent responsibility.[18] In particular, some will accept what this essay calls "full agent responsibility" (acting wrongfully, but blamelessly, in the evidence-relative sense) as a significant factor.[19]

The upshot of this discussion is that the responsibility dilemma as characterized by Lazar does not lead us to the conclusion he claims it provisionally supports—namely, that "the prospects for grounding the ethics of war in individual rights are poor: any theory of our rights to life that is sufficiently indiscriminate to work in the chaos of war is not discriminating enough to be a plausible theory of our rights to life."[20]

The takeaway lesson from this discussion is more modest. Individual moral rights do not enter the moral reasoning that determines what we ought to do only

---

18. Saba Bazargan argues that minimal culpability and agent responsibility might fail to generate forfeiture of the right not to be harmed but still favor attacking the minimally culpable harmdoers if someone must be attacked to prevent a very bad outcome. See his "Killing Minimally Responsible Threats," *Ethics* 125 (2014): 114–36.

19. Larry Alexander takes this line.

20. Lazar, "The Responsibility Dilemma," 213. However, in broad terms, the discussion in this essay upholds Lazar's insight, which is that the revisions to modern Just War theory proposed by McMahan and others lead to more far-reaching changes in our moral convictions in wide reflective equilibrium than the advocates of revision have tended to suppose. The dust has not yet settled on the project of rethinking the morality of self-defense and of Just War theory.

as constraints to be respected and honored. Individual rights are also goals to be promoted, and sometimes rights as goals trump rights in the role of constraints.[21]

The formulation of the point in the preceding paragraph is in a way misleading. The fact that aiming fire at an individual would significantly advance an important just cause and refraining from aiming fire at that individual would significantly retard that important enterprise can play a role in a deontological principle that balances several interacting factors to determine the degree of eligibility for being the target of such violence that is assignable to that individual. Great consequences hanging in the balance can override a deontological prohibition and render it the case that a bystander may be the legitimate target of attack. But soldiers (and civilians) on the side of the unjust cause are usually not mere bystanders. They will usually be causal contributors to the effort, agent responsible to some degree for these contributions, and, most important, culpable even if only to a small degree. One's small blameworthiness, insufficient by itself to render one a permissible target of attack, may interact with other relevant factors, and notably the amount of good that killing one will expectably produce. (Recall that terror bombing of Berlin during World War II might have been justified even though terror bombing of Buenos Aires, even with exactly the same good effect on the Allied war effort, would have been unjust killing.)

VIII.

The discussion in this essay has mostly set to the side epistemic considerations that at the end of the day will significantly affect what one is and is not morally permitted to do in the course of waging war. The considerations of individual blameworthiness and praiseworthiness that this essay urges are crucial to the determination of who may permissibly attack whom are largely opaque to participants and bystanders facing actual war. So besides a discussion of fundamental moral principles bearing on the morally proper conduct of war, we need a discussion of derivative, secondary moral rules, which more readily lend themselves to guiding the conduct of people facing war situations and trying to figure out what

---

21. This point holds for small-scale interactions involving small rights of few people in ordinary life, and also holds for large-scale interactions involving big important rights of many people in extraordinary events such as war. See Amartya Sen, "Rights and Agency," *Philosophy and Public Affairs* 11 (1982): 3–39. In the text I mention examples of situations in which refraining from acting against a person's right not to be harmed would have enormous bad consequences. However, I would hold that there can be examples in which an act that inflicts a modest harm against a rightbearer can be justified by modest benefits that would accrue to nonrightholders, even though no enormous consequences are at stake. What triggers the overriding of a person's right is that the ratio of (1) harm to nonrightholders if the right is not infringed to (2) the harm to rightholders if the right is infringed is sufficiently favorable.

morally they are permitted, required, and forbidden to do. These secondary rules will not require individuals to base their decision about what to do on information that they cannot obtain. So in a way the discussion in this essay is preliminary: a full resolution of the responsibility dilemma requires a discussion of derivative rules to guide conduct as well as of fundamental principles that fix what is morally right and wrong.

About such secondary rules I will say only that they are to be viewed as means to bringing it about that people's conduct approximates more closely to conformity to what the fundamental principles determine to be right and wrong. In settling the content of the secondary rules, the fundamental principles do not get tossed aside as irrelevant. Moreover, it is not at all obvious that a careful discussion of justifiable secondary rules of just warfare, rules for the practical guidance of conduct, would resurrect the traditional war convention centered on the moral equality of soldiers doctrine or anything close to it. I myself doubt this resurrection would occur. But this is a topic for another occasion.[22]

Addendum

In his excellent 2015 book *Sparing Civilians*, Lazar reworks the responsibility dilemma and suggests a resolution of it that differs substantially from the views I have been proposing. Looking briefly at Lazar's reworking and resolving promises to shed further light on the issues concerning what we owe to one another in the context of modern war.

Consider a stylized example of a war in which one side has a just cause sufficient to justify waging war on its opponent, which lacks such a just cause. Lazar notes that in actual and likely wars, the rights and wrongs determining which side, if either, has a just cause to fight, all things considered, will be murky and unknowable by ordinary combatants and noncombatants even if they make conscientious attempts to discover the relevant truths. But even if these determinations can be made, it will remain the case that there will be robust contingent reasons to maintain that combatants fighting for a just cause should attack only enemy combatants and refrain from attacking, or harming, civilians, and even though combatants fighting for an unjust cause ought not to be fighting at all, they have much stronger reasons to refrain from attacking or harming civilians

---

22. Notice that the war convention includes both the norm that soldiers fighting in declared wars and aiming fire at enemy combatants act permissibly regardless of the justice of the cause for which they fight and the norm that soldiers fighting in war should refrain from deliberately attacking bystanders and should take care not to impose disproportionate unintended but foreseen damage (collateral harm) on bystanders. The second norm might find its way into the set of justifiable secondary rules of war even though the first does not.

than enemy combatants. These moral facts justify an international law and norms regulating warfare that incorporate noncombatant immunity much as current actual practice does.

I have no horse in this race. Much of what Lazar argues for, I do not argue against. My commitments in this essay require opposing Lazar only insofar as he downplays the importance of culpability in determining who may shoot whom and insofar as he understands culpability differently than this essay has suggested.

What factors most often bring it about that it is morally far worse to attack noncombatants than combatants? One suggestion Lazar makes is that killing soldiers usually involves eliminative not opportunistic agency, killing soldiers the reverse, and killing by opportunistic agency is morally worse, other things equal, than killing by eliminative agency. The difference is that in eliminative killing the presence of the victims does not provide an opportunity for advantage, whereas in opportunistic killing the presence of the victims provides an opportunity to advance the agent's ends by killing them.

My response: generally speaking, to win a war one needs to induce the opposing country's political leaders to agree to stop fighting, and one's military efforts whether directed at combatants or noncombatants are aimed at inducing political leaders to give up the war enterprise, hence opportunistic. Objection: if one obliterates the enemy's military forces, this advances one's war aims, by eliminating an obstacle to overpowering the enemy, whatever the enemy's political leaders might do. Reply: in most wars one does not, or should not, aim to obliterate the enemy or destroy his government, but rather to induce enemy political leaders with authority to declare an end to the fighting.

Another differentiating factor invoked by Lazar is that combatants are generally not defenseless and vulnerable, whereas noncombatants are just that, and attacking the defenseless and vulnerable, among those not liable to be attacked, tends to be morally worse. The reason this is so is that we have special duties to protect the vulnerable, and attacks on noncombatants egregiously offend against this duty. Also, attacking the defenseless and vulnerable takes away their security, and opens them to domination, which is bad.

My response: if harms suffered by combatants and noncombatants would otherwise be equal, the extra cost of insecurity imposed on the latter is either not a harm at all if it is undetected, or if detected is usually of very slight account compared to harms arising from violent attack. If domination is bad, soldiers, being at war, are dominated by the military command structure of the forces they serve. If their country were not facing opposed troops prepared to do battle, the soldiers would not likely be under the thumb of this domination.

Lazar advances the surmise that most combatants, even if in fact fighting for a just cause that justifies their participation, are culpable by being insufficiently concerned to figure out whether or not their cause is just, hence somewhat blame-worthy by way of being negligent or reckless in making the decision to fight. This blameworthiness dampens the force of whatever reasons there are to refrain from attacking them.

My response: this may be so, but if so, does not necessarily establish asymmetry between civilians and soldiers so far as the wrongness of attacking them goes. Civilians are for the most part reckless or negligent in making their decisions whether or not to support a war their country is fighting and to contribute to its success in various noncombatant roles. Both civilians and soldiers may sometimes have straightforwardly wrongful motivations and reasons for their stance toward their country's wars. For example, they may exult at unjust aggression or seek revenge for imagined slights when taking revenge is wrong and culpable. (Some asymmetry may arise here when civilians correctly judge that whether or not they support their country's war will make absolutely no difference to what happens, so sustained expenditure of resources on their part to get the right answer concerning whether their cause is just is not morally required or even morally forbidden.)

The chief differentiating factor that makes killing civilians worse than killing soldiers is that attacking the former carries greater risk that one is attacking innocent people not liable to be harmed. According to Lazar, we should accept a high threshold for liability to be killed. This says that to be liable, (1) one must both make some causal contribution to a significant unjust threat and have "some degree of agential involvement" with that causal contribution, and also (2) the contribution or the involvement must be substantial. A substantial causal contribution must be a "necessary, sufficient, direct cause." Substantial agential involvement must go beyond simple McMahan responsibility and must involve significant culpability (blameworthiness). Noncombatants will generally not be making substantial causal contributions to any large unjust threat and those who are considering launching an attack on them will not be in a good position to assess their culpability. Combatants will generally be making substantial causal contributions of the relevant sort, so attacking a combatant carries a lesser risk that one is attacking a person who is not liable to be killed than attacking a civilian.

Although I have expressed doubt that making a causal contribution to an unjust threat is in itself any sort of factor that works toward rendering oneself a permissible target of attack, I do not claim to have done enough to undermine that common view, so I have no objection to Lazar's acceptance of the relevance of causal contribution. Same goes with agential involvement in the absence of culpability. Where we should definitely part company with Lazar is at the point where he asserts that causal contribution is necessary for liability to be attacked and that alleged culpability in the absence of causal contribution (or just unconnected to it) cannot suffice for liability to attack.

Lazar writes, "Suppose that you can save a saint from a threat only by killing a thief; the thief had nothing to do with the threat at all, but he has stolen in the past. The thief's bad character and past crimes are irrelevant to whether he is liable to be killed. He is not connected to this threat, so he cannot be liable to be killed to avert it." The claim here is that culpability divorced from causal contribution and agential involvement in a wrongful threat is irrelevant to the permissibility of killing the culpable person to avert the threat.

There is something right in what Lazar says here, but he bends the twig too far. He neglects the possibility, central to my claims in this essay involving fault forfeits first, that an individual may be culpable (blameworthy) with respect to a situation, without making a causal contribution to the wrongful threat, averting which justifies a violent response. In his example, the bad character and past crimes of the thief, unrelated to the threat now posed by some unconnected wrongful aggressor, do not (in my view) make him culpable with respect to this wrongful aggression situation. But he might be culpable by trying impotently to contribute to the wrongful aggression, or by being seriously disposed right now to make a significant contribution to this wrongful aggression if he had the opportunity to do so. These futile attempts and currently directed attitudes are relevant to the current situation, in which a person seeking to avert the wrongful aggression must impose violence on someone. (Suppose the person believes in the power of voodoo and magic chants and is summoning up her best harmful chants to unleash wrongful magical harm on the intended victim.) I say that being seriously culpable with respect to this situation, and more culpable than anyone else in this situation, in itself makes you the morally preferred target of violence if someone must be attacked to advance the just cause in the situation. The root idea here is that by sheer luck we might or might not be making a causal contribution, but what surely lies within our control is refraining from having seriously wrongful active dispositions toward those whom we are encountering in a situation we face. Failure to prevent an evil orientation of our will in the situation we are in can suffice to make us an eligible target and the morally most preferred target if there are several candidate targets who might be attacked to advance to just cause. However, Lazar's skepticism about the relevance of culpability unlinked to causal contribution alerts us to the need to clarify the so far fuzzy idea of being culpable "with respect to a situation" on which I here rely.

Lazar in his fine book has further suggestions supporting his claim that soldiers are generally more strongly morally bound to refrain from harming civilians than from harming enemy soldiers. For all I have said, he might be right about that claim. My concern has been to argue that *if* we must either judge some attacks on civilians to be permissible or become contingent pacifists, there might be moral grounds for relaxing the moral insistence on noncombatant immunity (so contingent pacifism can be rejected). Lazar claims to find other grounds for holding both that attacks on enemy soldiers in the course of fighting a just war can be acceptable and that attacks on civilians are almost always unacceptable. That's as may be. I have suggested that some of his arguments to this conclusion are one-sided, and do not support his position as tightly as he supposes. I have also urged that we should resist his implicit rejection of fault forfeits first. Culpability plays a role in setting the location of the boundary between permissible and impermissible killings and violent attacks more than most current Just War theorists, including Lazar, have realized.

5 DURESS AND DUTY

Victor Tadros

Introduction

Around July 16, 1995, Drazen Erdemovic acted as part of a firing squad, killing around seventy unarmed Bosnian Muslim men from Srebrenica, Bosnia and Herzegovina.* These killings were part of the mass execution of Bosnian Muslims at the military-run Pilica Farm in eastern Bosnia where hundreds of men were executed. The International Criminal Tribunal for the former Yugoslavia (ICTY) indicted Erdemovic for murder as a crime against humanity after he confessed to a journalist.[1] As part of his admission he said: "Because of everything that happened I feel terribly sorry, but I could not do anything. When I could do something, I did it." The reason he could do nothing else, he claimed, was that he was threatened with execution along with the other victims. Erdemovic was convicted and sentenced to five years imprisonment.

The case raised a number of difficult questions. My focus is solely on the availability of the defense of duress. The majority held that duress was never a defense to a charge of crimes against humanity. Two of the five judges, Cassese (presiding) and Li, dissented on this issue. Cassese, drawing on the law of a range of jurisdictions, outlined four strict conditions for the availability of the defense:[2]

---

* I am grateful to audiences at the Graduate Conference in Political Philosophy and the Not Just Law II conference at Warwick University and at the War Conference at the University of California San Diego. I am especially grateful to Dana Nelkin, who was my respondent at San Diego, for her excellent comments, and to Dick Arneson, Saba Bazargan, Helen Frowe, Adil Haque, Seth Lazar, Jeff McMahan, and Sam Rickless. I am also grateful to the Leverhulme Foundation for a major research fellowship that allowed me to do further work on this essay.

1. *Prosecutor v Drazen Erdemovic* IT-96-22 (October 7, 1997).

2. Par. 16.

1) The act charged was done under an immediate threat of severe and irreparable harm to life and limb.
2) There was no adequate means of averting such evil.
3) The crime was not disproportionate to the evil threatened: the crime committed under duress must be the lesser of two evils.
4) The situation leading to duress must not have been voluntarily brought about by the person coerced.

The majority followed the common law view that duress is never a defense to murder.

My question is whether and when a person who kills under duress acts permissibly—whether duress justifies rather than whether it excuses. The answer to this question is important in evaluating the law. But the law is concerned with duress as an excuse as well as a justification.

Section I offers a conceptual analysis of duress as a justification. Section II outlines two objections to duress as a justification to killing. Section III argues that these objections are not always decisive where killing is a foreseen side effect of the principal's action. Section IV argues that they are also not always decisive where the person killed was doomed to die. Section V argues that the objections outlined in Section II can be met in part in standard cases of duress. Some support is thus offered to the dissenting judges, though not to Cassese's principles themselves.

I. Duress as a Justification

Pro tanto wrongdoing is not always blameworthy. Those who act wrongly may lack responsibility; they may be excused; or they may be justified. Duress might justify or it might excuse. Some doubt that duress ever justifies wrongdoing.[3] But defenders of this view don't deny that threats can sometimes justify wrongdoing. For example, X's sincere and credible threat that he will shoot D's child if D does not illegally park his car renders D's illegal parking permissible. In fact, D would act wrongly were he not to park—doing so would result in the death of his child. Some deny that this case is a duress case. They use a different defense label, such as "lesser evil," to refer to it.[4] I will use the label "duress" to refer to it.

Standard duress cases have the following features:

---

3. See, for example, J. McMahan, *Killing in War* (Oxford: Oxford University Press, 2009), 113.

4. G. P. Fletcher and J. D. Ohlin, *Defending Humanity: When Force Is Justified and Why* (Oxford: Oxford University Press, 2008), 123, writing in the context of the *Erdemovic* judgment.

1) X threatens D that if D does not *v*, X will *w*.
2) D *v*s to avoid X *w*ing.
3) It is pro tanto wrong for D to *v*.
4) But for X's threat it would be wrong for D to *v*.

Duress justifies where X's threat is sufficiently credible and grave to render it permissible for D to *v*. Duress excuses if D wrongly *v*s all things considered, but X's threat diminishes or eliminates D's blameworthiness for *v*ing.

When duress excuses wrongdoing depends in part on when it justifies wrongdoing: the further D's conduct is from being justified, the more powerful the excuse D needs. For example, being threatened with a broken foot is terrifying. It might excuse breaking another person's foot. But it will not typically excuse homicide. This is not because the extent to which the threat is terrifying depends on what the person is asked to do. It is because the threat of a broken foot is nowhere near serious enough to justify killing.

Evaluating when duress excuses requires us to engage in the difficult task of assessing the psychological impact of duress. Duress in the context of war is often multifaceted and systematic. Living with the constant threat of death not only to oneself but also to those one loves may corrupt a person's moral psyche. The extent to which this excuses very serious wrongdoing is a difficult matter of judgment.

As Primo Levi suggests, those of us who lack the relevant experiences may be ill placed to judge:

> Before discussing separately the motives that impelled some prisoners to collaborate to a varying extent with the Lager authorities, it is necessary however to declare that before such human cases it is imprudent to hasten to issue a moral judgement. It must be clear that the greatest responsibility lies with the system, the very structure of the totalitarian state, the concurrent guilt on the part of the individual big and small collaborators (never likeable, never transparent!) is always difficult to evaluate. It is a judgement that we would like to entrust only to those who found themselves in similar circumstances, and had the possibility to test on themselves what it means to act in a state of coercion.... The condition of the offended does not exclude culpability, and this is often objectively serious, but I know of no human tribunal to which one could delegate the judgement.[5]

Armchair evaluation of duress as a justification is somewhat easier—it does not require an understanding of the psychological impact of duress.

---

5. Primo Levi, *The Drowned and the Saved*, trans. R. Rosenthal (London: Abacus, 1988), 28–29.

Here are two features of duress that I set aside. If X forms a conditional intention to *w* if D does not *v*, X's threat is sincere. If X will succeed in executing this intention if D does not *v*, X's threat is credible. Doubts typically arise about both sincerity and credibility, weakening the case for the defense. For example, did those threatening Erdemovic really intend to shoot him? Would they have executed that threat? Doubts about the answer to either question weaken Erdemovic's defense.

Second, a person who is threatened may not be motivated by the threat. D might *v* simply because he wishes to. Some claim that D's motivation cannot be relevant to the permissibility of D's conduct. Bad intentions, they claim, cannot make a permissible act wrongful.[6] If this is right, duress justifies even when the threats made are causally ineffective.

The better view is that duress justifies only if D acts in order to avert the threat. Consider the penalty for disobeying orders in Nazi Germany known as *Sippenhaft* (kin liability), which warranted killing those who disobey orders and their families. This practice provided the basis of a claim of duress in the *Stalag Luft III* case following World War II, which concerned eighteen members of the SS who were accused of killing fifty members of the RAF. The court did not believe that the members of the SS were acting under duress.[7] However, even if the eighteen were threatened, the defense is not available to those who acted only because they were fully committed to the Nazi cause. Were this not so, given how systematic threats were in Nazi Germany, many Nazis would have been exonerated.[8]

II. Objections to Duress as a Defense to Killing

Duress sometimes justifies pro tanto wrongdoing, I argued. Can it justify killing? The majority in the *Erdemovic* case, following the law of England and Wales, thought not. Duress cannot even *excuse* homicide in the law of England and

---

6. For influential arguments for the irrelevance of intention to permissibility, see J. J. Thomson, "Self-Defense," *Philosophy and Public Affairs* 20 (1991): 283; J. J. Thomson, "Physician-Assisted Suicide: Two Moral Arguments," *Ethics* 109 (1999): 497; F. M. Kamm, *Intricate Ethics: Rights, Responsibility, and Permissible Harm* (Oxford: Oxford University Press, 2007), chap. 5; and T. M. Scanlon, *Moral Dimensions: Permissibility, Meaning, Blame* (Cambridge, Mass.: Harvard University Press, 2008).

7. As Judge Cassese emphasizes in *Erdemovic* par. 24.

8. This was also the view held in the Nuremburg Trials. See K. J. Heller, *The Nuremberg Military Tribunals and the Origins of International Criminal Law* (Oxford: Oxford University Press, 2011), 303–4. For a more complete exploration of the significance of intentions, see V. Tadros, *The Ends of Harm: The Moral Foundations of Criminal Law* (Oxford: Oxford University Press, 2011), chap. 7; and "Wrongful Intentions without Closeness," *Philosophy and Public Affairs* 43 (2015): 52–74.

Wales.[9] The defense is unavailable even if D was an accomplice rather than a principal. It is also unavailable as a defense to attempted murder.[10] The law has many critics. Duress ought at least to be made available as an *excuse* to murder, many claim, even if killing under duress is never justified.[11] Some may object, though, that killing under duress is so far from permissible conduct that the legal position is warranted. Why might this be thought true?

a. Collaboration

If D responds to X's threat, D carries out X's wrongful intentions. D thus helps X fulfill his evil plan. D, it might be argued, thus wrongfully collaborates with evil. Collaborating with evil might be thought gravely wrong.

Two arguments might support this view. The *agent-relative argument* claims that D owes it to himself not to collaborate with evil. The *victim-centered argument* claims that D owes it to V, the person whom D will harm, not to participate in a plan that treats V as insufficiently important.

I doubt the force of the agent-relative argument. The best way to articulate it is as follows.[12] People identify with distinctive activities, goals, and commitments. Collaborating with evil may conflict so powerfully with those activities, goals, and commitments that the person will corrupt herself by collaborating. She may have a self-regarding duty not to corrupt herself in this way. Her integrity, to put the point in another way, is threatened by collaborating with evil, and she may have a duty not to threaten her integrity.[13]

This way of developing the agent-relative argument is unusual in its reliance on self-regarding duties. But, while this is not often noticed, this idea is crucial to the argument: integrity may provide us with a reason, but not a duty, to refrain from collaborating with evil. If collaborating with evil threatens our integrity, and our integrity is important to us, we may be permitted not to collaborate with evil, even where collaboration will benefit innocents. We can refrain from collaboration if the costs to our integrity are too high. But even if so, it does not follow that

---

9. *R v Howe* [1987] AC 417, overruling *DPP v Lynch* [1975] AC 653.

10. *R v Gotts* [1992] 2 AC 412.

11. See, for example, A. Ashworth, *Principles of Criminal Law*, 6th ed. (Oxford: Oxford University Press, 2009), 213–14; D. Ormerod, *Smith and Hogan's Criminal Law*, 13th ed. (Oxford: Oxford University Press, 2011), 360–61.

12. I am grateful, here, to Larry Temkin for helpful discussion.

13. The role of integrity in this context was first highlighted in B. Williams, "A Critique of Utilitarianism," in *Utilitarianism: For and Against*, ed. J. J. C. Smart and B. Williams (Cambridge: Cambridge University Press, 1973). Williams, it should be said, was not very clear about what he meant by integrity or why it might be morally important.

it is wrong for D to respond to X's threat. A person wrongly threatens her integrity only if doing so violates a self-regarding duty, not merely a self-regarding reason.

To explore whether there is such a duty, let us begin with the self-regarding reason a person may have not to collaborate. We can then see whether the person has a duty to do what she has reason to do. Many will feel the force of the reason against collaboration: were D to give in to X's threat D would subordinate himself to X's will while abhorring the end that X has set for himself. D, it might be argued, has a powerful reason against forging this relationship with X. In refusing to respond to X's threats, D secures his independence from X's will. This comes at a price—the price of the threat being carried out. Sometimes this price may be too high to make it permissible for D to secure his independence in this way. Nevertheless, D secures his independence from X, which has great value. Significant costs may be worth bearing in order to achieve this.

Does this reason amount to a duty? Perhaps. Bending himself to X's will too easily is demeaning. Perhaps self-respect requires (pro tanto) a person to execute the intentions of others only if their ends can be shared, or at least tolerated. Let us suppose that this is true. Even if this is true, the duty that I have just referred to is defeasible. I doubt that it is typically sufficiently powerful to render it wrong to act under duress when lives are at stake.

Furthermore, even if this self-regarding duty renders it wrong for D to collaborate with X, it does not imply that D wrongs V by collaborating with X. This suggests that the importance of the agent-relative argument may not extend to international criminal justice: it is more difficult to justify publicly condemning and punishing a person for violating self-regarding duties than other-regarding duties.

For these reasons, our focus should be on victim-centered arguments. But victim-centered arguments against collaboration are harder to find. D need not *endorse* X's intention, or share the disrespect that X shows to V—the fact that he acts on the threat tends to suggest otherwise. Perhaps it might be argued that D disrespects V by creating the impression that he endorses X's intention. But even if this could be wrong, it is not very gravely wrong. And it may be clear to everyone, including V, that D is only acting under duress.

b. Two Nonconsequentialist Principles

A stronger argument claims that killing under duress violates stringent nonconsequentialist principles. It is sometimes wrong to kill an innocent person to save one's own life—so clearly wrong that doing so would be difficult to excuse. Consider:

Human Shield: X is attempting to shoot D. D grabs V, an innocent bystander, and uses V as a human shield. X shoots V several times killing her.

D wrongly uses V as a human shield to prevent himself from being killed. This seems so clearly wrong that D's conduct is hard to excuse. D, along with X, murders V.

To support this verdict, notice that D violates two well-established moral doctrines. The Doctrine of Doing and Allowing (DDA) claims that it is more difficult to justify killing a person than refraining to save a person. Killing a person is justified only if doing so saves more people from being killed. This is not true in *Human Shield*. Hence, D wrongly kills V. The *means principle* claims that there is an especially stringent prohibition on harmfully using a person as a means to save others.[14] If D uses V as a human shield, D uses V as a means to save his own life. Hence, D wrongly kills V.

Obviously, the DDA and the *means principle* are controversial. I will not aim to justify them here.[15] They offer powerful support to the restrictive law of duress in England and Wales. Consider:

Standard Duress: X threatens D that if D does not kill V, X will kill D.

Standard Duress seemingly shares morally salient features with *Human Shield*. D kills rather than allowing V to die, and D uses V to save his own life. The killing of V is the means by which D influences X's intentions, averting the threat that he

---

14. For reasons beyond the scope of this essay, I think it better to refer to the *means principle* here than the more familiar Doctrine of Double Effect. There are various interpretations of this principle. My own interpretation is outlined in *The Ends of Harm*, chaps. 6 and 7, and more recently in "Wrongful Intentions without Closeness." For related views, see W. Quinn, "Actions, Intentions and Consequences: The Doctrine of Double Effect," in *Morality and Action* (Cambridge: Cambridge University Press, 1993), 185; J. McMahan, "Revising the Doctrine of Double Effect," *Journal of Applied Philosophy* 11 (1994): 201; P. A. Woodward: "The Importance of the Proportionality Condition to the Doctrine of Double Effect: A Response to Fischer, Ravizza, and Copp," *Journal of Social Philosophy* 28 (1997): 140; F. M. Kamm, *Intricate Ethics: Rights, Responsibilities, and Permissible Harm* (Oxford: Oxford University Press, 2007), chap. 3; I. A. Smith, "A New Defense of Quinn's Principle of Double Effect," *Journal of Social Philosophy* 38 (2007): 349; D. K. Nelkin and S. C. Rickless, "Three Cheers for Double Effect," *Philosophy and Phenomenological Research* 89 (2014): 125–58.

15. Let me, though, respond to one objection to the *means principle*. Kai Draper, in "Double Effect and the Laws of War" in this volume, suggests that the *means principle* cannot be justified because there is no significant intuitive difference between using V's body to prevent deaths of others (Push) and using a car with V in it to prevent deaths of others (Push Car II), if V will be killed. I think that there is a fairly strong intuitive difference between these cases, but I am also doubtful that our intuitions about these cases should move us too strongly. In the second case we have an inclination, that may well be unwarranted, not to discriminate between "using the car" and "using the car with a person in it." For this reason, it is difficult to trust our intuitions about the second case. Draper relies almost solely on intuition, and does not deeply explore arguments that have been offered in favor of the *means principle*. Even if his intuitions are widely shared, which I doubt, he has not discharged the burden of showing that the otherwise highly plausible *means principle* is false.

faces from X. This, it might be argued, is no different from using V to save his own life in cases such as *Human Shield*.[16] If D's conduct in *Human Shield* is inexcusable, isn't this also true of *Standard Duress*?

I will suggest that while these arguments are powerful, three countervailing arguments militate in favor of permitting the duress defense to killing in at least in some cases. First, a person who kills under duress may not treat his victim as a means. The DDA applies in these circumstances, but the more stringent *means principle* does not. Second, killing a person who is already doomed to die is easier to justify, even if that person is killed as a means. This factor was important in *Erdemovic*. Third, in *Standard Duress*, unlike *Human Shield*, although the person killed is used as a means, she is not killed opportunistically, in a sense to be explained, rendering the killing less problematic.

III. Duress and Side Effect Killing

Killing as a side effect rather than intentionally is sometimes murder. Consider:

Insurance. D plants a bomb in his shop in order to destroy it for the insurance money. He detonates the bomb, certain that V, a passerby, will be killed.

D foresees V's death as a certain side effect of his action rather than intending it. The law of England and Wales plausibly holds that D murders V.[17]

It is easy to see how killing under duress need not be intentional. X threatens D to act in a way that will kill V. D intends to act in that way in virtue of the fact that if D executes X's intention, X will not carry out the threat. Whether V's death is the means by which X's threat is averted, though, depends on whether X

---

16. Jeff McMahan picks out these two features of morality as reasons to doubt the validity of the duress defense as a justification or a complete excuse to killing in war. About the standard case of duress where X threatens you with death unless you kill V, he writes: "First, to accede to the demand of the person who threatens you would involve *killing*, whereas to refuse would involve allowing someone—yourself—to be killed. And it is, and always has been, widely accepted that the moral presumption against killing is in general stronger than the presumption against allowing someone to be killed (that is, failing to prevent someone from being killed). Second, killing the innocent third party would involve *intending* a harmful death, while refusing to kill him would not. And it is, and always has been, widely accepted that the moral presumption against bringing about a harmful death as an intended effect is in general stronger than the presumption against bringing about a harmful death as a foreseen but unintended effect." J. McMahan, *Killing in War*, 113.

17. See *R v Woollin* [1999] 1 AC 82. *Woollin* has the distracting feature that side effect killings are included within the definition of intention. In principle, the jury has the latitude not to call this a murder. They would almost certainly convict in this case though.

intends V's death. If X does not intend V's death, D need not intend V's death. In such a case, V's death is not the means by which X's intention is fulfilled.

Consider:

Insurance Threat: X wants his shop blown up for the insurance money. He threatens D that if D does not detonate a bomb that X has planted, X will kill D and four other members of D's family. Detonating the bomb will certainly kill V, a passerby.

V's death is a side effect of the execution of D's intention to blow up the shop. Furthermore, V's death is not the means by which X's threat to D and his family is averted. Hence, the *means principle* is not engaged.

Does the DDA render it wrong for D to kill V? The DDA is normally thought less stringent than the *means principle*. It is at least sometimes permissible to kill a person as a side effect to avert a lethal threat to more people. For example, it is permissible to turn a trolley away from five people toward one who will certainly be killed. It may not always be permissible to kill one person as a side effect of saving five. Consider Philippa Foot's example: an antidote could be created that will save five lives but creating it will also give rise to lethal fumes that will kill one person. It is to some extent intuitive that it is wrong to create the antidote even though the killing of the one person is a side effect of the act that saves the five.

I am unsure about the relevant differences between these cases. Some claim that it is more difficult to justify creating a new threat than diverting an existent threat.[18] But creating a new threat is also sometimes permitted. For example, in the context of a just war, it is intuitively permissible to bomb munitions factories even if civilians will be killed as a side effect. Doing so creates a new threat rather than merely diverting a threat.

Whatever the right view on this matter, I find it intuitive that D is permitted to blow up the shop to save himself and his family in *Insurance Threat*. One reason is that D avoids a threat to his family, and he has a duty to protect them. Another is that although D creates a new threat, V is already engaged in the situation, as a result of having been identified by X.

---

18. Those who find this idea morally significant include J. A. Montmarquet, "On Doing Good: The Right and the Wrong Way," *The Journal of Philosophy* 79 (1982): 439; P. Foot, "Killing and Letting Die," in *Moral Dilemmas* (Oxford: Oxford University Press, 2002), 78–87; and J. J. Thomson, "The Trolley Problem," in *Rights, Restitution, and Risk: Essays in Moral Theory* (Cambridge, Mass.: Harvard University Press, 1986), 94–126. For doubts, see W. Quinn, "Actions, Intentions, and Consequences: The Doctrine of Doing and Allowing," in *Morality and Action* (Cambridge: Cambridge University Press, 1993), 159–60; F. M. Kamm, *Morality, Mortality*, vol. 2: *Rights, Duties and Status* (Oxford: Oxford University Press, 1996), 162–66.

This example has implications for soldiers who are threatened to participate in unjust wars. It may be pro tanto wrong for a soldier to go to war, or to commit a particular act of war, because the harm caused as a side effect will be disproportionate. Even if duress is not a defense to engaging in a war that lacks a just cause, it may sometimes be a defense to engaging in disproportionate war.

Perhaps it might be argued that the threat will never be sufficiently grave to outweigh the deaths that a soldier will cause as a side effect. Against this, remember that a soldier participating in a war will be uncertain about the harms that he will cause. Suppose that a soldier is threatened that if he does not engage in a disproportionate war he will spend the rest of his life in jail. He goes to war and kills a civilian as a side effect. Let us also suppose that, were it not for the threat that the soldier faced, the risk to the civilian would have rendered the act of war disproportionate. It follows that were it not for the threat that the soldier faced, the soldier would have committed an unjustified homicide—the equivalent of what, in English law, is called manslaughter. Nevertheless, the soldier may have been permitted, all things considered, to engage in the act of war. Duress would be a defense to an act that would otherwise constitute a wrongful killing.

IV. Killing Those Who Are Doomed to Die

Erdemovic's killings have this notable feature: as his victims were to be shot by firing squad, they were almost certain to have been killed regardless of whether Erdemovic did the killing. What is the significance of this feature?

a. Overdetermined Death

Bernard Williams's famous *Jim and the Indians* case makes this problem familiar. Here is a summarized version:

> *Jim and the Indians.* Jim finds himself in the central square of a small South American town. The captain has tied twenty Indians against a wall. He is about to kill them. The Indians have been randomly selected to remind people of the disadvantages of protesting. As Jim is an honored visitor, the captain makes him an offer that if he kills one Indian from the group then, as a special mark of the occasion, the other Indians will be set free. Otherwise all twenty will be killed. There is no other way for Jim to save anyone. The Indians and other villagers beg Jim to accept.[19]

---

19. Bernard Williams, "A Critique of Utilitarianism," 98–99.

Most people think that Jim is at least permitted to kill one Indian. Many think that he is required to do so.

Central to explaining these judgments is this. Compare:

(1) Jim selects and kills one Indian; with
(2) Jim does nothing.

Jim selecting and killing one Indian preempts the captain killing twenty. Hence, (1) renders no Indian worse off overall than (2). But (1) renders nineteen Indians much better off than (2). Many people conclude that as long as the Indian killed is selected fairly, Jim does nothing wrong all things considered in killing an Indian.

Nevertheless, as Williams suggested, *Jim and the Indians* is a troubling case. Williams thought it a failing of utilitarianism, and other versions of consequentialism, that it could not explain why the case is troubling. For consequentialists killing the one Indian is pure benefit. But, Williams thought, Jim's conduct is troubling because killing an Indian would damage Jim's integrity. This, he claimed, was closely related to the fact that Jim would do the killing. It is not simply because Jim would be killing rather than letting die that explains our uneasiness, Williams claimed. It is rather that in killing there would be a conflict between Jim's actions and the projects that he is committed to and that he values.[20] While, for Williams, this did not necessarily render the conduct wrong, it should at least give us pause for thought. Consequentialists don't pause.

For reasons outlined above, I doubt integrity is very significant in this context. Williams's claim that we should feel uneasy about the permissibility of Jim killing one of the Indians can be vindicated though. The mere fact that no one is made worse off, and some are made much better off, by Jim's act does not render that act trouble-free. Sometimes it can be wrong to act in a way that will render no one worse off. Suppose that there is only one Indian who is doomed to die. Jim can kill this Indian or let the captain do so. If Jim kills the Indian, he will receive a reward of some jellybeans that will otherwise go to waste. The Indian is no worse off than he would be were the captain to kill him, and Jim is better off in virtue of having received jellybeans. Yet it is surely wrong for Jim to kill.

Now consider:

Duress (Doomed Variation): X threatens D that if D does not kill V, X will kill D. X will also immediately kill V.

---

20. Ibid., 116–17.

As in *Jim and the Indians*, if D kills V, no one is worse off and someone is much better off—in this case D. Even though we should also be troubled by this case, I believe that it is permissible for D to kill V. This seems so even if V does not consent to D killing him.

One way to reinforce this verdict is to consider V's perspective more closely. V will certainly be killed: either by D or by X. Suppose that V would prefer to be killed by X than D. Suppose also that V is able to select his killer. If V selects D as his killer, D's life will be saved. V's preferences, in this case, do not seem decisive. V is required to select D as his killer given that this will save D's life. Why should V have this duty? V's autonomy is already very severely constrained—he will certainly be killed almost immediately. Shouldn't we at least permit him to choose the death he prefers? Not if this will result in D's death.

Furthermore, were V able to select his killer, not only would he have a duty to select D, he would have an enforceable duty to do so. In determining whether a duty is enforceable, various considerations are relevant. Reasons that favor rendering a duty unenforceable include the importance to V of being able to make the right decision without being in the shadow of a threat, the importance to V of learning from mistakes, the costs that may be imposed on V if others attempt to enforce the duty, and the basic interest that we all have in being free from interference by others. The most important consideration that counts against a duty being unenforceable is the importance of the value that gives rise to the duty. In this case, the source of the duty is the importance of protecting D from being killed. D's life is easily sufficient, I think, to render V's duty enforceable.

Hence, if D kills V, D's act is one that V would have a duty to bring about were V able to do so, and V could be forced to execute that duty. If D kills V, D shows sufficient respect for V, even if he acts against V's preferences. I do not say, I should emphasize, that a hypothetical duty to authorize is *always required* to render killing permissible. Furthermore, if *actual* authorization can be secured, D ought to secure it. It respects another person more to treat their authorization as important even when it is not required. Compare taking, rather than asking for, another person's fire hydrant when it is required to put out a fire. But in the absence of actual authorization, the fact that V would have an enforceable duty to authorize D to kill him provides a powerful reason in favor of permitting D to kill V.

b. Self-Selection and Collaboration

This argument is unavailable in a related case. Consider:

Choose Oneself: X threatens twenty people, who are identical in all morally salient respects, that he will kill them all unless any one of them kills the other nineteen.

The one who kills the other nineteen will be saved. Each person is separated from the other nineteen and they cannot communicate with each other. Each can kill the other nineteen simply by pressing a button. The person who presses fastest will survive.

Let us suppose that D, a member of the twenty, kills the other nineteen. He is then saved. Does D act wrongly?

Evaluating this case helps us to evaluate collaboration in Nazi concentration camps. Primo Levi explained that collaborating improved one's chances of surviving the camps:

> The privileged prisoners were a minority within the Lager population, but they represent a potent majority among survivors; in fact, even if one does not take into account the hard labour, the beatings, the cold, the illnesses, it must be remembered that the food ration was decisively insufficient even for the most frugal prisoner: the physiological reserves of the organism being consumed in two or three months, death by hunger, or by diseases induced by hunger, was the prisoner's normal destiny. This could be avoided only with additional food, and to obtain it a large or small privilege was necessary; in other words, a way, granted or conquered, astute or violent, licit or illicit, to lift oneself above the norm.[21]

Levi's case involves many empirical and normative complications that *Choose Oneself* lacks. It is not clear whether more people survived the camps as a result of collaboration. Perhaps collaborators each increased the number of deaths overall. Some collaborators also only deprived others of resources rather than killing them in a more direct way.

Choose Oneself raises fewer moral considerations. Nevertheless, there are similarities between Levi's analysis of the Lager and *Choose Oneself*. In the Lager, there was no real prospect of fairly selecting who collaborates. A person must select herself to be "above the norm." If no one does this, Levi implies, more will die. But selecting oneself renders others worse off—it deprives each person of an opportunity to select herself to be "above the norm," and thus to save herself.

Suppose that the twenty could find a fair procedure for selecting the person who will kill the other nineteen. Each person would have a strong reason to participate in such a procedure. Each person would be better off ex ante than she would be were no one selected: each would have a one in twenty chance of survival

---

21. Levi, *The Drowned and the Saved*, 26.

as opposed to zero chance of survival. Furthermore, no one will be worse off ex post than she would be were no one selected. Each person who is killed would immediately have been killed anyway. Finally, one person would be much better off ex post than she would be were no one selected. These considerations militate strongly in favor of permitting the twenty to operate a fair procedure for selecting one killer. In such circumstances, it seems wrong for any person to press the button without setting up a fair procedure.

Where a fair procedure cannot be set up through mutual agreement, as in *Choose Oneself*, individuals ought to model such a procedure as best they can. How can they do this? It might be argued that it is fair for each person to press as quickly as possible. I doubt this is fair. It advantages those who are unscrupulous, who reason quickly, who press quickly, and so on. Perhaps it might be argued that it is a matter of luck whether one has these characteristics, and so the procedure that relies on them, being random, is fair. This seems false. Consider the systematic effects of people being permitted to rely on their quick-pressing skills and tendencies over the course of their lives. The slow, indecisive, and conscientious will systematically lose out to the fast, decisive, and unscrupulous. We can expect that people with the favorable characteristics will have secured many other advantages for themselves over the course of their own lives already. For this reason, procedures that do not rely on advantageous characteristics that people have are fairer.

Another possibility: each person could put his name in a hat with nineteen blank pieces of paper in it (assuming each has a hat and paper). Only if his name comes up will he press the button. Otherwise he refrains.[22] This suggestion has the following deficiency: it is possible that no one among the twenty selects the piece of paper with his own name on it. If this occurs, all twenty will be killed.

Another solution: each person should press the button only at the moment when, from the evidence that he has, he will have a one in twenty chance of being saved. That would give him the chance of being saved that he would have under a fair procedure. If he does this, it might be argued, he respects the other nineteen by refraining from taking for himself more than his fair chance of survival.

This solution is also problematic. Imagine that D, one of the twenty, knows that the other nineteen are committed pacifists. They will *definitely* refrain from pressing the button themselves. In that case, at any moment that D presses the button, his probability of surviving, from his evidential perspective, is one. If D is not permitted to press the button until his prospects of survival are one in twenty, he is never permitted to press the button, and all twenty will be killed. The pacifism of the nineteen cannot condemn D to death.

---

22. I thank Matthew Clayton for this suggestion, which he does not endorse.

A better solution: each person must act in a way that will give an equal chance of survival to those who wish to have such a chance of survival. If there are ten committed pacifists and ten who want an equal chance of survival, D should press the button at the moment when he has a one in ten chance of surviving. This is the maximum chance that D can have of survival consistent with providing an equal chance to those who want it.

This solution, though, does not take account of the possibility that there might be an unscrupulous person among the group who will certainly press as quickly as possible. For example, suppose that D knows that E is unscrupulous and will certainly attempt to save his own life by pressing immediately. E is faster than all of the others except D. It might be argued that D, in these circumstances, is permitted to press. He has two options: either save himself or allow E to save himself. E, it might be argued, forfeits his right to a chance in virtue of his intention to deprive the other eighteen of their chance of survival. D thus does not act wrongly by saving himself.

In the light of this, consider collaboration in concentration camps. Suppose that collaboration does not increase the number of deaths overall. However, by collaborating, a person may deny others a chance to collaborate. If one person takes the position of an administrator in a concentration camp, that position is not open to others. By taking this position, this person may disadvantage the others by denying them an opportunity to collaborate. Each person ought to provide a fair opportunity of collaboration to those others who want to collaborate.

Even if collaboration did not increase the number of deaths in the camp, many collaborators will have acted wrongly. Collaboration may have been wrong because collaborators unfairly raised themselves above the norm at the expense of others. Had they done so fairly, collaboration might have been permitted.

V. Manipulation, Opportunism, and Duress

In standard cases of duress, the arguments developed in the previous section do not apply. For example, in *Standard Duress*, V is safe if D does nothing. *Standard Duress* may seem no different from *Human Shield*—both the DDA and the *means principle* are implicated in both cases.

Yet, while killing under duress does seem difficult to justify, and may be unjustified in *Standard Duress*, it is unintuitive that *Standard Duress* is on a par with *Human Shield*. Suppose that *Standard Duress* is revised so that the threat that X poses to D is not only to D but also to four members of D's family. I find it intuitive that D may kill V. Yet using an innocent person as a human shield seems wrong even to protect oneself and four members of one's family. Here I suggest two important differences between these cases.

a. Agency and Responsibility

First, in killing V, D would be carrying out X's intentions, not pursuing his own aims.

Kamm argues that in these circumstances, X has full responsibility for the killing. In virtue of this fact, D lacks some degree of responsibility. This is so, she suggests, partly for a complex retributivist reason. If D kills V, X will deserve to suffer for his crimes. When X threatens D, there is a special reason for D to kill V: if D kills V, X will then deserve to suffer. As X has threatened D, Kamm suggests, D deserves to suffer. There is what we might call a "meta-retributivist" reason for D to kill V.[23]

Kamm's explanation is doubtful. We should generally doubt retributivism.[24] Meta-retributivism is even more difficult to believe. Here is a better approach. Consider more carefully the relationship between X's intention and the intention that D forms and executes. D forms and executes the intention to kill V only because X has the intention that D forms and executes the intention to kill V. The content of D's intention, in this case, largely depends on the content of X's intention. D would form and execute *any* intention that X wished him to form and execute. At least, this is true within broad limits—D would not kill all of his family and others in virtue of the threat that X poses to him and his family.

Here is another way to understand this. D's first order intention to kill V is formed in virtue of a second order intention: to form and execute the intention that X intends D to form and execute. This idea is neatly captured in cases where X first poses the threat to D and his family, and D responds by saying, "I'll do whatever you want."

Forming a second order intention to form and execute the intentions that another person wants one to form and execute is a central component of becoming another person's Agent. Agency, in the sense we are interested in, involves a relationship between an Agent and director where the director intends to issue instructions to the Agent about what to do and the Agent intends to do what he is instructed to do.

It might seem that whether one is an Agent can make no difference to what one is permitted to do for the following reason. D needs to decide whether to act

---

23. Kamm, *Intricate Ethics*, chap. 10. See, also, *The Moral Target: Aiming at Right Conduct in War and Other Conflicts* (Oxford: Oxford University Press, 2012), chap. 5. Kamm herself denies that it is permissible to kill one to save five in cases of this kind (*Intricate Ethics*, 306). Kamm treats this case as similar in important respects to using another person as a means to the good (see *Intricate Ethics* 337n7). "Redirecting" X might, though, be permitted. See *Intricate Ethics*, 307.

24. See, further, V. Tadros, *The Ends of Harm*, chap. 4.

as X's Agent. In deciding whether to do this, D must consider what he will be instructed to do. If D will be instructed to act wrongly, D ought not to become X's Agent. If X instructs D to act wrongly, D's act cannot become permissible in virtue of the fact that D acts as X's Agent. For any consideration that renders acting in this way wrong were D not X's Agent would count in exactly the same way against D becoming X's Agent. For example, if it is wrong for D to kill V as a means to save five were D not X's Agent, D also has a decisive reason not to become X's Agent. For were D to become X's Agent, D would form an intention to follow X's instruction to kill V as a means to save the five. As it is wrong for D to do this, it is wrong for D to become X's Agent.

I begin by showing that this argument at least sometimes fails. Notice that a director sometimes has a right to do wrong. The reasons that militate in favor of him having such a right also militate in favor of his being permitted to seek help to act wrongly. If so, acting as the Agent of the person who has a right to do wrong is not wrong.

Consider:

Rock and Roll. X wishes to play loud rock music on her stereo. Her physical disability prevents her bending down to turn on her stereo. D is X's home help. X instructs D to turn the music on loudly. This disturbs V, X's neighbor. X is unmoved by this.

Let us suppose both that it would be wrong for X to put her music on this loudly and also that it would be wrong for other people to prevent her from doing this—there is good reason for X to have a liberty right to play loud music, even when this wrongs V. It may also be permissible for D to help X to execute her intention to do this.

This view seems attractive for the following reason. We have a powerful reason to ameliorate the extent to which X's liberty is restricted as a result of her disability. Allowing X to have D act as her agent secures this aim. If D forms the second order intention to do what X wishes her to do, X effectively acquires an ability to achieve her ends—she has a tool that is responsive to her instructions. If X instructs D to put the music on, X acts wrongly. D, though, does not act wrongly. It is *only* X and *not* D who is morally responsible for the wrongful disturbance caused to V.

This demonstrates that it is sometimes permissible for an Agent to carry out an instruction that it was wrong for the director to issue. Furthermore, it demonstrates that this is sometimes true in virtue of the fact that Agency eliminates responsibility for wrongdoing: the director's responsibility for the wrongful act that the Agent helps her to perform negates the Agent's moral responsibility for it.

This discussion, though, provides limited support to the importance of Agency in duress cases. The reason is that the argument depends on D's powerful reason to ameliorate the restriction on X's liberty. This is not true in cases such as *Standard Duress*. D has no reason to enhance X's liberty to kill V by deciding to act as X's Agent.

We need a different argument for why Agency can sometimes make a difference to responsibility. It will help us to understand the issues better if we consider an Agent's decision to form a second order intention to follow the instructions of the director. Consider:

Inchoate Duress: X sincerely and credibly threatens D that if D does not do what X instructs D to do X will kill D's child.

D has a good reason to form a conditional intention to do what X instructs him to do. Within some limits—wide limits—D ought to do as X tells him. For example, if X tells D to tie X's shoelaces, or to go to the shops for milk, and so on and so forth, D ought to do these things. There are some things that D clearly ought not to do if X instructs him. He ought not to kill two of his children to save the one child threatened by X, for example. This is a condition on the second order intention that D ought to form in the face of X's threat. D should think: I will do some range of actions (let us call them "permitted actions") if instructed to do them but I will not do some other range of actions (let us call them "prohibited actions") if instructed to do them.

If X threatens D to become X's Agent and X's threat is sincere, credible, and serious, D has good reason to become X's Agent by forming a conditional intention to do what X commands. Our question is: what is the range of prohibited actions that ought to condition D's intention to act as X's Agent?

To help answer this question, consider the circumstances in which we would be required not to provide another person with a tool that will be used for killing. In forming the intention to act on another person's instructions, one makes oneself into the other's tool. If one can provide a tool for another person in order to avert a threat, perhaps one can also make oneself into a tool for another person in order to avert that threat. But providing another person with a tool does not seem stringently controlled by the *means principle*. Consider:

Sword: X wishes to kill V with a sword. Only D has access to the sword. If D does not provide X with the sword, X will kill D and four members of his family.

Even though D "does" rather than "allows" in this case, D's act seems permissible. D does not use V as a means to avert the threat.

Perhaps it makes a difference, in duress cases, that the person doing the killing *is herself* the tool that is used to do the killing. I doubt that this feature is terribly significant. Compare:

Human Club: X wishes to kill V. He can do this by using D as a human club, but only if D holds his body rigid. X will swing D at V, killing V.

D *makes himself* X's tool. This still seems permissible. In deciding to hold his body rigid, D does not use V as a means to save the five in the objectionable way that V is used in *Human Shield*.

Making oneself another person's Agent is different from making oneself into a human club. In making oneself into an Agent, one forms an intention to form and execute the intentions one is instructed to form. When these intentions are carried out, the harm that one imposes on others is imposed intentionally (or at least, one has the intention to affect others in a way that will harm them).

Nevertheless, perhaps the conditions under which one may make oneself the Agent of another are not terribly dissimilar to the conditions under which one may make oneself into a tool for the use by another. When one acts as an Agent, one treats oneself as a tool for the other's use. This may also negate, to some extent, the responsibility that one has for one's own actions. Perhaps the moral difference between supplying a person with a tool and turning oneself into a tool by making oneself the other person's Agent is not so great. If D is entitled to provide X with a sword in *Sword*, this suggests, D is also permitted to kill V if that is the only way to avert the threat to himself and four members of his family.

I remain unsure about this argument. I am tempted to think it has some force. In making oneself another person's Agent, it is the content of the second order intention—the intention to form and execute the intentions one is instructed to form and execute—that one is committed to. The content of one's first order intention is simply "whatever the director commands one to have." One can sometimes have good reason to give priority to such a second order intention, as we can already see from cases such as *Rock and Roll*. Perhaps in duress cases, one has a similar reason to give one's second order intentions priority in guiding one's actions—doing so is necessary to avert a significant threat. This distancing can perhaps diminish one's responsibility for the content of these first order intentions at least to some extent.[25]

---

25. This also helps to support Kamm's view, defended in *Intricate Ethics*, chap.10, that it makes a difference whether the person acting is responding to an offer from the threat maker, or whether she instigates the offer. It does so, though, on different grounds to those she offers.

b. Opportunism and Manipulation

There is another important difference between *Standard Duress* and *Human Shield* that I initially crudely characterized. In *Human Shield*, V is simply a bystander. If V is used as a means he is compelled to be involved in a scenario that he otherwise has no involvement in. In *Standard Duress*, in contrast, V is already involved in the threat that is posed to the five. The threat to the five comes about in virtue of the fact that X has targeted V.

To assess this fact, there are three different features of cases like *Human Shield* that might make killing especially wrong. First, if D kills V, D uses V to save the five—his killing is manipulative. Second, if D kills V, V will have provided D with an opportunity to save the five. Hence, if D kills V the five will have benefited from V's presence at the scene. In contrast, if D does not kill V, the five are no worse off than they would have been had V not been present at the scene. Let us say that if D kills V, D acts *opportunistically*—he exploits an opportunity created by V's presence. Third, V makes no causal contribution to the threat that the five face. Hence, if D kills V, he does not eliminate a threat that V makes a causal contribution to. D thus does not act *eliminatively*.[26]

Each of these features of *Human Shield* may have normative significance. First, a person can object to being used as a tool to serve an end. It is especially wrong, it might be argued, to use a person to serve one's ends. Each person is entitled to set ends for herself. She may not have her ends imposed on her by others. Using a person is a way of imposing ends on a person. It treats her as though she exists to serve these ends. This is inconsistent with her status as an end-setter.

Second, a person has a more powerful complaint against others exploiting opportunities that exist only in virtue of her presence. A person should not benefit from my existence in a way that harms me. If anyone is to benefit from my existence, it should be me.

Third, a person may object to being harmed if she has made no contribution to the threat that others face. If harming a person merely neutralizes a threat that she poses, harming her is easier to justify. A person can often be expected to internalize the costs of her own existence or presence. She should aim to ensure that her existence or presence is not harmful.

Obviously, there is much more to say about these ideas than I have space for here. I have only sketched an account that I hope reveals that they have some

---

26. For the distinction between opportunistic agency and eliminative agency, see W. Quinn, "Actions, Intentions, and Consequences: The Doctrine of Double Effect," *Philosophy and Public Affairs* 18 (1989): 334–51, at 344.

intuitive force. They are also subject to qualifications and limits that I cannot explore.

In *Standard Duress*, like in *Human Shield*, if D kills V, D uses V. If I am right in my characterization of what is wrong with manipulative agency, V might object that he has been used to serve the end of motivating X not to kill D at the cost of his life. This, he might argue, is not an end that he is required to serve. However, D does not exploit an opportunity to avert a threat that exists only in virtue of V's presence. If V had not existed, X would not have posed the threat to D. Furthermore, if D kills V, D eliminates a threat that is the result of V's existence.

The last two facts can also come apart.[27] The reason is that causal contribution and counterfactual dependence can come apart. Consider:

One of Two: X needs a new heart. A and B have compatible hearts. X threatens D that if D does not kill either A or B, X will kill D and four members of D's family.

The presence of A and B causes X to threaten D. However, X would have threatened D if either A had not been present (for B's heart will suffice) or B had not been present (for A's heart will suffice). Neither A nor B, considered alone, makes a difference to D's predicament. Nevertheless, A makes a causal contribution to the threat that D faces.[28]

This case is difficult to evaluate, and my response is tentative. The fact that A and B make a causal contribution to the threat is, I think, itself sufficient to distinguish *One of Two* from *Human Shield*. A and B are both involved in the threat as members of the group of people who can provide X with a heart, and hence which motivates X to threaten D. However, D's justification for killing either A or B in *One of Two* may be weaker than standard duress cases. And the justification for killing may be even weaker for much larger groups—for example if a whole crowd of people had a suitable heart.

---

27. I was prompted to think about this issue by comments made independently by Dana Nelkin and Bob Myers.

28. There is a dispute in the philosophy of causation about whether it is true that A causes the threat. In cases where two events are sufficient to produce a certain outcome that in fact comes about, and neither preempts the other, the most commonly accepted view is that both events make a causal contribution to the outcome. See J. Woodward, "Psychological Studies of Causal and Counterfactual Reasoning," in *Understanding Counterfactuals, Understanding Causation: Issues in Philosophy and Psychology*, ed. C. Hoerl, T. McCormack, and S. R. Beck (Oxford: Oxford University Press, 2011), 35.

Overall, although killing in duress cases is manipulative, and this counts heavily against it, it does not have other morally salient features that we find in standard cases of manipulative harming. Killing the person need not be opportunistic, and can be eliminative. This provides some support for the permissibility of killing under duress.

Conclusion

My aim has been to show that there are circumstances in which duress can justify killing a person where that killing would otherwise be wrong. Furthermore, I have aimed to show that the restriction on harming a person under duress is not as strict as the restriction on harming others as a means. There is also much more to say about duress as a justification than I have said here. Even my modest results seem important in helping to support Cassese's dissent in *Erdemovic*. A blanket restriction on duress as a defense to homicide, even to crimes against humanity, seems to me unwarranted, at least if the law aims to track morality reasonably closely.

6 CAN STATES BE CORPORATELY LIABLE TO ATTACK IN WAR?

François Tanguay-Renaud

States as Collectives and Liability: An Underexplored Starting Point

Under the influence of Jeff McMahan's groundbreaking work, many recent writings in Just War theory have taken a fundamentally individualistic turn in their approach to the morality of war.[1] It is individuals' actions that make wars unjust, and it is individuals' liability and moral value that govern how wars should be fought. Collectives' existence, rights, or liability have no salient moral role to play, and insofar as they figure in discussions of the morality of war, it is merely as shorthand for deeper individualistic complexities. Such radical reductive individualism is generally asserted in reaction to a longstanding theoretical tradition according to which the morality of war applies primarily to the acts of collective entities—namely, states—and only derivatively to the acts of individuals, such that otherwise familiar principles of individual morality do not apply in that context.[2] To be sure, one of the most strident rallying cries of individualist theorists is that traditional war doctrines that ascribe irreducible moral salience to

* I wish to thank Vincent Chiao, Helen Frowe, Adil Haque, Seth Lazar, Victor Tadros, Helga Varden, and Ekow Yankah for their comments in the context of two workshops where this essay was presented. I also thank the editors of this volume for their written comments. This research was made possible by a grant from the Social Sciences and Humanities Research Council of Canada.

1. See Jeff McMahan, *Killing in War* (Oxford: Oxford University Press, 2009), as well as, for example, Helen Frowe, *Defensive Killing* (Oxford: Oxford University Press, 2014).

2. The loci classici of this tradition include Jean-Jacques Rousseau, *The Social Contract*, ed. and trans. Gerald Hopkins, in *The Social Contract and Other Political Writings* (Cambridge: Cambridge University Press, 1997), I.4.9; Michael Walzer, *Just and Unjust Wars* (New York: Basic Books, 1977).

states almost invariably end up overlooking crucial differences in the moral position of individual participants in wars—including differences that stem from the justice or injustice of their respective causes and, among unjust participants, from the kind and degree of their involvement in warfare.

The appeal of this line of criticism lies primarily in its promise of greater moral discernment. Accordingly, theorists who champion it ought to be especially wary of overgeneralizations and non sequiturs. Indeed, even if traditionalist doctrines such as the moral equality of combatants and civilians' absolute immunity are flawed and ordinary individual distinctions are as central to the morality of war as they are to morality more generally, it does not necessarily follow that states are mere shorthand in evaluations of how wars should be fought. If one is prepared to hold, as many do, that at least some organized collectives, such as some commercial corporations and non-governmental organizations, can make *additional* moral differences in the world—that is, moral differences that are not fully reducible to those of their individual members—why would it not also be the case for states? McMahan himself recognizes that "there is no reason to suppose that states, or any other kinds of political collectives, are fundamentally different morally from collectives that are not political in nature," and that "the principles governing collective violence in war should be the same as those governing collective action in domestic contexts."[3] If that is true and, in war or otherwise, states, like corporations and NGOs, can, for example, engage in distinctively collective wrongdoing or otherwise make themselves liable to adverse actions qua collectives, then a full account of the morality of war may be well advised to take such facts into account. That is, war theorists may have to account for this collective reality *alongside* all the complex and important individual moral distinctions at play. Unlike what much of traditional Just War theory and contemporary individualist retorts would have us believe, the resulting moral picture may then be more, not less, complex.

My goal in this essay is to begin to investigate one salient moral difference that states qua group agents may intuitively be thought to make in war, assuming that such agents exist. My focus will be on the idea of liability to attack, central to much recent individualist Just War theorizing. Those liable to attack, McMahan contends, "would not be wronged by being attacked, and would have no justified complaints about being attacked."[4] This leads me to ask: insofar as states are corporate group agents, might they ever intelligibly be said to be liable in this sense qua groups? If so, could such corporate liability ever make a difference in an over-

---

3. McMahan, *Killing in War*, 156.

4. Ibid., 8.

all argument about the permissibility of attacking a state? In this essay, I argue that, if some states are indeed responsible corporate agents, the possibility of their liability to attack is at least intelligible and, in some cases, may be morally determinative. However, I also contend that, insofar as one is committed to the principle of value individualism (and perhaps even otherwise), cases in which state corporate liability is morally salient are likely to be rare and restricted to very specific sets of circumstances.

I take as my point of departure Christian List and Philip Pettit's account of group agency,[5] which, in my view, is currently the most developed and intuitively plausible available. The account holds, first, that groups such as states can be conversable agents in their own right, in the manner of individual human beings. That is, they can be constituted in ways that make it possible to reason and do business with them over time qua groups—for example, by entering into treaties or contracts with them, reasonably expecting that these will be honored. For such conversability to be possible, the group needs, of course, to be responsive to the attitudes and inputs of its individual members. However, it must also be responsive in a way that secures group sensitivity to reason over time, with a minimum of consistency and coherence. According to List and Pettit, these features can obtain when the group functions in keeping with an adequate normative framework, or constitution. A constitution is adequate in this sense when it sets out a decision procedure that ensures that the organized group's judgments, as well as action-directing attitudes and plans are, on the whole, functionally independent, as opposed to a mere reflection, of the corresponding judgments, attitudes, and plans of group members. Thus, autocratic decision procedures, according to which decisions are merely those of an individual dictator and no real group decisions are taken, are clearly inadequate. In such cases, there is no conversable group agent—only the dictator himself.

What a constitution must ensure is the group's relative autonomy, in the sense of enabling it to form judgments, attitudes, and plans that cannot fully be reduced to those of one or more group members. One might think of some forms of majoritarian democracy in such terms. For the sake of simplicity, consider the following three-person example, where A, B, and C are deciding whether $X\&(Y\&Z)$. If A believes $X\&(Y\&\neg Z)$, B believes $X\&(\neg Y\&Z)$, and C believes $\neg X\&(Y\&Z)$, then if the group votes on each of X, Y, and Z in turn, the group will hold that $X\&(Y\&Z)$ although none of the members believes this.

---

5. Christian List and Philip Pettit, *Group Agency: The Possibility, Design, and Status of Corporate Agents* (Oxford: Oxford University Press, 2011).

An additional issue arises here, as it does with other decision-making procedures for aggregating individual judgments into group judgments.[6] Broadly stated, individual responsiveness—in my example, to the beliefs of A, B, and C—may, over time, compromise the minimal rational consistency that we expect from agents proper. So, for conversable group agency to be possible, a process must also be in place to ensure that the group keeps track of where its accumulating decisions are taking it, and can respond appropriately to that information. In other words, balances and checks must be in place to make sure that, over time, the group can revise its corporate judgments so as to restore reasonable consistency.

One of the great strengths of this kind of account is that it rests on the non-mysterious premise that group agents derive all their matter and energy from their individual members. It is through their individual members that organized groups can access evidence and gain the understanding required to make evaluative judgments about the reasons for action and normative options they face. The overall contention, though, is that, by jointly committing and adhering to an adequate constitution, group members can generate a single, relatively autonomous, and enduring corporate agent that, when faced with normatively significant choices, is capable of making irreducible and reasonably consistent judgments about how it should respond—about what is good and bad, right and wrong. This corporate agent, which in an important sense has a mind of its own, may then formulate objectives, make decisions, and develop strategies and plans to implement these over time, all in a saliently irreducible way. It may also control for the execution of such plans by arranging things so that some individuals are directed, or empowered, to perform relevant tasks, while others are identified as possible back-ups. As List and Pettit argue, a corporate agent that arranges for action in this way is fit to be held responsible, and may appropriately be blamed, as "the source of the deed" or the "planner" at its origin.[7] Of course, the individuals who give life to such an agent still have to answer for what they do in making corporate agency possible. They remain moral agents in their own right. However, the entity they maintain also has to answer as a whole for what it does at the corporate level.

As complex organizations that deal diachronically with their members as well as with other organizations and individuals, endure alterations in membership,

---

6. In *Group Agency*, chaps. 2–3, List and Pettit consider various other premise aggregation procedures, sequential priority decision procedures, as well as more complex distributed premise-based procedures among subgroups.

7. List and Pettit, *Group Agency*, chap. 7. For a discussion, expanding beyond List and Pettit's work, of the various kinds of multilevel causal control and structural control that make group responsibility salient, over and above the responsibility of individual enactors, see Anders Strand, "Group Agency, Responsibility, and Control," *Philosophy of the Social Sciences* 43 (2013): 201–24.

and even changes in political regimes, modern states (or at least some of them) are prime candidates for long-lasting irreducible corporate moral agency and responsibility. Their constitutions typically include principles of governance, institute multilayered decision-making procedures, and impose the kinds of balances and checks necessary to foster relative organizational autonomy and sufficient rational consistency over time. Common examples of relevant decisional constraints include the separation of powers between the executive, the legislative, and the judiciary, bicameral legislatures, judicial review of administrative and legislative action, stare decisis, enforceable bills of rights, elections, federal division of powers, constitutional conventions such as ministerial and cabinet responsibility, impeachment procedures, and the like. No doubt, modern states depend on their individual members to make decisions and act, but by committing and adhering to their state's constitutional framework to a reasonable extent, such individuals can bring about genuine state moral agency and responsibility. Indeed, for List and Pettit, states qua corporate agents may even appropriately be described as persons, insofar as "person" is understood in the sense of an agent capable of appropriately responding to reasons, and performing in the space of obligations.[8]

As controversial as this and previous claims may be,[9] I will henceforth assume, *arguendo*, the soundness of the account to this point. That is, even if we accept that some states are irreducible group agents, or persons, and can be responsible for, say, unjust or otherwise wrongful actions and be blamed for them, can these states also be liable qua groups to adverse consequences? In other words, can their moral agency, or performative personhood, not only make them susceptible to judgments of responsibility and blame, as is often alleged, but also to liability, including liability to attack?

I. State Corporate Liability to Attack?

a. Liability to Attack

The idea of liability to attack is central to much individualistic Just War theorizing.[10] At its core lies the thought that, if one is liable to attack, one is not wronged

---

8. List and Pettit, *Group Agency*, chap. 8. They defend this account of personhood against accounts grounded in phenomenal consciousness, which, they concede, would not extend personhood to corporate agents.

9. Jeff McMahan himself rejects them: "Aggression and Punishment," in *War: Philosophical Perspectives*, ed. Larry May (Cambridge: Cambridge University Press, 2008), 67–84, at 83.

10. For an extended discussion of moral liability in this volume, see Richard Arneson, "Resolving the Responsibility Dilemma." See also Jeff McMahan, "Liability, Proportionality, and the Number of Aggressors."

by it, and may not complain about it on that basis. Liability so understood is not a justificatory panacea: it is neither a necessary nor a sufficient condition for the permissibility of attacking someone. For example, it may be wrong to attack a person who is liable to it insofar as it would wrong others, who would be harmed as a side effect. It may also be permissible to attack those who are non-liable, say, as a means of preventing substantially worse harm. Still, establishing that one is liable to attack is a distinctive and important step in an overall argument about the permissibility of attacking him or her.

How is liability established? Accounts diverge. For McMahan, liability corresponds to the loss or, more precisely, the forfeiture of a right. A "person's being liable to attack," he contends, "*just is* his having *forfeited* his right not to be attacked, in the circumstances."[11] Thus, one's liability to attack arises through some action—some responsible act or omission. Usually, McMahan argues, such liability arises through action that constitutes responsible wrongdoing—most notably, the responsible posing of an unjust threat of harm. Although an aggravating factor, culpability is not required for liability, as in the case of the homeowner who mistakenly threatens to shoot the identical twin of a mass murderer, known to break into people's homes and kill them on the spot, when the twin brother shows up at his doorstep. Despite being excused for his wrongful threat, McMahan holds, this homeowner is liable to defensive attack. Yet liability is importantly not an all-or-nothing affair. For example, it would wrong a person who is morally responsible for an unjust threat if he or she were merely attacked for fun, or simply because attacking them would do more good than harm in a way that bears no relation to their wrong. A person is liable to attack, McMahan insists, only when attacking this person is necessary for the prevention or correction of a wrong for which the person is morally responsible, and the harm that the attack would cause this person is not excessive in relation to the realization of one of those aims. Still, in war, where unjust threats will often be to individuals' lives, and be overly burdensome or impossible to avert without seriously harming or even killing those responsible for them, attackers may well be liable to such a fate.

Others, like Victor Tadros, conceive of liability more expansively. Like McMahan, Tadros thinks of it as tethered to preventive or corrective goals, and as coming with internal necessity and proportionality constraints. Still, according to him, the concept does not so much track the loss of rights as situations in which one does not have a right in the first place. The most important way in which one lacks a right not to be attacked for the sake of some relevant goal is, he

---

11. McMahan, *Killing in War*, 10.

suggests, when one has an enforceable duty to bear the harm that would result from the attack, for the sake of that goal.[12] Assume, for example, that one has a duty to rescue a child drowning in a pond at a minimal cost to oneself—say, incurring a bad cut on one's leg that will leave a visible scar (or perhaps even, per Tadros, losing a finger)—but that one is unwilling to do so. Assume further that the child could be rescued by throwing the unwilling person into the pond, and that this attack would only cause the person to incur the said minimal cost. Tadros argues that the unwilling person is liable to this attack. She is liable to it in the sense that she has an enforceable duty to rescue the child and, accordingly, has no right not to be harmed in this way for the sake of the child. When the stakes are higher, one may also be liable to much more than such a minimal cost. For example, Tadros contends that, were someone the only person able to save a very large number of lives, he may have an enforceable duty to do so at the cost of his life. Were he unwilling or unable to discharge this duty, he would then be liable to be killed as a means of saving the other lives at stake, even though he is not responsible for what is threatening them.

Culpability without responsibility can also ground liability to attack for Tadros. Consider the following hypothetical:

> Evelyn hires a hitman to kill Wayne. Fred also hires a hitman to kill Wayne. Both hitmen arrive at the same time. Because of where they are standing, Wayne can only use Fred as a shield against Evelyn's hitman and Evelyn as a shield against Fred's hitman. He manages to do that, resulting in the deaths of Evelyn and Fred.[13]

Tadros contends that it is permissible for Wayne to use Evelyn and Fred in this way, given that they are both liable to it. Since Evelyn culpably chose to set her murderous threat in motion, she has a duty to prevent Wayne from being killed by it, even at the cost of her life. So does Fred. Still, by hypothesis, neither can discharge this duty by themselves, such that each has a derivative duty to try to get someone else to do it for them. Tadros argues that since each can avert the threat that he or she culpably created by forming and executing an agreement with the other, to the effect that he or she will avert the threat that the other has created, each has a duty to do so. If either or both are unwilling, Wayne can do to them what they have a duty to do. That is, he can use the two as shields to avert the

---

12. See Victor Tadros, "Duty and Liability," *Utilitas* 24 (2012): 259–77.

13. Victor Tadros, *The Ends of Harm: The Moral Foundations of Criminal Law* (Oxford: Oxford University Press, 2011), 192.

threats that he faces even if, in so doing, he harms each of them as a means of averting a threat that he or she is not responsible for creating.

Tadros does not deny McMahan's contention that one's moral responsibility for an unjust threat can engender one's liability to attack, including liability to be seriously harmed or even killed in the process. However, since he believes that liability rests on enforceable duties to bear harm, and that such duties can be grounded in many other considerations than moral responsibility, his conception is more expansive and multifaceted. For him, considerations of beneficence and culpability can also ground liability to attack quite independently of considerations of moral responsibility, and so might considerations of causation and benefit.[14]

Here is not the place to adjudicate between these two leading accounts of liability. More would need to be said about them, and perhaps other contenders, before any sound verdict can be reached. Still, I believe that the two are sufficiently representative to allow for a meaningful discussion of the issue of corporate (group, collective) state liability to attack.

b. The Basis for Extending Liability to Attack to States

To recap, it follows from the account of corporate agency considered that states that meet relevant organizational criteria can have reasons, including duties—of beneficence, justice, not to harm, etc.—that apply to them qua groups, and to which they can respond appropriately qua groups. When they fail to do so, they, like other moral agents, may be responsible for wrongdoing (understood as a breach of duty). In the context of war, such wrongdoing might include the creation of unjust threats of harm. Since, as group agents, states can make choices and plan for action and, in so doing, may exhibit irreducible attitudes such as intentionality, recklessness, or negligence, they may even culpably give rise to such wrongful threats.

Moreover, it seems to follow from the account that, as corporate entities with goals of their own for which things can go well or badly over time—and, thus, which can plausibly have interests[15]—states may also conceivably have rights. They may have rights in the sense of interests sufficiently important to ground

---

14. Tadros, "Duty and Liability," 269–77; Victor Tadros, "Causation, Culpability and Liability," in *The Ethics of Self-Defense*, ed. C. Coons and M. Weber (Oxford: Oxford University Press, 2016).

15. On organized group agents as interest holders, see further Rachael Briggs, "The Normative Standing of Group Agents," *Episteme* 9 (2012): 283–91.

duties in others.[16] One common objection to this claim is that groups should never be thought to have any moral value prior to, or independent of, the good or interests of their individual members. Thus, their rights should not be ascribed any value per se. Assertions to the contrary, the objection typically goes on, served as normative entry points for some of the worst Nazi and communist atrocities of our times. They did so by paving the way for arguments that the corporate rights of groups, understood separately from those of individuals, could simply trump them.[17] While alluring, this (rather crudely formulated) objection does not undermine the possibility of morally important corporate rights that are irreducibly held by states. One possibility is that, though important, corporate rights, however valued, are always less stringent than individual rights, or at least less stringent than core individual rights to life, against torture, not to be harmed, and so forth, which are characteristically at stake in war. Another possibility is that, while corporate rights, however valued, might at times defeat important individual rights, they did not do so, contrary to what was alleged, in the specific historical circumstances contemplated by the objection.

List and Pettit opt for a different line of argument that is more aligned with familiar liberal or republican commitments. They reject outright that the rights and interests of organized groups can ever be valued independently of those of individual persons. After all, they claim, such groups are merely social arrangements that individuals create and maintain, through coordinated efforts, to serve social ends, and it would seem somewhat circular to factor in these groups' own interests when assessing their value. That is, List and Pettit's account allows for the possibility of corporate rights while endorsing the widely shared principle of value individualism, according to which the worth of corporate agents (and, indeed, of anything else) must ultimately be appreciated in terms of their contributions to human (or, at least, sentient) life and its quality.[18] Their point, I take it, is that to meet the common objection, an account of state corporate rights can make clear that the moral value and strength of these rights may only be derived from how they serve individuals' good or interests—even if only in a mediated

---

16. On this understanding of rights, see Joseph Raz, *The Morality of Freedom* (Oxford: Oxford University Press, 1986), chap. 7. As Raz himself recognizes, one is capable of having rights in this sense "if either his well-being is of ultimate value or he is an 'artificial person' (e.g. a corporation)" (166). Note that, unlike Raz, I do not claim here that individual human beings have no rights grounded in other considerations than interests.

17. See further David Rodin, *War and Self-Defense* (Oxford: Oxford University Press, 2003), 143–44.

18. List and Pettit, *Group Agency*, 182; Christian List and Philip Pettit, "Episteme Symposium on *Group Agency*: Replies to Gaus, Cariani, Sylvan, and Briggs," *Episteme* 9 (2012): 293–309, at 307–8.

and irreducible way.[19] Consider the oft-discussed irreducible rights of states against the interference of external actors in their internal affairs, namely, their sovereignty rights. States plausibly have such rights, at least in part due to their interests in developing and seeing through their group plans. Insofar as they do have such rights, they also plausibly have some moral stringency. However, when it comes to assessing it, value individualism ought to take center stage. For example, the rights' stringency may be evaluated based on the desirability, for individual members, of seeing their state's group plans realized given the importance of collectively organized territorial governance that is close to the governed and, in our morally plural world, can better reflect and support the development of valuable local understandings, cultures, and traditions. Furthermore, insofar as there are no other entities able to govern as effectively and impartially, and secure important public goods such as these and others, failure to recognize states' sovereignty may be quite counterproductive for individuals. External meddling may result in all sorts of harmful mistakes and abuses that make things far worse for them.

Such theoretical refinements should go some way toward assuaging the concerns of individualistic theorists who are reminded of traditional Just War theorists' "domestic analogy," according to which states are analogous to individual persons, and are governed by the same moral principles as them.[20] Recall, though, that this analogy never comes alone for Just War traditionalists. They also think that war occurs primarily between states, and that it is primarily morality as it applies to *them* that governs it. Consequently, individual participants in war are largely eclipsed from key aspects of their theories. Taking their view seriously seems to entail that individuals are, at most, embodiments of their states, and the harms they suffer are, at most, non-lethal harms to the larger collective entity. For individualists, a key problem with such reasoning is that, while we may intelligibly say that attacks on states can wrongfully "harm them"—in the sense of violating "their rights" or otherwise setting back "their interests"—such talk is at most metaphorical and dangerously so. It is dangerous insofar as it is taken as a basis to argue that it is the rights and interests of states qua distinct persons that should be morally commanding in war, as opposed to those of individuals. Surely, individualists counter, wartime attacks on states generally involve the killing and serious harming of individuals, and these facts are sufficiently important not to be disregarded in favor of an exclusive focus on states, or unduly discounted as mere

---

19. See further Dwight Newman, *Community and Collective Rights: A Theoretical Framework for Rights Held by Groups* (Oxford: Hart Publishing, 2011), esp. chap. 5.

20. The expression is used by Walzer in *Just and Unjust Wars*, 58.

expendable parts of them.[21] I find this rejoinder compelling. If attacks on states are to be justified in terms of state liability, the explanation for it must give individuals' rights and interests their due.

So, for some individualists, List and Pettit's suggestion that states can be *real*, as opposed to metaphorical, corporate agents—even persons—with important irreducible duties and rights will likely trigger alarm bells. Still, the latter's account can avoid traditionalist oversimplification. Pace List and Pettit themselves, it may perhaps even do so by recognizing the non-circular possibility of some non-individualist valuation of corporate states and their rights—some may prefer to speak of impersonal value.[22] It may, insofar as it also clarifies how such valuation can relate to individuals' distinct rights and interests without denying them their proper stringency. Admittedly, the idea of impersonal collective valuation— independent of how human lives-in-being (or, at least, sentient beings) are affected by the collective object of value—remains philosophically fraught, especially among self-proclaimed individualists. So this suggestion will likely meet significant resistance. Note, however, that the account can also avoid traditionalist oversimplification by unwaveringly holding onto the received wisdom of value individualism, as List and Pettit themselves suggest and as I will assume from now on. I do so both for the sake of simplicity and as an attempt at rapprochement with individualists, but also because I believe (though cannot argue here) that even if some states have impersonal corporate value, this value is likely insignificant as compared with the value of individual interests generally at stake in wars, such as life and bodily integrity.

Thus, following List and Pettit, states qua group agents can have irreducible rights, but these rights may be lost, or otherwise run out, in virtue of how states relate to individuals.[23] A state may, for example, have no sovereignty-based complaint against various types of external interferences aimed at thwarting its

---

21. See especially Jeff McMahan, "What Rights May Be Defended by Means of War?" in *The Morality of Defensive War*, ed. Cécile Fabre and Seth Lazar (Oxford: Oxford University Press, 2014), 115–56.

22. Think, for example, of their aesthetic value in the abstract. See further Derek Parfit, *Reasons and Persons* (Oxford: Oxford University Press, 1984).

23. Incidentally, such value individualist thinking about the relative moral importance of states qua group agents goes some way toward addressing Marko Milanovic's query, which Larry May highlights in his contribution to this volume. "If human rights accrue to human beings solely by virtue of their humanity," Milanovic asks, "why should these rights evaporate merely because two states [...] have engaged in armed conflict?" Insofar as value individualism is true, even if states are distinct moral agents with rights of their own, these must always be understood in terms of how they serve the rights of individuals, and never as unrelated substitute for them. In other words, human rights remain at the heart of the morality of war, in spite of states' involvement.

violations of its individual members' human rights.[24] It may also have no justified sovereignty-based complaint against some external interferences aimed at averting its unjust threats to foreign populations. May we then intelligibly hold that a state is, qua corporate entity, liable to such interferences? It seems to me that we may.

II. The Moral Salience of State Corporate Liability to Minimally Harmful Targeted Attacks

An important tension here is that a state's corporate liability to an external interference does not entail that individuals, who may be harmed in the process, are also liable to it. Such individuals may not be morally responsible in any way for the unjust threat that gives rise to their state's liability. Neither may they be causally responsible or culpable for it, or even beneficiaries of it. Still, this objection is contingent. Some external interferences aimed at averting a state's unjust threat may be sufficiently well tailored to impact only what is irreducibly the state's own—namely its decisions, plans, policies, and their materialization—without harming individuals, or only occasioning negligibly small harm to them. Think of some sufficiently well-designed arms embargoes geared at thwarting a state's aggressive intentions. Or consider foreign tanks temporarily crossing an aggressive state's border, or military aircrafts flying into its airspace, in a preventive show of force. Think also of more invasive targeted bombings of unmanned weapons-storage or missile-launching facilities, or of empty military airport runways soon to be harnessed for unjust offensives. All else being equal,[25] state corporate liability to such incapacitating or otherwise preventive interferences—which, note, include attacks—may not only be intelligible, but also morally unproblematic.

An important payoff of recognizing the possibility of such liability is tied to the eventuality that a state's unjust threat may emanate from an irreducible decision. Remember the kind of multi-premise majority decision-making discussed above. Imagine that, when votes on successive issues are aggregated, they yield a corporate plan to launch an immediate unjust offensive that no individual actually endorses. Imagine further that no individuals, either voters or enactors of the states' plan, are sufficiently responsible for it—let alone culpable or benefiting—for their liability (assuming they have any) to be determinative of the permissibility of a

24. For two of many versions of this claim, see Joseph Raz, "Human Rights without Foundations," in *The Philosophy of International Law*, ed. Samantha Besson and John Tasioulas (Oxford: Oxford University Press, 2010), 321–37; Christopher Heath Wellman, "Debate: Taking Human Rights Seriously," *Journal of Political Philosophy* 20 (2012): 119–30.

25. By this I mean, in part, that harm to individuals occasioned by the interference would be, at most, negligibly small.

circumscribed yet necessary preventive attack of the kind just suggested. In such limited cases, their state's liability to attack might ground the relevant permission.

Some may be tempted to recharacterize this permission in terms of a liability-less "lesser evil" justification—say, because bombing the would-be aggressor state's military runway or weapons-storage facility would save many lives. This view has the appeal of simplicity. However, I believe there are at least two reasons why the possibility of morally salient state corporate liability should not be discarded. First, it will not always be unambiguous that bombing unmanned runways or storage facilities is a lesser evil. It may not be if, for example, such defensive bombings are carried out to prevent the unjust destruction of military installations or other state property whose value is, all things considered, not obviously greater. In such situations, state corporate liability may be a morally salient fact that helps fix the parameters of permissible preventive attacks on the unjustly threatening state. Second, lesser evil reasoning may be articulated without any attention to the involvement of irreducible state agency in the creation of unjust threats. Insofar as a group agent is, in fact, a source of such threats, and such behavior affects its moral standing, subtler moral reasoning that reflects it is likely preferable.

Others, still, may question the point of recognizing state corporate liability from the angle of redundancy. They may contend that the voters and enactors of the state's unjust threat in my scenario have really brought this threat about jointly, irrespective of whether their actions ultimately translated into those of an irreducible corporate agent. If, indeed, they are jointly responsible for the threat, they may also be jointly liable for it. Could such joint liability not play the limited demarcation role that I have so far been ascribing to state corporate liability, in relation to non-harmful attacks on military facilities? Here are some grounds for doubting it. First, to be successful, this move would require a sound account of how the joint liability of some individual decision-makers and enactors implies the permissibility of destroying *state* property. Even if such an account can be provided—say, through arguments from representation or trusteeship—joint liability may still not exhaust the space of state corporate liability. By hypothesis, no individual voter in my scenario intended the unjust threat, and all may have actively opposed it. Thus, it is hard to conceive of such voters as intending or desiring that they together bring about the unjust threat, a condition commonly deemed necessary for non-corporate joint action and responsibility.[26] Assuming

---

26. See, e.g., Michael Bratman, "Shared Agency," in *Philosophy of the Social Sciences: Philosophical Theory and Scientific Practice*, ed. Chris Mantzavinos (Cambridge: Cambridge University Press, 2009), 41–59; Philip Pettit and David Schweikard, "Joint Actions and Group Agents," *Philosophy of the Social Sciences* 36 (2006): 18–39. One may wonder whether voters intending or desiring that they together bring about *a* decision on a given set of issues is sufficient to ground their joint agency and responsibility in respect of what is actually decided. While I doubt it, I cannot provide a defense here.

that no one vote would have made a difference, there may also be relevant issues of causal overdetermination in respect of each voter. Let us also stipulate that none of them would benefit from the threat in any significant way. Finally, for the sake of simplicity and effective exposition, let us assume that, in the state in question, a quick-reaction electronic system is in place to compute the votes and give immediate effect to time-sensitive operational military plans such as the one decided upon—say, by initiating, without further human intercession, the targeted launch of automated missiles. Though farfetched, this last set of facts avoids muddying the example with distracting questions of individual liability that could arise from the responsibility or culpability of enactors of the plan. Along with the voting scenario described, this hypothetical specification helps show that, in some conceivable though limited cases, state corporate liability might have a morally salient role to play.

III. Fleshing Out Individualists' Powerful General Objection to State Corporate Liability

Now, despite what I said in the last section, preventive military action against a state will almost always involve the deliberate killing or severe harming of individuals, on a significant scale. After all, this is what we have commonly come to mean by "war"—likely because, most often, it is hard to imagine bringing a state to desist from unjust aggressive designs by means of attack without harming at least some of its individual members. The key individualist objection to the moral salience of state corporate liability in this context can perhaps most clearly be articulated in terms of Tadros's understanding of liability. Underlying my earlier description of his account is Tadros's attempt to meet the nonconsequentialist objection against intentionally using—or worse, harmfully using—individuals as a means to achieve some good. This important objection is generally defended on the basis of individuals' ultimate value as beings independent from each other, who each have an intrinsic right to set their own ends. It is in response to this objection that Tadros contends that individuals can permissibly be harmfully used if they have enforceable duties—and, thus, are liable—to bear harm for the sake of some goal. Admittedly, List and Pettit do argue that corporate agents are relatively independent, or autonomous, from their individual members. However, nowhere do they even speculate about the possibility of such agents' ultimate valuation; their commitment is to value individualism. Insofar as they are correct (or that the impersonal significance of states is comparatively trivial), it would seem paradoxical to claim that states qua group agents can have morally salient enforceable duties to sustain attacks, when those who are targeted as means of enforcement are mostly their individual members, often at the cost of their lives or bodily integrity. Shouldn't the inquiry be the other way around, focusing instead on ultimately valuable individuals and their liability, as opposed to the liability of an entity whose value is derivative from theirs (or is otherwise too insignificant to play any salient role)?

The point can also be made in McMahan's idiom by emphasizing that, while it may sometimes be consistent with value individualism for corporate rights (and their loss) to take priority over specific individual rights, such prioritization is only permissible when it better serves individuals' interests or good otherwise understood. Prioritizing corporate rights and their loss when assessing the permissibility of attacks targeting individuals is likely to do precisely the reverse, since a state's forfeiture of sovereignty rights may well not automatically entail that targeted individual members also lose their individual rights not to be harmed. To know whether they do, we need a more particularized approach to determining the permissibility of attacks that tracks individuals' liability and its grounds.

Again, individuals' liability is not a justificatory panacea. If, as in cases of attacks targeting what is the state's own, some individual members end up being harmed or killed as unintentional side effects, the salient moral question may be whether these individuals' rights could permissibly be overridden, or otherwise delimited, for the sake of some intended greater good. I am also not denying the possibility that such greater good may sometimes be irreducibly collective in nature—think of the value of a just or a solidaristic community—and that it may be entwined with the existence of states qua corporate agents. Notice, however, that the point about overriding is not a point about liability so much as a point about competing values. Nor is the following point so much about states' corporate liability as it is about group values and their importance. Given the limited focus of my inquiry on state corporate liability, it seems methodologically important to keep these distinctions in mind.

Should my conclusion then be that, while state corporate liability to an attack may be morally relevant to its permissibility when the attack does not involve harm to individuals, or perhaps no significant harm to them, it is irrelevant or, at most, overshadowed by individual considerations when it does? List and Pettit's account of corporate agency would not stand in the way of this conclusion. Unlike traditionalist collectivist accounts, their argument does not preclude assessments of individual liability arising from what individuals do in making state corporate agency possible, or otherwise. Thus, some voters in my earlier scenario may have intended to bring about the unjust threat, and done everything they could to ensure its materialization. Given their actions, not only in voting but also in convincing others, they may, at least partly, have been morally and causally responsible, even perhaps culpable, for this unjust threat. In light of the importance of the threat, they may even have been liable to defensive attack. Military enactors of the threat may, too, have been liable in virtue of their responsible and culpable contributions. If that is correct, our next question must then be whether a state's corporate liability can ever *add* anything salient to the individualist moral picture when assessing the permissibility of deadly or significantly harmful attacks in war.

IV. A Limited Democratic Rejoinder?

Could it be, for example, that, in respect of at least some states that meet the conditions of group agency, their corporate liability may ground individual members' liability to attack in a general way? The suggestion is not new, although some of its more famous articulations blatantly fail to meet the individualists' objection. Think here of Rousseau's controversial contention that only the democratic state remains once the social contract that creates it is entered into by the multitude of individuals, such that, by definition, the state's collective will is also the will of each individual member.[27] Given this blunt conflation, it is unsurprising that Rousseau holds that "war is then not a relationship between one man and another, but a relationship between one State and another, in which individuals are enemies only by accident ... any State can only have other States, and not men, as enemies."[28]

There are more nuanced versions of the democratic proposal. For example, in his recent work on non-domination, Philip Pettit himself suggests that while a state can be a responsible corporate agent in its own right, its individual members can also aspire to control it jointly.[29] They can aspire to do so in domains in which our world's existing arrangements allow states at least some discretion as to action, and in a way that makes individual members' share in the joint control equal. For such equally shared joint control to obtain, a number of conditions must be met. Crucially, individual members, enabled by a suitable constitution, must exercise equally accessible, unconditioned, and efficacious influence over the state, which pushes it to act in a direction equally acceptable to all. The overall claim is that, when such conditions are met, individual members actually control their state's will, even if they leave matters of detail to the corporate luck of the draw. This argument may have implications for liability. Could we not hold that individual members of such a democratic state would have no justified complaints against their state being subjected to a bloody attack aimed at preventing its unjust threat,

27. Rousseau, *The Social Contract*, I.6, II.12.

28. Rousseau, *The Social Contract*, I.4.9.

29. Philip Pettit, *On the People's Terms: A Republican Theory and Model of Democracy* (Cambridge: Cambridge University Press, 2012), chaps. 3–5.

given that its liability to it must, in a very real sense, also be theirs in an equal measure (in virtue of their equal joint control)?

The idea that control of a liable agent entails the controllers' liability is a multifaceted one that I cannot unravel here. Instead, let me point out a number of key difficulties with the argument that are relevant to my inquiry. These difficulties exist over and above the obvious criticism that no existing state comes even remotely close to meeting Pettit's desiderata of popular control. In all current so-called democracies, popular control is limited and unequally exercised, such that control-based generalizations about liability are morally hazardous. Still, since Pettit's conditions are explicitly meant to be achievable, let us take him at his word for the sake of argument.[30]

Note, first, that if a state's individual members actually control it, and this control gives rise to their liability to attack, then the key to the permissibility of the attack seems to be their joint individual liability, not their state's corporate liability. As Pettit makes clear, there is a distinction between the unincorporated plurality of citizens who jointly seek to control their state, and the state qua self-governing singular corporate entity that they may not succeed in controlling.[31] If, when they do not control their state, they are not liable for its wrongs and, when they do control it, they are liable for them, it seems to be their control-derived liability, not their state's liability, that is operative.

Second, the fact that an individual member has as good an opportunity as all others to exercise some control over his state does not mean that he actually controls it (or even that he has a consistently effective ability to do so). This point holds true even if, as Pettit suggests, there is a system of contestation in place that allows individuals to test state decisions for how the process in which they are generated respects the value of equal access to influence. For if the state ultimately does things that one bitterly and proactively opposes—for example, launches unjust military offensives—one must surely regard them as things one does not control. Arguably, what Pettit has in mind is joint popular control of the *general* direction of a state's actions over time, where each individual member might "win some" but also "lose some." However, what if one of my "losses" relates to my state's one-off creation of a serious unjust threat to the population of another state? Would my share in the control of my state's otherwise nonbelligerent direction suffice to make me liable to be harmed, and possibly killed, to avert this threat? Assuming that I lack any other relevant responsibility, culpability, and so forth, for the threat, and would not even benefit from it, it is intuitively doubtful. This,

30. Ibid., 180.

31. Ibid., 285–88.

I believe, is because it is such facts about me qua individual that remain morally commanding. Our intuitions may be somewhat different when a state's popularly controlled *general* direction is one of unjust belligerency. However, even if, in such a case, we can accurately say that this direction is controlled by all, my earlier point still holds. Joint individual liability may provide all the explanation we need.

Note, finally, that Pettit's control argument is explicitly limited to adult, able-minded, and more or less permanent residents of democratic states. Children, visitors, and those who are genuinely unable to control their state are excluded ab initio.[32] Therefore, assessments of the permissibility of attacking them must proceed separately from any general control-based arguments about joint or corporate liability, if their rights are not to be unduly disregarded.

Then again, I may have unfairly stacked the deck against the relevance of state corporate liability to lethal or significantly harmful attacks by focusing on a suggestion that rests on *individuals'* actual control. Indeed, a similar worry also arises in respect of all arguments grounded in individuals' voluntary choice to join a state or in their actual consent, explicit or tacit, to accept responsibility for its actions. Since, typically, not every member of a state will have so chosen or consented, let alone have had a genuine opportunity or otherwise been able to do so, individualized assessments would still be called for and ready generalizations remain questionable. Notice, however, that this kind of objection may not hold as firmly against arguments based on what is sometimes referred to as "necessary popular authorization." If, for example, one were able to argue successfully that no individual member could reasonably oppose their corporate state's actions, because they generally could or should not do without them, then it may be possible to maintain that when the state's corporate liability is engaged, theirs also is ipso facto.

Consider, as a way of orienting our thinking, the following proposal, inspired by aspects of the Kantian and broader republican traditions, which I have broken down into deliberately rough and suggestive premises. I offer it, without being committed to it, as a provocation that may help us see how such an argument could unfold:

(1) *Justice as individual independence.* The ideal of justice corresponds to social conditions in which each individual is treated with the respect with which she should be treated. According to one prominent version of this view, justice prevails when each is treated as an equally valuable independent

---

32. Ibid., 138.

being who may set her own ends for herself, unless she does so in a way that is inconsistent with equal independence for all.[33]

(2) *Corporate state agency as required for justice.* Given the difficulty of bringing about and maintaining such a condition in every relevant aspect of individuals' lives, the coordination of a state qua corporate agent is required. Such a state is required for justice, since the many complex, interconnected, and dynamic tasks necessary to make it possible could not be discharged by any one individual or by an unorganized plurality, even with the assistance of an impersonal apparatus of disciplining rules and routines. The tasks in question include establishing and adjusting just laws that, among other things, identify substantive and coherent basic liberties; ensuring that sufficient resources and adequate infrastructures are in place to sustain everyone's independence; protecting people against the invasion of their independence, whether in particular relationships or on a more general front; and so forth. What is needed to discharge such tasks is a state (or whatever else one may want to call it) qua collective agency, made up of numerous specialized officials and subsidiary agencies, yet speaking with a unified voice, acting to a coherent set of ends and, insofar as it fails, remaining sensitive to the need to restore harmony. To be effective, this state also needs to have the power to secure coercively the order it establishes, as well as a recognized claim to exclusive authority to govern it.[34]

(3) *The high value of justice.* Justice is extremely valuable given that a life lived under the subjection of another's private will (think of the life of a slave or of an ongoing victim of torture), or even the ongoing threat of subjection to it (think of life in the state of nature), is a critically impoverished life.[35]

(4) *Individual members' stringent duty of justice to support and own up to the state's endeavors.* Therefore, for their own sake and the sake of others, individual members of a reasonably just corporate state all have a stringent (and, arguably, enforceable) duty to support its endeavors, plausibly at considerable costs to themselves. They have such a duty insofar as their state's interpretation and rendering of justice is reasonable. This last proviso is necessary since reasonable mistakes are an inevitable concomitant of moral agency in our world, and the value of a reasonable approximation of justice may more than make up for such deviations.

When such a reasonably just state launches an unjust offensive against another state on the mistaken, yet understandable assumption that it is necessary to defend its

---

33. For a detailed articulation of this view, see Arthur Ripstein, *Force and Freedom: Kant's Legal and Political Philosophy* (Cambridge, Mass.: Harvard University Press, 2009).

34. For a defense of this position, see Pettit, *On the People's Terms*, esp. 132–36.

35. Again, see Ripstein, *Force and Freedom*.

internal order and individual members, the argument so far may seem to invite the conclusion that the latter are liable to share in the costs. While their state may clearly be deprived of a right against forceful interference as a result of the offensive, they, too, as a result, may generally be deprived of their right against attack. They may be so deprived on account of their duty to support and own up to their state as an enabler of justice, when it succeeds as much as when it reasonably errs.

Interestingly, those who otherwise defend state corporate liability on similar lines tend to deny, often without saying much more, that the kind of argument considered can successfully ground a general liability as severe as a liability to harmful attacks.[36] Why? One might think that, on its own, the general duty to support the conditions of justice—in the form of a state qua corporate agent—is not sufficiently important to ground a general liability to be killed or seriously wounded. Indeed, recall that, by hypothesis, individual members may not have consented to (or been able to consent), voluntarily affirmed, or otherwise identified with the state or its wrongdoing, and may not have had any responsibility for or culpable connection to the existence or subsistence of either. Still, is it really so implausible to think that justice, itself so valuable to human life in society, can, at least sometimes, be sufficiently important on its own to ground individuals' general liability to attack—whether the value is understood as in *(1)* or, expansively, to include the coordination and distribution of resources with a view to elevating individuals beyond minimally decent conditions of well-being, or even as also having some impersonal value? Furthermore, even if justice so understood is not sufficiently important on its own, could it not be so, at least sometimes, when coupled with other important public goods the realization of which depends on states' corporate agency?[37]

The key point to make here is that, even if a plausible argument to this effect could be developed, other even more formidable obstacles stand in the way of the line of argument considered. One relates to the premise that, in today's world, justice and other relevant values depend for their realization on the corporate agency of organizations akin to those I have been referring to as corporate states.

---

36. See especially Anna Stilz, "Collective Responsibility and the State," *Journal of Political Philosophy* 19 (2011): 190–208. At one point, Stilz seems to claim that individual state members cannot permissibly be harmfully targeted in response to their state's harmful wrongdoing insofar as they are not individually to blame for it. As we have seen, though, blameworthiness tends not to be regarded as a condition sine qua non of liability to attack. On the state being constitutive of what justice requires, see further Anna Stilz, "Authority, Self-Determination, and Community in *Cosmopolitan War*," *Law and Philosophy* 33 (2014): 309–35.

37. Cf. John M. Parrish, "Collective Responsibility and the State," *International Theory* 1 (2009): 119–54.

If, alternatively, an individual Hobbesian-like sovereign or, say, individuals acting through states (or other organizations) with no corporate agency of their own can realize these values, or if no organizations whatsoever are required to realize them, then the part of the argument that rests on state corporate agency becomes superfluous. In other words, the argument may only be misleadingly tethered to the corporate idea with which I have been concerned. Individuals' general liability to attack may still arise, at least in part, from their membership in a given state, but contentions to this effect might then be able to sidestep altogether the corporate question.[38]

In the end, though, even if a claim about state corporate agency and justice like the one in (2) can withstand close scrutiny, an even more germane objection remains: is the line of argument considered really one about state corporate liability at all? Is it not instead an argument about when state corporate injustice or other relevant state action may partake in grounding *individuals'* liability to attack? Arguably, (4) betrays this fact by suggesting that if state corporate liability ipso facto engages individual members' liability, it is because they have a strong and potentially enforceable duty to support and own up to the endeavors of their reasonably just state. The question then arises of whether the idea of state corporate liability to attack does any salient moral work, over and above its tracking of individuals' liability. While, as I suggested earlier, the answer may sometimes be affirmative in cases where individuals are not at risk of being significantly harmed by an attack on the liable state, the reverse seems to be true when significant individual harm is at stake. In such contexts, even if state corporate agency may constitute an important premise in liability assessments (say, as a condition of justice), it is individuals' duties and rights that seem to remain commanding—just as individualist theorists claim they should be.

This worry may well be fatal to the prospects of a salient moral category of state corporate liability to (most) attacks in war. Compound it with the other controversies mentioned, as well as with the fact that the line of argument considered is strictly limited to states of a certain type (i.e., reasonably just corporate states), and the relevance of the category seems ever more questionable (at least when significant harm to individuals is at stake). Could this conclusion be the price to pay for accepting individualists' core insight against Just War traditionalists, and for refraining from departing from value individualism in unacceptably radical ways? I am tempted to think it is.

---

38. Prominent arguments adopting this strategy include Frances Kamm, "Failures of Just War Theory," in *The Moral Target: Aiming at Right Conduct in War and Other Conflicts* (Oxford: Oxford University Press, 2012), 36–80, at 64–72; Tadros, "Duty and Liability," 271–77.

Conclusion: The Wider Relevance of State Corporate Agency

Thus, even if it is intelligible and may otherwise be morally useful, the idea of state corporate liability seems, at most, of very limited relevance to the morality of war. This conclusion will likely please many individualist theorists—including those who think that, although it matters that wars are not fought by lone individuals but groups of them, individualist concepts such as individual complicity, vicarious individual liability, individual associative duties, and joint individual liability are sufficient to account for attendant moral complexities. Still, even if my conclusion and analysis are correct, these theorists should not be too quick to claim victory. State corporate agency and responsibility may still have an important role to play in the morality of war. An important upshot of my discussion, I believe, is that it not only helps identify what this role is not, but also orient where we should look next.

For one thing, if, as queried above, some values of great importance can only be realized through the intercession of corporate agents, such values may ground important duties in individuals to constitute, support, and influence these agents—and correspondingly limit these individuals' rights. Insofar as the said duties are enforceable, the question may then be asked whether they may be enforced through attacks in war. Here, the issue is clearly one of individual liability, as opposed to corporate liability, but it remains intrinsically connected to the possibility and value of corporate agency. The line of argument sketched in the previous section is only one of many conceivable arguments that merit further exploration along such lines.[39]

Furthermore, if states qua corporate agents can perpetrate wrongs that are distinctively their own, then a question arises as to whether individuals may participate in such wrongs in ways that enhance their individual liability. The suggestion is sometimes encountered that individuals' wrongful complicity in corporate wrongdoing can be distinct from wrongs these individuals perpetrate as principals, when contributing to corporate agents' decisions and their implementation.[40] No doubt, even if this suggestion is correct, some difficult work remains to be done about how to differentiate properly accomplice from principal wrongdoing, especially in the context of single individual actions enacting corporate decisions.

---

39. Much insightful work on individuals' duties tied to the possibility of corporate agents is currently being developed, and may usefully be applied to the Just War theory context. See especially Stephanie Collins, "Collectives' Duties and Collectivization Duties," *Australian Journal of Philosophy* (2012): 1–18.

40. On such "organizational complicity," see Chiara Lepora and Robert E. Goodin, *On Complicity and Compromise* (Oxford: Oxford University Press, 2013), chap. 7. See also Anders Strand, "Group Agency, Responsibility, and Control."

For example, could a soldier's murder of an enemy at gunpoint double up as an act of complicity in a wider state aggression, and could his or her liability to attack be impacted as a result?

Such further paths of inquiry contingent on the possibility of state corporate agency are tantalizing, and hold the promise of a more fruitful integration of a salient corporate dimension in the morality of war. Of course, insofar as individualized considerations can best account for the puzzles raised here, or if the ideas of corporate agency and corporate responsibility ultimately turn out to be mistaken, then the inquiry will inevitably be of limited value. Since the jury is still out, though, I hope to have helped provide at least some focus for further investigations.

III THE LAW OF WAR

7

TARGETING AL QAEDA

LAW AND MORALITY IN THE US "WAR ON TERROR"

Andrew Altman

Introduction

The United States is at war with al Qaeda and other terrorist organizations. So the American public, and the rest of the world, have been told by the US government since the attacks of September 11, 2001. The administration of President George W. Bush said that the United States was engaged in a "global war on terror," a war authorized by Congress and alleged to be permissible under the law of war and the "inherent right" of self-defense recognized by the UN Charter.[1] The Obama administration retired the phrase "global war on terror," while still insisting that the country was at war with al Qaeda and associated organizations and that lethal attacks against those groups were sanctioned by the law of war and the nation's right of self-defense.[2] John Brennan, counterterrorism advisor and later director of the CIA under President Barack Obama, succinctly put the view of both the Obama and Bush administrations, stating that the attacks on al Qaeda and associated groups were "legal, ethical and wise."[3]

---

1. In his address to a joint session of Congress on September 20, 2001, President Bush said, "Our war on terror begins with Al Qaeda, but it does not end there. It will not end until every terrorist group of global reach has been found, stopped and defeated." "Address to the Joint Session of the 107th Congress," *Selected Speeches of President George W. Bush 2001–2008*, 68; available at http://georgewbush-whitehouse. archives.gov/infocus/bushrecord/documents/Selected_Speeches_George_ W_Bush.pdf.

2. Scott Wilson and Al Kamen, "'Global War on Terror' Is Given New Name," *Washington Post* March 25, 2009, http://articles.washingtonpost.com/2009-03-25/ politics/36918330_1_congressional-testimony-obama-administration-memo.

3. "U.N. to Probe Errant U.S. Drone Attacks," http://www.upi.com/Top_News/ US/2012/10/26/UN-to-probe-errant-US-drone-attacks/UPI-59031351236600/. In the first term of President Obama's administration, approximately three hundred drone

On the other hand, critics of those attacks have asserted that, under the rules of international law, the United States has not been at war with al Qaeda and cannot claim the legal privileges that go with being at war. Moreover, the critics claim that the nation's lethal operations against al Qaeda are not legally justifiable as self-defense and that the killings violate the proscription in international human rights law against the arbitrary taking of life. And, for good measure, the critics add that the killings are counterproductive, because they antagonize the local population and incentivize individuals to join forces with the groups against which the United States is fighting. The critics' view could be summed up simply by reversing each part of Brennan's statement: the US attacks are illegal, unethical, and unwise.

In this essay, I examine the legality and morality of the US attacks, often called "targeted killings," and my argument rejects much of the position of the US government. The critics are right in claiming that the law of war and the right of self-defense do not provide legal or ethical license for the US policy of targeted killings, as that policy has been carried out during the post-9/11 period. However, neither critics nor defenders of US policy have grasped that the issue turns on the question of how international law does, and should, distribute the risk to innocents that arises from the activities of violent non-state groups operating across borders *and* from the actions of states to counter those activities.[4] Nor have critics or defenders appreciated the gravity of the normative and conceptual challenge of formulating a legal norm that would fairly distribute the risks. At this point in the debate over targeted killing, no viable answer to that challenge is even on the horizon.[5]

---

strikes were conducted in Pakistan, as compared to fewer than fifty during the entire Bush administration. Strikes also dramatically increased in Yemen, from one under President Bush to seventy-two in President Obama's first term. See http://securitydata.newamerica.net/drones/pakistan-analysis.html and http://securitydata.newamerica.net/drones/yemen-analysis.html.

4. I use "innocents" as a shorthand for persons who have not done anything to make themselves morally liable to lethal attack.

5. The unfolding nature of the "war on terror" has made it a bit of a legal and moral moving target. The US attacks on al Qaeda in Afghanistan during the months immediately after September 11, when the Taliban ruled the country, present a different set of issues than the attacks on al Qaeda subsequent to the overthrow of the Taliban. And the attacks in Afghanistan present different issues than those conducted in Pakistan and Yemen, as well as those against Islamic State forces in Syria, Iraq, and elsewhere. My concern here is with US attacks against transnational terrorist groups, where the attacks are conducted outside of a so-called "hot battlefield" (a delimited geographic area in which organized military forces confront one another).

The term "terrorist," as both an adjective and noun, is far from unproblematic. In what follows, I use "terrorist" in a stripped-down sense to characterize politically motivated and indiscriminate attacks on a civilian population that are calculated to create a substantial toll in deaths and/or severe physical injuries and to produce widespread fear among the population. See Michael Walzer, *Just and Unjust Wars*, 3rd ed. (New York: Basic Books, 2000), 197–203.

When the issue of targeted killing first arose in public forums, the discussion was about the killing of named persons who had been identified by US intelligence organizations as senior figures in the operations of al Qaeda or affiliated groups and placed on "kill lists" by the executive branch. These killings, which came to be called "personality strikes," were much like assassinations, although the US government argued that, because the United States was at war with al Qaeda, the killings were not, under the law, assassinations.[6] In more recent years, it has been revealed that US forces have engaged in another form of targeted killing, so-called "signature strikes," which are actually much more like war as ordinarily conceived. In signature strikes, the targeted persons are not on kill lists and have not been identified by name. However, on the basis of intelligence information, the persons are said to behave in their daily affairs in a manner that indicates that they are active members of al Qaeda or some similar group. Their "signature" behavior functions as if it were the uniform of an enemy force, opening them to lethal attack, in the eyes of the US government.

Although there are important operational differences between personality and signature strikes, my concern is not with those differences. Both kinds of strikes involve the exercise of lethal force, and the US government has defended both kinds of targeted killing on grounds that do not differentiate between them. It is that defense that will be the focus here.[7]

Most targeted killings have occurred in Pakistan, and there has been much discussion of whether that country has consented to US attacks. Reports based on *Wikileaks* suggest that, at one point, Pakistan did consent to at least some of the attacks. See Tim Lister, "Wikileaks: Pakistan Quietly Approved Drone Attacks, U.S. Special Units," *CNN: US*, December 2, 2010, http://www.cnn.com/2010/US/12/01/wikileaks.pakistan.drones/index.html?_s=PM:US.

However, it is uncertain that there has been continuing consent. See Stanford University International Human Rights and Conflict Resolution Clinic and New York University Global Justice Clinic, *Living Under Drones*, chap. 4, note 605 and accompanying text, available at http://chrgj.org/wp-content/uploads/2012/10/Living-Under-Drones.pdf. As for Yemen, the other country in which a large number of strikes have taken place, it seems that, prior to its overthrow in early 2015, the government consented to US drone strikes. See Mark Mazetti and Mark Landler, "Drone War Rages On," *New York Times*, August 3, 2013, A4.

6. US law, under Executive Order 12333, prohibits assassinations. In this article, I do not examine the legality of targeted killing under US law.

7. The United States has also engaged in "double-tap" strikes, which are signature strikes in which there is an initial strike and then a follow-up attack aimed at persons who go to the aid of individuals hit in the initial strike. The rationale for such strikes is that those who go to the aid of the initial targets are themselves likely to be enemy fighters. Double-tap strikes appear to pose an especially great risk to civilians, as compared to single strikes. See http://chrgj.org/wp-content/uploads/2012/10/Living-Under-Drones.pdf.

I. The Combatant Privilege

The law of war, now called "the law of armed conflict" (LOAC) by most international lawyers, licenses the deliberate killing of human beings in situations where, absent such law, the killings would count as murder and the perpetrators would be liable to legal punishment under the law of the local jurisdiction. This license to kill makes LOAC an especially controversial and contested part of international law, and, in recent years, the most intense controversies have centered on the US policy of killing reputed members of al Qaeda and associated groups, whether the attacks are conducted by armed unmanned aerial vehicles ("drones") or by the military means of Seal Team 6 in their assault against Osama bin Laden. American officials in both the Bush and Obama administrations have argued that the killings are licensed by LOAC.

The Hague Conventions of the late nineteenth and early twentieth centuries codified the existing law of war. The conventions did not explicitly mention the combatant privilege, but its existence was clearly implied. In any case, two important claim-rights explicitly included in Hague IV (1907) were, in effect, aspects of the privilege as it had come to be understood: the right of a belligerent to prisoner-of-war status upon capture by the enemy (Annex, Article 3) and the right to repatriation upon the conclusion of hostilities (Annex, Article 20). In the absence of the privilege, soldiers would have been subject to the local law of the jurisdiction in which they fought, and their use of lethal force against their enemy would (absent special circumstances) have amounted to the crime of murder. In such a case, the soldiers could have legally been treated as common criminals and would have lacked, for example, any right to "be treated as regards board, lodging, and clothing on the same footing as the troops of the Government who captured them" (Annex, Article 7). The soldiers might also have lacked, depending on the jurisdiction, the right to "complete liberty in the exercise of their religion, including attendance at the services of whatever church they may belong to" (Annex, Article 18), and they would certainly not have had the right to repatriation upon the end of hostilities.

Moreover, Hague IV enumerated certain requirements that could only be understood as conditions that soldiers needed to satisfy in order to possess the privilege of attacking enemy belligerents. Those requirements demanded that soldiers "be commanded by a person responsible for his subordinates;...have a fixed distinctive emblem recognizable at a distance;...carry arms openly; and...conduct their operations in accordance with the laws and customs of war" (Annex, Article 1). The Hague conditions for holding the combatant privilege, it should be noted, were formal, in the sense that the substantive justice or morality of the cause in which a soldier fought was irrelevant to satisfying them.

Combatants pursuing egregiously immoral goals could still possess the privilege, as long as they were part of a chain of command, wore distinctive emblems, and so on. This aspect of the law of war was retained, even after the Hague requirements were subsequently modified, and it is generally regarded as an important feature of the distinction between the rules governing when the resort to war is legal (*jus ad bellum*) and the rules dictating which means and methods of warfare are legal (*jus in bello*).

The combatant privilege remained implicit in international treaties governing armed conflict until well after World War II. The Geneva Conventions (1949) do not mention the privilege, and it was not until Additional Protocol I to those conventions (1977) that we find an explicit acknowledgment of the privilege: "Members of the armed forces…(other than medical personnel and chaplains…) are combatants, that is to say, they have the right to participate directly in hostilities."[8] This recognition of the privilege was rightly seen as an important part of articulating a basic rule of the law of war as it had developed in the nineteenth and twentieth centuries, namely, that belligerent parties "shall at all times distinguish between the civilian population and combatants and… shall direct their operations only against military objectives" (Article 48). This rule, also known as the "principle of distinction,"[9] makes practical sense only if some version of the combatant privilege is part of international law. The principle implies that a special class of persons, that is, combatants, not only has an extraordinary legal license to kill but also lacks the normal legal immunity against being intentionally killed.[10]

It is important to note that the privilege of belligerency is not an unconditional license to kill enemy combatants, regardless of the incidental damage that might be caused to noncombatants in the process. The privilege is qualified by a principle of proportionality that prohibits an attack when it "may be expected to cause incidental loss of civilian life, injury to civilians, damage to civilian objects, or a combination thereof, which would be excessive in relation to the concrete and direct military advantage anticipated."[11] LOAC does not further specify what

---

8. *Protocol Additional to the Geneva Conventions of 12 August 1949, and Relating to the Protection of Victims of International Armed Conflicts (Additional Protocol 1)*, 1977, Article 43, Par. 2, available at: http://www.icrc.org/ihl.nsf/INTRO/470.

9. Gary Solis, *The Law of Armed Conflict* (Cambridge: Cambridge University Press, 2010), 251.

10. LOAC does not permit attacks against wounded and sick soldiers, among certain other non-civilians, who are regarded as being hors de combat.

11. *Additional Protocol I*, Article 57, Paragraph 2b.

counts as excessive, and, in practice, the military commanders on the ground have wide discretion to make that determination.

The combatant privilege also operates in tandem with LOAC's principle of military necessity. In Franz Lieber's classic formulation of the principle, "military necessity admits of all direct destruction of life or limb of armed enemies and of other persons whose destruction is incidentally unavoidable in the armed contests of the war."[12] And in the "Hostage Case" after World War II, the court held that such necessity "permits a belligerent, subject to the laws of war, to apply any amount and kind of force to compel the complete submission of the enemy with the least possible expenditure of time, life, and money."[13]

II. From War to Armed Conflict

Under the law of war as it existed through the end of World War II, the combatant privilege came into play only when a state of war existed between two sovereign nations. A state of war was a legal situation brought about only when a nation undertook, via declaration, to be at war against another nation. But, in the aftermath of World War II, major changes were made in the legal regime regulating warfare. One of those changes, codified as Common Article 2 of the Geneva Conventions (1949), provided that the terms of the conventions "shall apply to all cases of declared war or of any other armed conflict which may arise between two or more of the High Contracting Parties, even if the state of war is not recognized by one of them." Jean Pictet's commentary provides the rationale for this revision in the legal regime: Common Article 2 "fills the gap left in earlier Conventions, and deprives the belligerents of the pretexts they might in theory invoke for evasion of their obligations. There is no longer any need for a formal declaration of war, or for recognition of the state of war, as preliminaries to the application of the Convention.... The existence of armed conflict...brings [the Convention] automatically into operation."[14] Indeed, in the years since the adoption of the Geneva Conventions, international lawyers have come to routinely use the phrase "law of armed conflict" rather than the traditional "law of war" to mark the fact that the current rules regulate the use of military force, whether or not such force amounts to war. As a recent report of the International Law

---

12. *The Lieber Code of 1863*, Article 15, http://www.au.af.mil/au/awc/awcgate/law/liebercode.htm.

13. *US v. Wilhelm List*, in International Military Tribunal, *Trial of Major War Criminals* (Washington, D.C.: US Government Printing Office, 1948), 1253–54.

14. Jean S. Pictet, *Commentary: The Geneva Conventions of 12 August 1949*: Vol. 1 (Geneva: International Committee of the Red Cross, 1952), 32.

Association has put it, "In international law, the concept of armed conflict has largely replaced the concept of war."[15]

Scholars and jurists also now commonly use the phrase "International Humanitarian Law" (IHL) to refer to that part of LOAC that regulates conduct during an armed conflict, that is, *jus in bello*, as opposed to the rules governing when the resort to armed force is permissible, that is, *jus ad bellum*. The phrase, IHL, is meant to highlight the idea that a fundamental animating purpose of LOAC is to reduce the devastation and suffering that would otherwise occur in armed conflict and that, as Pictet puts it, "the principle of respect for human personality...is at the root of all the Geneva Conventions."[16] Talk of humanitarian law makes explicit and emphasizes the law's aim of diminishing the human suffering of armed conflict.

Another innovation in the legal regime established by the Geneva Conventions was the introduction of the concept of non-international armed conflict (NIAC). Prior to the war, the rules of warfare applied only to interstate conflicts: the law did not recognize or address violent conflicts between a state and a non-state party. However, Common Article 3 of the conventions changed the legal landscape by prescribing certain rules "in the case of armed conflict not of an international character occurring in the territory of one of the High Contracting Parties." For the first time, the law of war imposed rules on the conduct of armed hostilities between a state and a non-state entity. On the other hand, the requirements of Common Article 3 were quite minimal: to "treat[ ] humanely" all persons who were "taking no active part in the hostilities" and to care for "the wounded and sick."

Additional Protocol I (1977) to the Geneva Conventions subsequently extended the full coverage of the conventions to "armed conflicts in which peoples are fighting against colonial domination and alien occupation and against racist régimes in the exercise of their right of self-determination" (Article 1, Par. 4). Additional Protocol I also clarified (and modified) the Hague IV conditions for a "right to participate directly in hostilities," that is, for having the combatant privilege. The privilege is held by persons who are members of an armed force "under a command responsible [to one of the belligerent parties]...for the conduct of the members" and possessing an "internal disciplinary system which...shall enforce compliance with the rules of international law applicable in armed conflict" (Article 43, Par. 1). All combatants have the obligation "to distinguish themselves from the civilian population when they are engaged in an attack or in a military operation preparatory to an attack" (Article 44, Par. 2). Aside from

---

15. International Law Association, The Hague Conference, Use of Force Committee, "Final Report on the Meaning of Armed Conflict in International Law," 2010, 33, http://www .ila-hq.org/en/committees/index.cfm/cid/1022.

16. Pictet, *Commentary*, 38.

some exceptional circumstances, combatants who violate such an obligation forfeit their privilege.

Additional Protocol II (1977) placed NIAC under a more demanding set of rules than the minimal requirements of Common Article III. This protocol applied "to all armed conflicts which are not covered by [Additional Protocol I]…and which take place in the territory of a High Contracting Party between its armed forces and dissident armed forces or other organized armed groups which, under responsible command, exercise such control over a part of its territory as to enable them to carry out sustained and concerted military operations and to implement this Protocol" (Article I, Par. 1).

III. The Connection Between Legal and Moral Issues

In the wake of the attacks of 9/11, the Bush Administration stated that the United States was in a "global war on terror" against al Qaeda and any organization or country that supported or gave haven to al Qaeda. Congress passed a joint resolution, the *Authorization for the Use of Military Force* (AUMF), which provided that "the President is authorized to use all necessary and appropriate force against those nations, organizations, or persons he determines planned, authorized, committed, or aided the terrorist attacks that occurred on September 11, 2001, or harbored such organizations or persons."[17] Although AUMF was not a formal declaration of war, we have seen that such a declaration is no longer necessary under international law to create a condition in which the privileges and obligations of LOAC come into play. But the administration's use of "war" signaled its view that US forces had the privilege of belligerency in killing Taliban and al Qaeda members. Moreover, the administration held that, because al Qaeda's members failed to carry their arms openly and the organization had no disciplinary mechanism for ensuring that the members observed such legal rules as the principle of distinction—indeed, the organization conspicuously flouted that principle and other rules—al Qaeda's forces lacked the combatant privilege. Accordingly, their use of lethal force amounted to the crime of murder.

The Obama Administration retained this basic picture of hostilities with al Qaeda. Thus, early in his first term, President Obama stated: "Now let me be clear. We are indeed at war with al Qaeda and its affiliates."[18] And even when the

---

17. *Authorization for the Use of Military Force*, http://news.findlaw.com/hdocs/docs/terrorism/sjres23.enr.html.

18. "Remarks by the President on National Security," National Archives, May 21, 2009, https://www.whitehouse.gov/the-press-office/remarks-president-national-security-5-21-09.

president spoke in his second term about the possible end of the conflict with al Qaeda, he continued to refer to the conflict as a war: "Under domestic law, and international law, the United States is at war with al Qaeda, the Taliban, and their associated forces. We are at war with an organization that right now would kill as many Americans as they could if we did not stop them first. So this is a just war—a war waged proportionally, in last resort, and in self-defense."[19]

The questions of whether US forces have a privilege of belligerency with respect to al Qaeda and whether the United States is in an armed conflict with that group are, in the first place, legal questions. But they are legal questions that have moral implications. Consider the privilege of belligerency. If US forces have that privilege, then there is a presumptive case that it would be morally wrong for them to be prosecuted and punished for their targeted killings, were they to fall into the hands of the authorities of the states where the killings took place. It would be presumptively wrong because, if US forces have the privilege, then the killings are not violations of the law of the states in which they occur. The principle of *nulla poena sine crimine* (no punishment without a crime) captures not only a key part of the rule of law but also a presumptive requirement of morally justified punishment. That it would be morally wrong to prosecute persons holding the privilege does not entail that such persons are beyond moral criticism for their conduct. Nonetheless, US forces involved in targeted killings could make at least a presumptive moral case against being prosecuted, if they have the combatant privilege. On the other hand, if US forces lack any legal privilege to kill, then prosecution and punishment by local authorities, assuming other due-process conditions are met, would be morally permissible.[20] Some U.S. targeted killing operations are carried out by ground troops, like the Seal Team that killed Osama bin Laden, and the possibility of such troops falling into the hands of a government that is inclined to prosecute them is not unrealistic. Any locals who might help in the operations would also face the possibility of arrest and prosecution.

19. "Remarks by the President at the National Defense University," National Archives, Washington, D.C., May 21, 2009.

20. The armed drones that have been used in Pakistan belong to the CIA, raising the question of whether CIA personnel could have a combatant privilege. The short answer is no. President Obama's own Office of Legal Counsel concluded, in a once-secret memo that only became publicly available in the wake of a lawsuit against the administration, that CIA personnel who operate lethal drones "are not entitled to the combatant's privilege." See Office of Legal Counsel, U.S. Department of Justice, "Memorandum for the Attorney General Re: The Applicability of Federal Criminal Laws and the Constitutions to the Contemplated Lethal Operations Against Shaykh Anwar al-Aulaqi," July 16, 2010, https://www.aclu.org/sites/default/files/assets/2014-06-23_barron-memorandum.pdf, 33n44. The OLC pointed out, however, that the CIA's lack of the privilege of belligerency did not make the agency's killings punishable under LOAC.

It is true that most US targeted killings are done by unmanned armed drones, with the drone operators working thousands of miles away from the locations in which their targets are killed. Such operators face no realistic chance of arrest and prosecution. But the moral point remains: if they have the privilege of belligerency, then there is a presumptive moral case against prosecuting and punishing them for the killings.

Additionally, the question of whether US soldiers have the privilege of belligerency is part of a broader moral issue that has often been raised in debates over US policy with respect to al Qaeda: is the United States placing itself above international law and playing by a set of rules different from those by which it judges other states? Among common *moral* criticisms is that, notwithstanding the claims of the government, the United States has quite deliberately placed itself above the law. The gravamen of the criticism is not simply that US officials are hypocrites, but that the country has a moral obligation to abide by the terms of LOAC. And the criticism has not gone unnoticed by officials. In defending administration policy regarding al Qaeda, Harold Koh, an international law expert who had been dean of Yale Law School prior to his appointment by President Obama as legal adviser to the State Department, insisted the administration was "following universal standards, not double standards."[21]

The simplest case for the existence of a moral obligation to abide by the rules of LOAC rests on the claim that the United States has agreed to the rules, so that its moral obligation to obey is a promissory obligation. But I think that Ronald Dworkin has put his finger on an additional and more compelling ground of the moral obligation. Dworkin is dealing with international law in general, but his argument has special force when it comes to the law governing armed conflict. The argument rests on the "principle of salience," namely, that "if a significant number of states, encompassing a significant population, has developed an agreed code of practice, either by treaty or by other form of coordination, then other states have at least a prima facie duty to subscribe to that practice as well," with the proviso that this duty holds only if general observance of the code would "improve the legitimacy" of each state and of "the international order as a whole."[22] Recognizing the moral force of something akin to Dworkin's principle of salience

21. Harold H. Koh, "The Obama Administration and International Law," March 25, 2010, http://www.state.gov/s/l/releases/remarks/139119.htm. After leaving office, Koh expressed some criticism of the administration but it was directed not at the substance of administration policy, but rather at the lack of transparency. See Koh, "How to End the Forever War," May 7, 2013, https://lawfare.s3-us-west-2.amazonaws.com/staging/s3fs-public/uploads/2013/05/2013-5-7-corrected-koh-oxford-union-speech-as-delivered.pdf.

22. Ronald Dworkin, "A New Philosophy for International Law," *Philosophy and Public Affairs* 41 (2013): 2–30, at 19.

does not require accepting his further claim that the principle provides a better account of the sources of international law than the traditional positivist principle of state consent.

The reason why Dworkin's principle has particular moral force when it comes to LOAC is that the rules of that body of law provide a highly salient instrument for coordinating the actions of states in way that can substantially diminish the unjust harm that states would otherwise inflict in the course of armed conflict. As compared with a wholly uncoordinated condition, or even the less robustly coordinated condition prior to World War II, LOAC dramatically improves the "legitimacy of…the international order as a whole." As Dworkin recognizes, this improvement does not mean that changes to LOAC are out of order. The Geneva LOAC regime contained important and justified revisions in the preexisting law of war, and further revisions might well be called for. But LOAC is what we have now, and it is all we have now. Accordingly, in light of Dworkin's principle of salience, there is a strong case that the rules of LOAC establish presumptive moral obligations.

IV. Armed Conflict with al Qaeda

If there is no "armed conflict," as that term is used in LOAC, between the US and al Qaeda, then LOAC does not confer on US soldiers a privilege of belligerency. The repeated insistence by both the Bush and Obama administrations that the United States is at war with al Qaeda is their way of saying that there is just such an armed conflict. And the existence of an armed conflict might seem all but self-evident. As legal scholar Jens Ohlin argues, "al Qaeda attacked the United States and continues to attack the United States and its allies, and in turn the United States and its allies are trying to destroy al Qaeda and kill its members. If that isn't an armed conflict, then nothing is."[23]

However, even granted that there is an armed conflict between the United States and al Qaeda, it is doubtful that LOAC grants a privilege of belligerency to US armed forces engaged in the conflict. Common Article 3 is the part of LOAC most directly relevant, and it does not say anything about who holds the privilege of belligerency but only lays down rules of minimally humane treatment that must be followed in any armed conflict involving a non-state party and taking place on the territory of a state party. In virtue of agreeing to the conventions, each of the state parties has undertaken the obligation to ensure that those minimal standards are met: Pakistan, for example, has undertaken to ensure that the

---

23. Jens David Ohlin, "The Duty to Capture," *Minnesota Law Review* 97 (2013): 1268–1342, at 1282.

standards are met in any armed conflict on its territory, and the United States has undertaken to ensure that the standards are met in any NIAC in which they are engaged. Nothing follows about whether some outside state has a privilege to conduct hostilities against a non-state party in Pakistan or whether US forces have the privilege in operations that they conduct in Pakistan. The applicability of the article to hostilities with al Qaeda only means that, whether or not US forces have a privilege of belligerency, international law imposes certain limits on how the armed conflict can be conducted.

It might be argued that there would be an anomaly in applying Common Article 3 restrictions to a conflict without also recognizing the privilege of belligerency for the parties to the conflict. The restrictions of LOAC in general are part of a package deal in which there are obligations on one side, namely, the obligations imposed by the various restrictions on how a conflict may be fought, and privileges on the other, namely, the privilege of belligerency. So if the United States has any Common Article 3 obligations when it engages in hostilities with al Qaeda on Pakistan's territory, then the United States must also have a privilege of belligerency in conducting those hostilities.

I do not deny that the obligation/privilege package does characterize the overall structure of LOAC. In general, states have undertaken to observe a certain body of restrictions on their use of armed force and, in return, their combatants can be granted a privilege to kill enemy combatants. However, it does not follow that there is a privilege of belligerency that accompanies every conflict to which the obligations of LOAC apply. One might regard as anomalous the combination of "obligations + no privilege" that I am suggesting exists for certain NIACs. However, the combination could also be regarded as one of the sensible steps taken by the Geneva Conventions toward reducing the human suffering of war. And the standard view of international lawyers is, in fact, that the rules governing NIACs do not grant a privilege of belligerency.[24]

V. International Human Rights Law

Thus far I have argued that LOAC does not grant US forces a combatant privilege when they conduct targeted killings against al Qaeda and other terrorist groups. Many critics of US policy go further and assert that the killings violate international human rights law (IHRL). Thus, a critical report coming out of Stanford and New York University Law Schools holds: "Targeted killings...cannot be lawful under IHRL, which allows intentional lethal force only when necessary

---

24. See Solis, *The Law of Armed Conflict*, 191.

to protect against a threat to life, and where there are no other means, such as capture or non-lethal incapacitation, of preventing that threat to life. There is little public evidence that many of the targeted killings carried out fulfill this strict legal test."[25]

IHRL is laid out primarily in several international conventions, the most relevant of which, for current purposes, is the *International Convention on Civil and Political Rights* (ICCPR). Article 6 of the convention provides: "Every human being has the inherent right to life. This right shall be protected by law. No one shall be arbitrarily deprived of his life." The UN Special Rapporteur on extrajudicial killings gives the following gloss on IHRL norms: "A State killing is legal only if it is required to protect life (making lethal force proportionate) and there is no other means, such as capture or nonlethal incapacitation, of preventing that threat to life (making lethal force necessary)."[26] The Rapporteur points out that US targeted killings do not meet the two requirements.

It must be noted that the proportionality and necessity requirements here are quite different, and much stricter, than the proportionality and necessity requirements that are part of LOAC. IHRL proportionality looks to the threat posed by the person killed and demands that the killing be justifiable on the basis of the degree of threat. And IHRL necessity demands that killing be the only way to avert the threat. By contrast, LOAC's doctrine of military necessity permits the killing of enemy combatants, even when they could be captured (assuming that they have not surrendered), as long as the killing contributes to the defeat of the enemy at the lowest cost. Moreover, LOAC's proportionality principle does not look to the degree of threat posed by an enemy combatant in determining the level of civilian causalities acceptable in attacking the combatant. Rather, LOAC proportionality looks to the anticipated military advantage of the attack. The result of these differences between IHRL and LOAC is that the license to kill is far narrower under the former than the latter.[27]

---

25. *Living Under Drones*, 117. Also see Michael Ramsden, "Targeted Killings and International Human Rights Law: The Case of Anwar Al-Awlaki," *Journal of Conflict and Security Law* 16 (2011): 385–406.

26. Philip Alston, "Report of the Special Rapporteur on Extrajudicial, Summary or Arbitrary Executions," Human Rights Council, UN General Assembly, May 2010, par. 32, http://www2.ohchr.org/english/bodies/hrcouncil/docs/14session/A.HRC.14.24.Add6.pdf.

27. I agree with Larry May's claim in this volume that, to the extent that IHRL displaces or dilutes LOAC's principles of proportionality and military necessity, it becomes increasingly difficult to argue that killing in the course of armed conflict is legally permissible or to avoid the conclusion that a kind of pacifism is legally required. And although May is right that there has been some movement in the direction of applying strict human-rights norms to the context of armed conflict, my own assessment is that such movement has been quite minimal and that LOAC's undiluted principles of proportionality and necessity remain very firmly entrenched.

It should be noted that the primary obligation that the ICCPR places on states is to ensure that persons within their own jurisdiction are protected by law from having their lives arbitrarily taken. That obligation is not violated by the US-targeted killings, simply because the killings take place outside of US jurisdiction and the obligation does not concern a state's extraterritorial conduct. However, it can be reasonably argued that ICCPR places on every state party an obligation to refrain from interference with the efforts of the other state parties to comply with its terms. Accordingly, even if US attacks on al Qaeda do not violate the nation's primary obligations under IHRL, they arguably violate secondary obligations to avoid interfering with the efforts of other states to provide due process protections.

Nonetheless, there is a line of argument that has been suggested by various US officials that we have not yet examined. The argument centers on the claims that targeted killings are a lawful exercise of the nation's right of self-defense and that, accordingly, US forces have the privilege of belligerency in carrying out such killings. If this line of thinking stands up, then the IHRL criticism of targeted killings could be circumvented, and so the criticism cannot stand alone but must depend on a further argument rebutting US claims about its right of self-defense.

VI. Self-Defense and the Distribution of Risk

Article 51 of the UN Charter reads: "Nothing in the present Charter shall impair the inherent right of individual or collective self-defence if an armed attack occurs against a Member of the United Nations, until the Security Council has taken measures necessary to maintain international peace and security. Measures taken by Members in the exercise of this right of self-defence shall be immediately reported to the Security Council." The US government has invoked this provision of the Charter in defending its killings of members of al Qaeda and associated organizations. The killings help to protect US citizens from al Qaeda's violent plans, and, as Harold Koh argued, despite IHRL's requirement of due process before life is taken, "a state that is engaged in an armed conflict or in legitimate self-defense is not required to provide targets with legal process before the state may use lethal force."[28]

Koh is right that legitimate self-defense does not require that due process be extended to the persons against whom defensive force is deployed. However, his implication that existing international law licenses targeted killings as a form of self-defense is problematic. An expert working group has stated what

---

28. Koh, "The Obama Administration and International Law."

many international lawyers regard as the "black-letter law" of self-defense: "the use of force is justified in self-defence only when force is necessary to bring an [ongoing] attack to an end or to avert an imminent attack."[29]

On the other hand, in the years since the attacks of September 11, one could argue that the traditional black-letter law of self-defense has undergone modification in light of a new understanding by (some) states of the threat of terrorism. The Bush Doctrine explicitly sought to change the traditional law, claiming the legal right to take lethal preemptive measures to stop a potential threat from becoming imminent. In its 2002 *National Security Strategy of the United States*, the administration declared that "we must adapt the concept of imminent threat to the capabilities and objectives of today's adversaries." It then made clear that adapting the concept meant that imminence would no longer be treated as a necessary condition for defensive action: "The United States will not use force in all cases to pre-empt emerging threats, nor should nations use pre-emption as a pretext for aggression. Yet in an age where the enemies of civilization openly and actively seek the world's most destructive technologies, the United States cannot remain idle while dangers gather."[30]

However, the Bush Doctrine was rejected by many states and scholars as incompatible with international law.[31] That a number of states would reject the doctrine should not be surprising, as many of them are vulnerable to preemptive attacks by states with more powerful and technologically advanced military forces. Thus, the widespread criticism that other states leveled at the United States for its 2003 invasion of Iraq, a war undertaken on the basis of the Bush Doctrine, reflected concerns that states had about any legal license for a state to embark on a preemptive attack. The criticism showed that the international consensus that would be needed for preemptive self-defense to be counted as part of existing international law was lacking.[32]

---

29. Nico Schrijver and Larissa van den Herik, "Leiden Policy Recommendations on Counter-terrorism and International Law" (April 1, 2010), Par. 41, http://www.grotiuscentre.org/resources/1/Leiden%20Policy%20Recommendations%201%20April%202010.pdf. Thanks to Steven Ratner for this reference.

30. *National Security Strategy of the United States*, September 2002, 15, http://www.state.gov/documents/organization/63562.pdf.

31. Among the few defenses of the doctrine by international lawyers was Abraham D. Sofaer, "On the Necessity of Pre-emption," *European Journal of International Law* 14 (2003): 209–26.

32. Admittedly, some of the international criticism of the invasion could be construed as saying that it was an improper application of preemptive self-defense, because the Iraqi government did not have weapons of mass destruction, as claimed by the Bush administration. But much of the criticism also rejected the idea of preemptive self-defense and regarded the invasion as an illustration of the grave abuses to which such a doctrine would be vulnerable.

Although the Bush doctrine clearly fails to reflect existing law, it is not clear that the traditional rules of self-defense continue to apply. Monica Hakimi has argued that, at the current time, the international law of self-defense is indeterminate when it comes to the lethal defensive actions taken by states against terrorist groups: "States have not coalesced around a legal standard on *when* [defensive] force [against non-State actors] is lawful."[33] My sense is that Hakimi is right and that there is insufficient agreement in state practice and in the beliefs about legality that accompany state practice to say whether international law permits targeted killing as a mode of self-defense. If anything is apparent in the years since 9/11, it is that states do not hold a uniform view of the matter, whatever might have been true prior to that time.

Still, we can raise the moral questions of whether the traditional rules of self-defense were justifiably abandoned by some states in light of terrorism and whether there is really any better alternative to those rules. Legal norms of self-defense should be able to make a practical difference to the actions of states by being sufficiently determinate to guide and coordinate those actions. Otherwise, states are effectively left in a pre-legal situation in which each one decides individually when self-defense is called for. The difficulties of formulating an alternative to the traditional rules that is both morally defensible and can make a practical difference are illustrated by the Obama Administration's various efforts to defend its targeted killing policy. Although the administration portrayed its arguments as showing that its policy was permissible under the existing law of self-defense, the arguments can be seen as part of an effort to reshape the law in a way that the US government would find reasonably acceptable.

During President Obama's first term, Harold Koh explained administration policy: "Whether a particular individual will be targeted in a particular location will depend upon considerations specific to each case, including those related to the imminence of the threat, the sovereignty of the other states involved, and the willingness and ability of those states to suppress the threat the target poses."[34] Notice that none of these considerations was said to be a necessary condition for a licensed extraterritorial attack. Even the imminence of a threat was simply taken to be a consideration presumably weighed in the balance on some non-specified scale. Accordingly, Koh's remarks failed to articulate a norm of self-defense with sufficient specificity to guide and coordinate the behavior of states. And the failure to be more specific about the norm of self-defense that the administration took

---

33. Monica Hakimi, "Defensive Force Against Non-State Actors: The State of Play," *International Legal Studies* 91 (2015): 1–31, at 4.

34. Koh, "The Obama Administration and International Law."

itself to be applying left rather empty Koh's claim that, in its international actions, the administration was "following universal standards, not double standards."[35]

It might well be true that the lives of US citizens would be put at increased risk in the absence of targeted killings against violent non-state groups that operate across borders. But the states in which such attacks take place can equally well argue that such killings put the lives of their own citizens at increased risk and that it is part of their right to national self-defense to stop the killings, if possible, and to put the killers on trial for murder, if they can be caught after the fact. Appeals to the right of self-defense cannot resolve such a dispute, without greater specification than what Koh provided of what the norm of self-defense allows.

It might be claimed that the right of states in whose territory violent non-state groups are located should give way to the right of the states engaged in an extraterritorial attack, on the ground that every state has the moral obligation to ensure that its territory is not used as a launching pad for non-state groups to organize lethal plots against other states. But even granting such an obligation, it does not follow that the states against which plots are directed automatically have a moral right—or should have a legal right—to launch an extraterritorial attack that puts at risk the lives of persons in the territorial state who are not involved in the plot. What is called for is some fair—or at least morally tolerable—distribution of the risks, and it is difficult to see that a tolerable distribution is one in which the risks are shifted almost entirely from the citizens of the state targeted by the plot to the citizens of the territorial state. The technological, military, and political dominance of the United States enables it to shift the risks in that way, and it is not difficult to understand that US officials would deploy the nation's dominance to that end. Their incentives are all directed toward counting the interests of Americans and disregarding or radically discounting the interests of the citizens of other states. But it is an unduly limited perspective that would fail to see that other states and their citizens cannot be reasonably expected to agree with the shift in risk that accompanies attacks on their territory by the United States.

Perhaps in partial response to such concerns, during his second term, President Obama was more specific than Koh about the content of the self-defense norm: "We act against terrorists who pose a continuing and imminent threat to the American people, and when there are no other governments capable of effectively addressing the threat. And before any strike is taken, there must be near-certainty that no civilians will be killed or injured—the highest standard we can set."[36] These criteria—imminence, absence of other governments to address the threat,

---

35. Ibid.

36. "Remarks by the President at the National Defense University."

and near-certainty of no civilian casualties—put some flesh on the bare bones of the norm of self-defense.

It might seem that the "near-certainty" standard would go a substantial way to meeting the reasonable concerns of the states on whose territories attacks by the United States or other states would likely take place. If the civilians (that is, persons not involved in the activities of violent non-state groups) of territorial states are not put at risk by the extraterritorial use of armed force, then it could no longer be argued that such force unreasonably shifts the risks of dealing with violent non-state groups onto the shoulders of those civilians. However, even if, in any given case, it is nearly certain that no civilians will be killed in a strike, over the run of cases, it is highly likely that there will be civilians killed.[37] For example, if "near certainty" means a .95 probability of no civilian causalities, then, for every one hundred cases, there will be five instances in which there will be civilian deaths—and, of course, there could be multiple civilian deaths in any or all of those five cases. Accordingly, the near-certainty standard can still involve a very significant imposition of risk on the civilian population of the state where the targeted killings are carried out.

The estimates of civilian deaths from US drone strikes in Pakistan are consistent with the risk that attends even the use of the near-certainty standard. The most conservative figures are from the University of Massachusetts Drone Project, which places the number of civilian deaths in Pakistan during the first five years of Obama's administration at 67. The Long War Journal counts 105 civilian deaths in the same period, and the New America Foundation puts the number at 153. The largest numbers come from the Bureau of Investigative Journalism, giving a minimum of 249 civilian deaths.[38]

---

37. In June 2011, John Brennan asserted, "Fortunately, for more than a year, due to our discretion and precision, the U.S. government has not found credible evidence of collateral deaths resulting from U.S. counterterrorism operations outside of Afghanistan or Iraq, and we will continue to do our best to keep it that way." Other officials made similar claims at the time. No organization independent of the US government that has studied targeted killings has found the claims credible, and the head of an independent organization that supports such killings characterized Brennan's assertion as "absurd." Scott Shane, "C.I.A. Is Disputed on Civilian Toll in Drone Strikes," *New York Times*, August 11, 2011, http://www.nytimes.com/2011/08/12/world/asia/12drones.html?pagewanted=all&_r=0. One reason for the administration's inability to find "credible evidence" of civilian causalities is that their counting method presumes that all military-age males in a strike zone are combatants, a presumption that is overcome only by posthumous evidence clearing them. Jo Becker and Scott Shane, "Secret Kill List Proves a Test of Obama's Principles and Will," *New York Times*, May 29, 2012, http://www.nytimes.com/2012/05/29/world/obamas-leadership-in-war-on-al-qaeda.html?pagewanted=all.

38. The data are available at http://umassdrone.org/pakistan.php; http://www.longwarjournal.org/pakistan-strikes/; and http://www.thebureauinvestigates.com/2012/07/02/resources-and-graphs.

It is true that the figures for 2013 show a marked decrease in the number of civilian deaths in Pakistan, with estimates ranging from zero to 14.[39] The decrease is undoubtedly due in large part to a sharp drop in the total number of drone strikes. At the same time, a December strike in Yemen reportedly killed at least six civilians, raising questions in the media about whether the Obama Administration is consistently adhering to a strict standard.[40] However, those questions should be posed in a context that explicitly recognizes that, even with a standard that requires of any given attack that there be a .95 level of certainty that no civilians will be killed, there will almost certainly be strikes that kill civilians, over the course of dozens of attacks.

Turning to the matter of imminence, the president's assertion that targeted killings are directed only at imminent threats is quite dubious. The Massachusetts project counts 306 attacks in Pakistan from 2009–12, with nearly 2,000 militants killed. Assuming that each attack aimed to stop a separate threat to the United States, then there were supposedly over 300 separate *imminent* threats against the United States emanating from Pakistan alone in four years, that is, over 300 threats that were about to be realized had the United States not acted first. With that many imminent threats, though, it would be remarkable if not a single one of them had slipped through the net, as it were, and succeeded in striking the United States. Yet there were no such successful strikes. It is entirely plausible that thousands of credible threats emanated from Pakistan over the period in question, but the data strongly suggest that the administration is playing fast and loose with the idea of imminence. And even if we focus on 2013, when the number of strikes was in the 30 to 50 range, it is difficult to believe that the administration was waiting until each of those threats became imminent before striking; for even if the methods of identifying imminent threats were 90 percent successful, the probability would still be very high that one of the several dozen imminent threats would have slipped through the net.

It might be argued that there are so many threats against the United States that preventing any of them from slipping through the net requires that they be derailed before they become imminent. As I have just noted, waiting until each threat is imminent would increase the risk that one of them will turn out to be

---

39. An estimate of zero-four civilian deaths for 2013 comes from the Bureau of Investigative Journalism (but it is unclear from the Bureau website how much of the year its figures cover), while an estimate of 14 comes from the Long War Journal. According to the Long War Journal, the year with the highest number of strikes in Pakistan was 2010, when there were 117. For 2013, the number was 27. The Massachusetts project counted 268 strikes in 2010 and 52 in 2013.

40. Mark Mazzetti and Robert F. Worth, "Yemen Deaths Test Claims of New Drone Policy," *New York Times*, December 21, 2013, A1 and A3.

successful, and the increased risk is arguably too high. Such an argument is not unreasonable, and it is likely part of what motivated the Bush Administration to adopt its doctrine of preemptive self-defense and the Obama Administration to make its implausible claims about imminence. However, the argument effectively abandons the imminence standard and raises the thorny question of what standard to use as an alternative. The Bush Administration abandoned imminence but did not replace it with any determinate norm that could serve as a salient point of coordination among states. The United States simply decided ad hoc which threats were sufficient to strike against and which were not, and, although this arrangement was satisfactory to the administration's advocates of unrestrained US sovereignty, it only reinforced the conclusion of many commentators that the nation was operating above the law, in violation of its legal and moral obligations. In the next section, I examine the suggestion that imminence be replaced with necessity as the central condition of legally permitted national self-defense.

VII. Necessity?

Several commentators have argued that the imminence standard is normatively defective and should be jettisoned in both law and moral thinking. For example, Russell Christopher argues that the standard has the unacceptable consequence that persons who are physically unable to respond quickly enough to defend themselves against imminent aggression are deprived of a right to effective self-defense. Christopher and other critics of imminence contend that what really counts in determining the permissibility of lethal defensive action is not how imminent the threat is but whether the lethal action is necessary to avert the threat (assuming that death or grave injury is what is threatened).[41] If such action is necessary, then it is not important whether the threat is imminent or not. Moreover, Christopher and the critics claim that imminence is not even a good proxy for necessity, as it is both under- and over-inclusive: not only are there situations in which defensive force is necessary prior to the point of imminence, as in the case of agents too slow to mount an effective defense if they wait until an attack is imminent; there are also situations in which defensive force is unnecessary

---

41. See Russell Christopher, "Imminence in Justified Targeted Killing," in *Targeted Killings*, ed. Claire Finkelstein, Jens David Ohlin, and Andrew Altman (Oxford: Oxford University Press, 2012), 253–84. Other critics of imminence include Larry Alexander, "A Unified Excuse of Preemptive Self-Protection," *Notre Dame Law Review* 74:1475–1505, at 1477; and Jeremy Horder, "Killing the Passive Abuser: A Theoretical Defense," in *Criminal Law Theory: Doctrines of the General Part*, ed. Stephen Shute and Andrew Simester (Oxford: Oxford University Press), 283–97, at 289–94.

even at the point of imminence, for example, when the aggressor has a last-second change of heart and decides not to aggress.

The criticisms of the imminence standard are not entirely without merit. However, they gloss over some key points. The imminence standard helps to lend a norm of self-defense sufficient determinacy to coordinate the behavior of states. Moreover, in light of the biases and epistemic limitations that can lead agents to misperceive or deliberately mischaracterize the threats they face, the relative clarity of the standard and the difficulty of satisfying it provide a safeguard against mistake and abuse. As Jeremy Waldron argues, if the imminence requirement were relaxed, it would be of crucial moral importance to have institutions in place that could provide a reliable check against the worst abuses.[42] Perhaps the UN Security Council could do the job, but it is far from clear that the council is a fit instrument for such a task.

If imminence were jettisoned and replaced with a necessity standard, a formulation of the latter standard would be needed that is sufficiently determinate to guide and coordinate the actions of states in their decisions about self-defense and to make a practical difference in their conduct, or else we would be back to a pre-legal situation. Simply saying that lethal action is permissible if necessary for self-defense is to say next to nothing without some account of what "necessary" means. Seth Lazar has shown that it is implausible to say that "necessary" means that the threat literally *cannot* be averted unless the lethal action is taken.[43] Even if God knows which threats can or cannot be averted by which lethal actions, it makes little sense to fashion human law from the perspective of an omniscient observer. Rather, the law should be fashioned from a human perspective, and that means one in which averting threats is a matter of probabilities across the range of alternative responses. Simplifying somewhat Lazar's proposal, a lethal attack against a threat is necessary if and only if, given the evidence that would be available to a reasonable person in the defender's position, any less harmful response to the threat would pose an excessively high risk of unjust harm (to the defender and/or other innocents), even when the likelihood of increased benefits (such as fewer collateral casualties) is taken into account.

A legal norm fashioned around this idea of necessity would clearly lack the crispness and specificity of an imminence standard. Perhaps it would be so indeterminate

---

42. Jeremy Waldron, "Justifying Targeted Killing with a Neutral Principle?" in Finkelstein, Ohlin, and Altman, *Targeted Killings*, 112–31, at 122. Also see Allen Buchanan's work on the interplay of legal norms and institutional capacity: "Institutionalizing the Just War," *Philosophy and Public Affairs* 34 (2006): 2–38.

43. Seth Lazar, "Necessity in Self-Defense and War," *Philosophy and Public Affairs* 40 (2012): 3–44.

as to fail in any intended action-guiding and coordinating role. On the other hand, there are LOAC norms that are less than crisp, for example, its rule of proportionality, which holds that attacks risking harm to civilians should not be undertaken if the harm would be "excessive in relation to the concrete and direct military advantage anticipated."[44] So it would seem premature to rule out a necessity standard.

Nonetheless, it would be highly questionable to maintain that the necessity standard, had it been law, would have licensed US targeted-killing policy as it has been practiced in the aftermath of 9/11. The number of civilian deaths from drone strikes, particularly over the period 2009–13, makes it difficult to believe that the policy has adequately weighed the harm done to non-US citizens. Instead, US policy appears to have shifted the risks of dealing with al Qaeda to the shoulders of the citizens of other states, with little regard for the interests of those citizens. So even if a necessity standard would have permitted some of the targeted killings, it is questionable that it would have permitted anything approaching the full scope of killings that US policy has undertaken.

It is also worth noting that a necessity standard provides no easy way around a difficult problem that we have encountered in examining the imminence requirement. The aggregate of threats from a group such as al Qaeda might be such that refraining entirely from lethal force against the group would pose an excessively high risk of unjust harm, even though, for any single threat, lethal force against it is not necessary. This is the analog for the necessity standard of a problem that confronts the imminence requirement, namely, that, even if no single threat is imminent, the aggregate of threats might be such that waiting for one of them to become imminent carries an excessively high risk that another slips through the net. The key normative challenge in formulating a defensible response to terrorist organizations such as al Qaeda does not derive from the fact that their members hide amid civilian populations but rather from the danger posed by the aggregate of their threats. Resolving this aggregation problem requires a principle for the distribution of risks that adequately weighs the interests of all innocents. Yet advocates of a necessity standard have fared no better than defenders of the imminence requirement in recognizing the need for such a principle, much less in telling us what that principle is.

Conclusion

I have argued that US targeted-killing policy is not licensed by any norm that international society has adopted as law. And the policy is ethically questionable

---

44. *Additional Protocol I*, Article 57.

because it appears to place an unreasonably high level of risk on citizens of the states where the killings are conducted. At the same time, the United States has a reasonable objection to existing international law, if the law is understood as requiring an imminent threat for the use of lethal force in defense against the threat. Even if each of the many separate threats posed by al Qaeda and other terrorist groups is not imminent, waiting until the threats become imminent might pose an unreasonably high risk for US citizens. How the law should address such an objection, and what would count as a morally defensible and practically feasible distribution of risks posed by violent groups and the efforts to stop them, are enormously difficult questions. Recognizing that US policy has not been morally or legally justifiable does not provide the answers to those questions, and much work remains to figure out what a defensible policy of targeted killing would be like.

8 KILLING WITH DISCRIMINATION

Adil Ahmad Haque

Introduction

Philosophical discussions of the law of armed conflict tend to focus on two legal norms. The first legal norm is that combatants may not intentionally kill or harm civilians not taking direct part in hostilities.[1] The second legal norm is that combatants may not unintentionally kill or harm such civilians except as a necessary and proportionate side effect of attacking legitimate military targets.[2]

Almost all philosophers writing on the ethics of armed conflict believe that these legal norms are morally justified. Most believe it is morally wrong to inflict intentional, unnecessary, or disproportionate harm on civilians.[3] Even those who believe that some civilians are morally liable to be killed or harmed generally believe that all civilians should remain legally immune from being killed or harmed, lest combatants mistakenly kill or harm the morally liable and the morally immune alike. Since I am a member of the former group, I will assume in this essay that civilians retain their ordinary moral right not to be killed or harmed unless and for such time as they directly participate in hostilities. Members of the latter group

---

1. Protocol Additional to the Geneva Conventions of 12 August 1949, and Relating to the Protection of Victims of International Armed Conflicts (Protocol I) art. 51(2), 8 June 1977, 1125 U.N.T.S. 3 (entered into force December 7, 1978) [hereinafter Protocol I] ("The civilian population as such, as well as individual civilians, shall not be the object of attack").

2. Protocol I, arts. 51(5)(b), 57(2)(a)(iii) & (b).

3. In this essay, all my moral and legal claims regarding civilians apply only to civilians not directly participating in hostilities, and all my moral and legal claims regarding combatants apply also to civilians directly participating in hostilities. Finally, Just War revisionists may modify my moral claims depending on the justice of the attacking force's cause.

may treat my moral claims regarding civilians as applying only to civilians who retain their ordinary right not to be killed or harmed.

This essay examines the moral justification of a different legal norm, one that has received little attention by philosophers. The law of armed conflict prohibits *indiscriminate attacks*, including the use of highly imprecise weapons. The V2 rockets employed by German forces toward the end of World War II are often cited as the paradigm case of unlawfully indiscriminate weapons. In recent years, international lawyers have argued that anti-personnel landmines, SCUD missiles, cluster munitions, white phosphorous, and Katyusha rockets are also unlawfully indiscriminate. Unfortunately, without a general account of what makes an imprecise weapon unlawfully indiscriminate, such weapon-specific arguments will remain inconclusive.

We might imagine that there are two questions here. First, how imprecise must a weapon be before it should be considered unlawfully indiscriminate? Second, what is the moral justification of the legal prohibition of indiscriminate weapons? In fact, I believe the first question cannot be answered independently of the second. Without taking a long detour into jurisprudential controversies, I will simply assert that when the content of a legal norm cannot be fixed solely by reference to positive legal materials, it is appropriate to resolve any residual legal indeterminacy through moral reasoning in light of the moral aims of that legal norm. Since positive legal materials do not identify a required level of precision, it is appropriate to conclude that a weapon should be considered unlawfully indiscriminate if its imprecision renders its use morally impermissible.

In this essay I will explore two possible justifications for the legal prohibition on the use of indiscriminate weapons. The prohibition may be justified instrumentally, as an indirect strategy of implementing more fundamental prohibitions on inflicting intentional, unnecessary, and disproportionate harm on civilians. However, I will argue that it is intrinsically morally wrong to use weapons that, either by their nature or by their use, are more likely to strike civilians or civilian objects than to strike combatants or military objectives. I conclude that the use of such weapons should be considered unlawfully indiscriminate.

I. Discrimination in the Law of Armed Conflict

Before examining the moral basis for the legal prohibition of indiscriminate weapons, we should first understand the nature of the legal prohibition itself. Article 51(4) of Additional Protocol I to the 1949 Geneva Conventions prohibits indiscriminate attacks, which it defines as

(a) those which are not directed at a specific military objective;
(b) those which employ a method or means of combat which cannot be directed at a specific military objective; or
(c) those which employ a method or means of combat the effects of which cannot be limited as required by this Protocol; and consequently, in each such case, are of a nature to strike military objectives and civilians or civilian objects without distinction.[4]

The first and third kinds of indiscriminate attack are morally impermissible for obvious reasons. Attacks that are not directed at a specific military objective include firing blindly into enemy territory and randomly dropping bombs over enemy territory after hitting or missing the original target.[5] Such attacks violate the basic legal principle that "constant care shall be taken to spare the civilian population" and the basic moral principle that soldiers must both *not try* to kill civilians and *try not* to kill civilians.[6] Similarly, methods (tactics) or means (weapons) of combat whose effects technologically cannot be controlled, such as biological weapons, morally cannot be unleashed.[7] There is no way to guarantee that the use of such weapons will satisfy necessity and proportionality.

It is only the second kind of indiscriminate attack, one that uses a tactic or weapon that cannot be directed at a specific military objective, that raises serious questions. For one thing, the text of the prohibition has not been and should not be read literally. Strictly speaking, a weapon "cannot be directed at a specific military objective" only if there is nothing one can do to increase the likelihood that the weapon will strike an intended target. If aiming the weapon makes it more likely to strike its intended target than, for example, to strike any equally distant point in the opposite direction, then in a limited sense it has been directed at a specific military target. Since such a narrow construction yields absurd results and defeats the intention of the parties, a broader construction is required. For example, the Red Cross Commentary explains that this prohibition applies to "long-range missiles which cannot be aimed *exactly* at the objective."[8] More generally, this provision has been understood to prohibit the use of weapons that

---

4. Protocol I, art. 51(4).

5. See Yoram Dinstein, *The Conduct of Hostilities Under the Law of International Armed Conflict* (Cambridge: Cambridge University Press, 2004), 118.

6. Michael Walzer, *Just and Unjust Wars* (New York: Basic Books, 1977), 155–56.

7. See, for example, Michael N. Schmitt, "The Principle of Discrimination in 21st Century Warfare," *Yale Human Rights & Development Law Journal* 2 (1999): 143, 147.

8. See, for example, International Committee of the Red Cross, *Commentary on the Additional Protocols of 8 June 1977 to the Geneva Conventions of 12 August 1949*, Yves Sandoz, Christophe

cannot be *accurately* or *reliably* directed at a specific military objective. This of course raises the question with which we began: how inaccurate does a weapon have to be before it becomes unlawfully indiscriminate? The provision does not say.

In addition, Article 51(5) goes on to declare the following types of attacks indiscriminate:

(a) an attack by bombardment by any methods or means which treats as a single military objective a number of clearly separated and distinct military objectives located in a city, town, village or other area containing a similar concentration of civilians or civilian objects;

and

(b) an attack which may be expected to cause incidental loss of civilian life, injury to civilians, damage to civilian objects, or a combination thereof, which would be excessive in relation to the concrete and direct military advantage anticipated.[9]

Attacks that violate 51(5)(a) are *directed at* neither military objectives (lawful) nor civilians (unlawful) but rather an *area* containing both. Put another way, the *object* of such an attack is neither the military objectives (lawful) nor the civilians (unlawful) but rather the area containing both. In my view, directing an attack at an area containing civilians is morally closer to directing an attack at civilians than to directing an attack at military targets and harming civilians as an unintended side effect. Put yet another way, making an area containing civilians the object of attack is morally closer to making civilians the object of attack than to making military objectives the object of attack and harming civilians as an unintended side effect. Since the focus of this essay is on indiscriminate weapons rather than indiscriminate targeting, I will not defend these claims further here. I will note only that the categorical prohibition on area bombing could also rest on the grounds that it almost always involves intentional, unnecessary, or disproportionate harm to civilians.[10]

Swinarski, and Bruno Zimmermann, eds., 1987, 621, emphasis added. ("The V2 rockets used at the end of the Second World War are an example of this").

9. Protocol I, art. 51(5).

10. In his contribution to this volume, Kai Draper argues that intentionally harming civilians as a means is not significantly harder to justify than unintentionally harming civilians as a side effect. Draper presents two cases in which "the only way to induce the enemy to surrender is to detonate an atomic bomb above a city, foreseeably killing tens of thousands of persons in the

Importantly for our purposes, an attack that violates 51(5)(b) does not nec-essarily violate 51(4): an attack might be expected to cause excessive harm to civilians even if it directs precise means and methods of combat with limited effects at specific military objectives. It is harder to say whether an attack that violates 51(4) necessarily violates 51(5)(b). On the one hand, an attack that is not directed at a specific military objective, or that employs weapons or tactics that cannot be so directed, *may be expected* to cause some harm to civilians and gain no military advantage, and thereby violate 51(5)(b). On the other hand, an attack may have positive *expected value* if the (less probable) military advan-tage sufficiently outweighs the (more probable) harm to civilians, and might thereby satisfy 51(5)(b). The language of 51(5)(b) is most naturally read to suggest that it is the *expected outcome* of an action (that is, the probable out-come) rather than the *expected value* of an action (that is, the difference between

---

city below.... In the first, the bomb is detonated in order to kill the inhabitants of the city. The enemy is expected to surrender immediately in order to avoid further losses of life. In the second, the bomb is detonated over the city in order to destroy the enemy's weaponry (unbe-knownst to its own civilian population, the enemy's leaders have distributed this weaponry across the city), and the loss of civilian life is foreseen but unsought. The enemy is expected to surrender immediately in order to avoid further losses of weaponry." Draper submits that the first bombing is not much worse than the second.

The second case seems to involve area bombing, which I have suggested is morally closer to intentionally harming civilians than to unintentionally harming civilians. On my view, Draper is right to think that his two cases are morally close, but he is wrong to think that these cases show that intentionally harming civilians is morally close to unintentionally harming civilians.

We should instead compare Draper's first case with a third case in which an atomic bomb is directed at a discrete military target that only an atomic bomb can destroy, the destruction of which is the only way to induce the opposing party to surrender. I find the first case much harder to justify than the third case, though I understand why this might seem unclear.

Let us suppose that either attack will kill ten thousand innocent civilians and save fifty thousand other innocent civilians from being killed by the adversary. Let us also assume *argu-endo* that it is permissible to unintentionally harm *one* innocent person as a side effect of saving *five or more* other innocent people from comparable harm but that it is only permissible to in-tentionally harm *one* innocent person as a means of saving *ten or more* innocent people from comparable harm. On these assumptions, the third attack is clearly justified, since it will save five innocent people for every innocent person it would kill (ratio) and will save at least five more innocent people than it will kill (difference). In contrast, the first attack may seem more ambiguous. The first attack will save fewer than ten innocent people for every innocent person killed (ratio); however, the first attack will save at least ten more innocent people than it will kill (difference). In other words, the first attack seems permissible if we *subtract* the number killed from the number saved but seems impermissible if we *divide* the number saved by the number killed.

On my view, the *ratio* (not the *difference*) between the number killed and the number saved is morally decisive. For example, it would be wrong to intentionally or unintentionally kill 10,000 innocent people to save 10,010 other innocent people. So the appearance that the first and third cases are morally close is an illusion.

the values of the possible outcomes, discounted by their probabilities) that determines its legal permissibility. Unsurprisingly, the drafting history of 51(5)(b) contains no evidence that the parties considered such matters when drafting the relevant language.

I argue in this essay that both the expected outcome of an attack and the expected value of an attack are relevant to its moral permissibility. If I am correct, then 51(4) and 51(5) should be interpreted in a way that tracks, as closely as possible, the moral norms that provide their strongest moral justification.

II. Intention, Necessity, and Proportionality

The use of imprecise weapons might be morally impermissible for at least three reasons. First, the attacking force may in fact *intend* to kill, harm, or terrorize civilians through the use of imprecise weapons. Second, the use of such weapons may be *unnecessary* if the party using the weapon could have used different, more accurate weapons instead. Third, the use of such weapons may be *disproportionate* in a morally important sense if the military advantage of striking the military target, discounted by the probability of striking the target, is outweighed by the harm of striking civilians, discounted by the probability of striking civilians.

Indeed, most actual uses of imprecise weapons inflict or risk inflicting intentional, unnecessary, or disproportionate harm on civilians and would be morally impermissible on those grounds. It is worth noting, however, that each concept (intent, necessity, and proportionality) contains certain ambiguities that would need to be resolved before they could be confidently applied in many cases.

For example, attacking forces clearly intend to harm civilians when they use imprecise weapons *in order* to harm civilians, particularly when their "primary purpose...is to spread terror."[11] However, attacking forces might also have a disjunctive intention, to strike either specific military targets or nearby civilians, and use imprecise weapons because they are indifferent between the two outcomes. In addition, attacking forces may use imprecise weapons *in order* to strike specific military targets only *because*, or *on the condition* that, even if their weapons miss their military targets they will harm and terrorize civilians, which the attacking force takes to offset the military cost of the attack. In the latter cases, the attacking force does not consider the possibility of harming civilians as an affirmative reason to launch the attack, but rather as a "defeater of a defeater" that offsets

---

11. Protocol I, art. 51(2).

reasons against launching the attack (such as expenditure of resources).[12] It is not clear whether the moral and legal prohibitions on intentionally attacking civilians apply to the latter cases. I suspect that they do apply, but I will say no more about these issues here.

It seems clearly true that, other things equal, it is morally impermissible to use a less precise weapon rather than a more precise weapon when the former will place civilians at greater risk than the latter. Of course, other things are not always equal. For one thing, the use of more precise weapons may place attacking forces at greater risk. For example, the alternative to using cluster munitions to render an area inaccessible to opposing forces may be to clear and hold that area with one's own ground forces. Yet the use of less precise weapons cannot always be justified by reference to the risks to one's own forces of using more precise weapons. As David Luban and I have argued elsewhere, though on somewhat different grounds, combatants ought to use more discriminating means and methods of combat unless doing so will increase the marginal risk to those combatants to a substantially greater degree than using less discriminating means or methods would increase the marginal risk to civilians.[13] Since I have addressed these issues at length elsewhere I will not do so again here.

Finally, some attacking forces may not have more precise weapons that can achieve the desired effect. For example, non-state armed groups that use primitive rockets against advanced militaries often do not have more precise weapons that deliver comparable explosive payloads. Yet the absence of precise weapons does not necessarily render permissible the use of imprecise weapons. Among other things, the use of imprecise weapons may be disproportionate in the sense defined above: the military advantage of striking the military target, discounted by the probability of striking the target, may be outweighed by the harm of striking civilians, discounted by the probability of striking civilians. Since proportionality is typically determined by comparing the military advantage and the civilian harm of a successful strike, I will refer to the probabilistic sense of proportionality as *e-proportionality* (for *expected value proportionality* or *expectable-proportionality*). As I will discuss at length below, the use of an imprecise weapon is impermissible if it is e-disproportionate, but even an e-proportionate attack may be impermissible if it is sufficiently imprecise.

---

12. See F. M. Kamm, *Intricate Ethics: Rights, Responsibilities, and Permissible Harm* (New York: Oxford University Press, 2007), chap. 4.

13. See Adil Ahmad Haque, "Killing in the Fog of War," Southern California Law Review 86 (2012): 63; David Luban, "Risk-Taking and Force Protection," in *Reading Walzer*, ed. Yithak Benbaji and Naomi Sussmann (New York: Routledge, 2014), 277–301.

III. An Instrumentalist Account

If the use of imprecise weapons is morally wrong only if it inflicts intentional, un-necessary, or e-disproportionate harm on civilians, then why have an independ-ent legal prohibition on the use of imprecise weapons? Why not rely on the dis-tinct legal prohibitions on inflicting intentional, unnecessary, or disproportionate harm on civilians?[14]

For one thing, combatants may better conform to those distinct prohibitions indirectly, by directly following the prohibition on using imprecise weapons. While combatants necessarily know if they are inflicting intentional harm on civilians, and generally know if they are inflicting unnecessary harm on civilians, they do not always know if they are inflicting e-disproportionate harm on civil-ians. Combatants might better avoid inflicting e-disproportionate harm on civilians by never using imprecise weapons than by trying to evaluate the e-proportional-ity of using imprecise weapons on a case-by-case basis. If so, then the legal prohi-bition of using imprecise weapons would be instrumentally morally justified.[15]

Of course, such a rationale for the legal prohibition of indiscriminate weap-ons could succeed only if the content of the prohibition could be identified inde-pendently of its underlying rationale. If combatants have to determine whether the use of a weapon would be e-disproportionate in order to determine whether it is unlawfully imprecise then they would be no better off following the prohibition on imprecise weapons than directly following the prohibition on e-dispropor-tionate attacks.

How might we identify the content of the prohibition of imprecise weapons without simply applying the prohibition of e-disproportionate attacks? One ap-proach would be to look to legal conventions, positive legal norms that specifi-cally prohibit certain weapons, such as biological weapons, on the grounds of their imprecision. These legal norms could be followed directly, without refer-ence to their underlying rationale.

We would, of course, want to know what leads states to recognize a weapon as unlawfully imprecise. Presumably, states will reject a particular weapon only if

---

14. One possibility might be that the legal prohibition of inflicting disproportionate harm does not extend to e-disproportionate harm. As I mentioned above, positive legal materials are in-conclusive on this point. Since e-proportionality is a morally important category, I would argue that the law should be interpreted broadly. But I will say no more about this here.

15. For another thing, third parties—including international organizations, international courts, military tribunals, the press, civil society organizations, and the general public—may find it easier to determine whether a weapon is unlawfully imprecise than to determine the intention with which it was used in a particular case. In this way the prohibition of intention-ally harming civilians may be better enforced indirectly, by directly enforcing the prohibition on imprecise weapons.

the use of that weapon is very rarely e-proportionate and the e-proportionate uses of the weapon are very rarely necessary to victory. When these conditions are satisfied, states will have much to gain and little to lose from agreeing with other states to abstain from using the weapon in future conflicts. Moreover, since states will accept or reject a ban on a particular weapon based on its military utility and its impact on civilians, such bans cannot be entirely dismissed as "merely conventional" or morally arbitrary.

One potential problem with relying on weapon-specific, categorical prohibitions is that such an approach prohibits only weapons that are, in legal terms, indiscriminate *by their nature* but not weapons that are indiscriminate *by their use*. This approach might not allow us to say, for example, that it is unlawful to use cluster munitions against infantry units traveling through cities and towns but lawful to use cluster munitions against tank formations far from civilian areas. Some states might resist a categorical ban on cluster munitions while admitting that international law should regulate their use. But perhaps even categorical prohibitions of specific weapons could be limited to their use in or near civilian areas.

There is another problem with the categorical approach, namely that it seems to justify specific prohibitions of particular imprecise weapons rather than the general prohibition of all imprecise weapons. Even if states do not ban a specific weapon by treaty, an international consensus that a weapon is unlawful due to its inaccuracy generates a norm of customary international law prohibiting the use of that weapon. Rather than providing the content of the general legal prohibition, state consensus on specific weapons simply generates specific legal prohibitions. There is a danger that, on the view we are exploring, the general prohibition of indiscriminate weapons will serve only as a preamble to the specific prohibitions that actually guide the conduct of combatants.

But perhaps this objection could also be overcome, say through the use of analogical reasoning. For example, we might argue that any weapon violates the general prohibition if it is as or more imprecise than those weapons that violate a specific prohibition. This would leave the general prohibition with some independent content.

So it is possible that a meaningful legal prohibition on imprecise weapons can be morally justified on instrumentalist grounds. Nevertheless, I will argue that this legal prohibition rests on an independent, non-instrumental moral foundation. I will argue that it is inherently morally impermissible for combatants to use weapons that are more likely to strike civilians than opposing combatants or military objectives.[16] The use of such weapons is morally impermissible

---

16. For current purposes, "strike civilians" means either directly striking civilians or harming civilians as a direct side effect of striking civilian property.

even if the attacking force does not intend to harm civilians, does not possess more precise weapons, and even if the expected military advantage substantially outweighs the expected harm to civilians. The legal prohibition of indiscriminate attacks may therefore rest on the inherent moral wrongness of the legally prohibited conduct, rather than on the instrumental value of the legal prohibition itself.

IV. Permissibility and e-Proportionality

We have already seen that the use of an imprecise weapon is morally impermissible, even if it is not intended to harm civilians and even if it is the most precise weapon available, if it is e-disproportionate. To see that even an e-proportionate use of an imprecise weapon can be morally impermissible, consider the following (skeletal) scenarios. The scenarios assume that all civilians who might be harmed or spared are members of the same political community and that the only relevant military advantage is the protection of civilians from the immoral and unlawful attacks of the other side.[17] Such a scenario might arise in the context of humanitarian intervention or in operations conducted on the territory of the attacking force. By describing military advantage solely in terms of civilian lives we are better able to recognize the effect of other moral considerations on our intuitive moral judgments.

Here is the first case:

30-70(i): If you strike the target you will save one hundred civilians from being killed. However, there is only a 30 percent chance of hitting your target and a 70 percent chance of missing your target and killing forty other civilians.

The expected number of deaths if you do not attack is 100; the expected number of deaths if you attack is 98 (.7 times 140); therefore the expected value of the attack is two saved lives. Launching the attack would maximize expected value—in this case, the number of survivors discounted by the probability of their survival. Yet launching the strike seems intuitively impermissible. Why? One reason might be that we are not merely comparing possible outcomes but possible actions, and the permissibility of an action is affected by its causal structure as well as by its causal consequences.

In a nod to Derek Parfit, I will refer to the number of civilians who would be saved by a successful strike, discounted by the probability of success, as the

---

17. Presumably, any relaxation of the final constraint may be offset by changing the number of civilian lives at stake.

number of civilians *expectably-saved*, and to the number of civilians who would be killed in a failed strike, discounted by the probability of failure, as the number of civilians *expectably-killed*.[18] If killing is substantially worse than letting die then presumably expectably-killing N civilians is substantially worse than failing to expectably-save N civilians. Indeed, if killing is X times worse than letting die, then a permissible attack would have to expectably-save X times more civilians than it would expectably-kill. Let us call such an attack *de-proportionate*, since it remains e-proportionate even after its deontic properties are taken into account.

The attack in *30-70(i)* expectably-kills 28 and expectably-saves 30. It follows that if killing is even slightly worse than letting die, then the attack in *30-70(i)* is de-disproportionate. Nevertheless, we cannot explain the impermissibility of indiscriminate attacks solely in terms of de-disproportionality. Consider the following case:

30-70(ii): If you strike the target you will save one hundred civilians from being killed. However, there is only a 30 percent chance of hitting your target and a 70 percent chance of missing your target and killing ten other civilians.

The expected number of deaths if you do not attack is one hundred; the expected number of deaths if you attack is seventy-seven (.7 times 110); therefore the expected value of the attack is twenty-three saved lives, much greater than in *30-70(i)*. Moreover, the attack in *30-70(ii)* expectably-kills seven and expectably-saves thirty. It follows that killing would have to be more than four times worse than letting die to render the attack in *30-70(ii)* de-disproportionate. It is not clear that killing is four times worse than letting die, yet the attack in *30-70(ii)* seems clearly impermissible. Certainly, the attack in *30-70(ii)* does not seem four times less wrongful or easier to defend than the attack in *30-70(i)*. This suggests, at a minimum, that something other than de-proportionality is at play.

Now let us vary the probabilities but make the expected value roughly the same as in *30-70(ii)*, and make the ratio of civilians expectably saved and expectably killed fall between those in *30-70(i)* and in *30-70(ii)*.

70-30: If you strike the target you will save fifty civilians from being killed. There is a 70 percent chance of hitting your target and a 30 percent chance of missing your target and killing fifty other civilians.

The expected number of deaths if you do not attack is fifty; the expected number of deaths if you attack is thirty (.3 times 100); therefore the expected value of

---

18. Derek Parfit, *On What Matters*, vol. 1 (Oxford: Oxford University Press, 2011), 160.

launching the attack is twenty saved lives, about the same as in *30-70(ii)*. Moreover, the attack in *70-30* expectably kills fifteen civilians and expectably saves thirty-five, a ratio between those in *30-70(i)* and *30-70(ii)*. Yet the attack in *70-30* intuitively seems much easier to defend. This intuitive judgment, in turn, seems to presuppose that the probability of killing civilians makes an independent contribution to the moral status of the attack, quite apart from its e-proportionality or de-proportionality. The following sections argue that both this intuitive judgment and its intriguing presupposition are in fact correct.

V. The Reasonable Belief Threshold

To understand why it is wrong to use imprecise weapons, we should imagine trying to defend the killing or harming of civilians as a result of using such weapons.

Imagine that you are a pilot. You fire a highly accurate missile at a legitimate military target located in a civilian area. In mid-air, the missile's guidance system malfunctions, the missile veers off-course, and strikes a group of civilians. You have killed these civilians, albeit unintentionally, and you must now explain why their deaths are not your fault. You cannot justify killing them, since they are not morally liable to be killed and their deaths did not prevent far greater harm to others. But you might offer the following excuse: not only did you not intend to kill any civilians, you reasonably believed that you would not kill any civilians, since the probability that you would kill civilians was less than the probability that you would strike your target and kill no civilians. Of course, this is not a complete excuse. In addition, you might also have to show that the probability of killing civilians was so low, and the military value of your intended target so high, that the expected value of your launching the missile was not only positive but quite substantial (substantial enough to override the moral asymmetry between killing and letting die).

Now imagine that, instead, you are a member of a non-state armed group. You fire a very inaccurate missile at a legitimate military target located in a civilian area. The missile misses its target and strikes a group of civilians. As before, you cannot justify killing the civilians. Moreover, you cannot offer the same excuse as before: you cannot say that you reasonably believed you would kill no civilians, because the probability of killing civilians was greater than the probability of striking your target and killing no civilians. Now, you may be able to say that the military value of your intended target was quite high and that the expected value of launching your missile was substantial. But, as I will argue in the next section, this latter claim is not enough to excuse your actions.

In general, an action is justified only if it is supported by an undefeated reason and excused if it is supported by an undefeated reason to believe that it is justified.

Indeed, "the paradigm excuse is...justified belief in justification."[19] Conversely, an action cannot be excused if it is based on defeated reasons to believe that it is justified or, conversely, if one has decisive reasons to believe it is unjustified. Since the use of an imprecise weapon will prove justified only if it strikes a legitimate target, the use of such a weapon is excusable only if the attacker has undefeated reasons to believe that the weapon will strike a legitimate target.

It follows that one cannot justify or excuse the use of a weapon if one's reasons to believe that weapon will strike civilians are stronger than (and thereby defeat) one's reasons to believe that the weapon will strike a legitimate military target.[20] Put another way, it is morally unjustifiable and inexcusable to use a weapon that will probably, or more likely than not, strike civilians.

The moral requirement of "justified belief in justification" explains the permissibility of the first attack and the impermissibility of the second attack. More broadly, this moral requirement sets a minimum standard of accuracy that every weapon must satisfy. Weapons that fall short of this "justified belief" standard should be considered unlawfully indiscriminate.

I have thus far described my position in terms of justification and excuse, concepts more familiar within criminal law theory than mainstream moral philosophy. My position could just as easily be expressed in a different idiom. Following Jeff McMahan, we might say that the killing of civilians with imprecise weapons is *objectively impermissible*, and that the use of such weapons is *subjectively impermissible* when it is unreasonable to believe that they will strike legitimate targets.[21] Following Derek Parfit, we might say that the killing of civilians with imprecise weapons is wrong in the *fact-relative* sense, and that the use of imprecise weapons is wrong in the *evidence-relative* sense when one has most or decisive reason to believe that they will strike civilians or civilian objects.[22]

---

19. John Gardner and Timothy Macklem, "Reasons," in *The Oxford Handbook of Jurisprudence and Philosophy of Law*, ed. Jules Coleman and Scott Shapiro (Oxford: Oxford University Press, 2000), 440, 444. ("The contrast here is between having reasons for action and having reasons to believe that one has reasons for action. It corresponds to the distinction, well known to all lawyers, between justifications and excuses. One *justifies* one's actions by reference to the reasons one had for acting. One's actions are *excused* in terms of the reasons one had for believing that one had reasons for action.") Obviously, an action can be excused on other, non-epistemic grounds. But it is moral excuse based on epistemic justification that concerns us here.

20. These reasons may be inductive in nature, based on the results of prior uses of the kind of weapon at issue, or they may be based on the relevant causal mechanisms and prevailing circumstances. The more frequently a weapon hit its target in the past, the stronger one's reason to believe it will hit its target in the future. If a weapon strikes its target most of the time then, holding all else constant, one has reason to believe it will strike its target on a particular occasion.

21. See Jeff McMahan, *Killing in War* (Oxford: Oxford University Press, 2009), 43.

22. See Parfit, *On What Matters*, note 18, 150–51.

Importantly, the reasonable belief requirement I am proposing may not be absolute. For example, the use of an imprecise weapon might be permissible if it would expectably-save one hundred times as many civilians as it could possibly kill, even if it would probably or most likely kill some civilians and save none. Indeed, assuming the use of the weapon is not intended to harm civilians, the deontological threshold for the permissible use of such a weapon will be lower than the deontological threshold for permissibly attacking civilians intentionally. For example, if it is permissible to intentionally harm N civilians to prevent comparable harm to $N(X)$ civilians, then it should be permissible to use an imprecise weapon that could harm as many as N civilians if doing so will expectably-save $N(X-Y)$ civilians. How much lower the threshold should be (the value of Y relative to X) is a question I do not yet know how to resolve. Fortunately, I need not resolve this question here and now.

VI. Cluster Munitions

The principles laid out so far clearly govern the use of projectile weapons that strike a single target, such as Katyusha rockets and Scud missiles, as well as landmines that trigger a single explosion. In contrast, cluster munitions are missiles or bombs that release smaller "bomblets" in mid-air, some of which will strike civilians or civilian objects and some of which will strike combatants or military objectives.

It may be tempting to think that the reasonable belief threshold should not apply to such weapons and that only necessity and de-proportionality should constrain their use. One might reason in the following way. Compare two scenarios:

A: Civilians and military targets are located very close to each other. Your only weapon is a guided missile. You launch the missile, destroying the military targets and killing the civilians as an unintended side effect.

B: The same civilians and the same military targets are now located apart from each other. Your only weapon is a cluster bomb. You drop the cluster bomb, and the bomblets strike the same civilians and the same military targets.

In *A*, the strike is permissible if it is de-proportionate. The only obvious difference between *A* and *B* is that in *A* combatants and civilians are killed by the same weapon strikes and in *B* they are killed by different bomblets. This difference may seem morally irrelevant, and one might conclude that in *B* the strike is also permissible if it is de-proportionate.

This reasoning, though superficially attractive, is mistaken. Compare *B* with:

C: Same as *B* except you can only drop the bomblets individually. Each bomblet strikes the same thing as in *B*.

Clearly, the reasonable belief constraint governs the action in *C*. It is impermissible to drop a bomblet unless one reasonably believes that bomblet will not strike a civilian or civilian object. The only difference between *B* and *C* is that in *B* the bomblets are dropped together and in *C* the same bomblets are dropped separately. This difference is certainly morally irrelevant. Therefore, on further reflection, the difference between *A* and *B* is morally relevant. If one cannot reasonably believe that most of the bomblets a cluster bomb contains will miss civilians and civilian objects then one cannot reasonably believe of any given bomblet that it will miss civilians and civilian objects. On such facts it follows that you cannot launch any individual bomblet and therefore cannot launch the cluster bomb itself. The use of cluster munitions is so difficult to justify because each cluster bomb is, in fact, not one weapon but many and the use of each weapon it contains must be justified on its own terms.

VII. Expectabilism and Rule-Consequentialism

Derek Parfit defines *Expectabilism* as the view that "when the rightness of some act depends on the goodness of the act's effects or possible effects, we ought to act, or try to act, in the way whose outcome would be *expectably-best*,"[23] where the expectably-best outcome is the outcome with the highest expected value. Interestingly, Parfit later offers "(E) everyone ought always to do, or try to do, [i] whatever would be most likely to make things go best, or more precisely [ii] what would make things go expectably-best."[24] However, as we have seen, [ii] is not a more precise formulation of [i] but is rather a quite different claim. In many cases, the act most likely to make things go best is not the act that would make things go expectably-best. (E) therefore gives conflicting advice.

Parfit also claims that *Expectabilism* is compatible with act-utilitarianism so long as *Expectabilism* is understood to use "ought" in the evidence-relative or belief-relative senses. This is incorrect. According to act-utilitarianism, an act is wrong in the evidence-relative sense if we have decisive reason to believe that it will make things go worse. If an act will probably make things go worse then this fact generally gives us decisive reason to believe that the act will make things go worse. Yet, as we have seen, an act that will probably make things go worse may

---

23. See Parfit, *On What Matters*, note 18, at 160.

24. Ibid., 374 (brackets are mine).

also make things go expectably-best, provided that the improbable good outcomes sufficiently outweigh the probable bad outcomes. It follows that an act that is required by *Expectabilism* may be wrong in the evidence-relative sense according to act-utilitarianism.

Of course, I have argued that the use of imprecise weapons can be morally impermissible even if such use would be expectably-best. Is *Expectabilism* false? How could it be morally impermissible to do what is expectably-best? Let me start by flipping the question around. Why ever seek the expectably-best outcome, rather than the probably-best outcome? Why ever do what will maximize expected value, rather than what will probably maximize actual value?

For example, imagine that you are offered a bet with a 30 percent chance of winning one hundred dollars and a 70 percent chance of losing ten dollars. Why take such a bet, when the likely outcome is that you will lose ten dollars? First, if you take the same bet a sufficiently large number of times, then over time your winnings will exceed your losses. Second, if you always take bets with positive expected value, then over time your winnings will exceed your losses. More generally, if you always do what maximizes expected value, then over time you will maximize actual value. In other words, by always doing what is expectably-best, you will perform a series of actions with greater actual value than the series of actions you would perform by always doing what is probably-best.

It therefore seems that, although Parfit presents *Expectabilism* as an aspect of act-consequentialism, *Expectabilism* is better understood as an aspect of rule-consequentialism. Act utilitarians are committed to always choosing the action most likely to produce the best outcome. In contrast, rule utilitarians are committed to always choosing the action that will produce the expectably-best outcome. Paraphrasing Parfit, everyone ought to follow *Expectabilism* because the universal acceptance of *Expectabilism* would make things go best from an impartial point of view.[25]

It would seem that, according to *Expectabilism*, the e-proportionate use of imprecise weapons is permissible, even when the weapons will probably strike civilians, because the universal acceptance of a rule permitting the e-proportionate use of imprecise weapons will make things go best (that is, result in substantially greater military advantage than civilian harm). Now, Parfit defines *Expectabilism* such that we ought to do what is expectably-best only "when the rightness of some act depends on the goodness of the act's effects or possible effects."[26] This suggests that we need not show that *Expectabilism* is false, but

---

25. Ibid., 375.
26. Ibid., 160.

merely that the permissibility of the e-proportionate use of imprecise weapons depends on more than the goodness of their actual or possible effects. If we can show this, then we can show that *Expectabilism* simply does not apply to the issue at hand.

Indeed, we have already seen that the permissibility of using imprecise weapons depends not only on their effects but also on how those effects are brought about. In particular, the most important bad effects of using imprecise weapons involve doings (notably killings), while the most important bad effects of not using imprecise weapons involve allowings (notably lettings die). These causal features of using imprecise weapons give us additional, deontic reasons not to use such weapons over and above any non-deontic, impartial reasons we might have to use or not use such weapons. It was for this reason that we introduced the concept of de-proportionality, to describe an attack in which the expected military advantage outweighs the expected harm to civilians by a sufficient proportion to override the deontic asymmetry between killing and letting die. But of course we are now exploring a stronger position.

It is generally accepted that an action that intentionally wrongs another person, that intentionally infringes her rights or breaches a duty owed to her, cannot be defended on rule-consequentialist grounds alone. For example, it would be morally impermissible to punish all crimes disproportionately for the sake of general deterrence, even if this would reduce both the aggregate harm caused by crime and the aggregate harm inflicted through punishment. In general, we cannot justify or excuse wrongs committed against one person solely in terms of the aggregate consequences of acting similarly in similar situations. We have to be able to defend our treatment of her to her, based on our reasonable beliefs about the impact of our action on her rights and welfare and on the rights and welfare of others.

For similar reasons, an action that one has most or decisive reason to believe will wrong another person also cannot be defended on rule-consequentialist grounds alone. Return to the two cases discussed in the previous section. The pilot can defend her attack by saying to any civilians killed, "I reasonably believed that I would strike my intended (legitimate) target and thereby prevent substantially greater harm to others." In contrast, the armed group member cannot defend her actions by saying, "I reasonably believed that I would miss my intended target, harm civilians, and prevent no harm to others; however, I also reasonably believed that if I and others like me launch similar attacks in similar situations then over time we will prevent substantially more harm than we inflict."

Why precisely does the latter defense fail? Is it because the defense ignores the separateness of persons, their dignity, or their inviolability? Or is it because the defense rests on a principle that those affected by its application could reasonably reject? Does the defense fail for some combination of these reasons, or for reasons that are not yet well understood? I am not yet in a position to say. Fortunately, we need not converge on a true theory of normative ethics in order to recognize a false theory of normative ethics. *Expectabilism* is plausible when only the welfare of others is at stake, but not when the rights of others are at risk.

Conclusion

It is almost certainly the case that no war has ever been fought in full compliance with the law of armed conflict. It is also probably the case that even a war fought in full compliance with the law would not be fully just. But by properly understanding the law's moral foundations we can better understand what makes war fought in violation of the law particularly unjust. Moreover, by clarifying what the law permits and forbids, we may help make war less unjust than it would be otherwise.

I have argued that it is almost always morally impermissible to use weapons that are more likely to strike civilians and civilian objects than to strike combatants and military objectives. Such weapons should be considered unlawfully indiscriminate. In addition, the legal prohibition of such weapons may justifiably remain absolute, since the use of such weapons will hardly ever be morally permissible and even a narrow legal permission to use such weapons may be abused far more than it is properly used. Finally, the use of weapons that are not unlawfully indiscriminate in this sense is still unlawful if the weapons are used with the intent to harm civilians, or if they place civilians at unnecessary, e-disproportionate, or de-disproportionate risk. This last point may seem surprising given the conclusions of the previous section, but it should not be. Although the law should not permit deontically impermissible acts on rule-consequentialist grounds, the law often should prohibit deontically permissible acts on rule-consequentialist grounds. If legally prohibiting e-disproportionate and de-disproportionate attacks will yield impartially better outcomes over the long term then the law is morally justified in doing so.

9

DOUBLE EFFECT AND THE LAWS OF WAR

Kai Draper

Introduction

In the Law of Armed Conflict (LOAC), a distinction is drawn between harming noncombatants directly (that is, as a foreseen consequence of attacking them), and harming them indirectly (that is, as a foreseen consequence of attacking military targets). The former is a war crime, the latter is not. Moreover, although under LOAC some acts that are *not* criminal are nevertheless prohibited, harming noncombatants indirectly is not even prohibited so long as the harm is minimized and there is an adequate military justification for the attack that inflicts the harm.[1]

What is the rationale for this legal distinction? On one view, which I shall call "the pragmatic view," even if the distinction has no intrinsic moral relevance, a reasonable basis for it can be found in the fact that it is apt to reduce the costs of war. The alternative of prohibiting any attack that foreseeably harms noncombatants would be less useful; for harming noncombatants indirectly is an essential feature of modern warfare, and so prohibiting it would serve only to undermine respect for LOAC. Thus, on the pragmatic view, the foundation for the legal distinction between directly

---

1. Article 85 of Additional Protocol I (Protocol Additional to the Geneva Conventions of 12 August 1949, and relating to the Protection of Victims of International Armed Conflicts, 8 June 1977) states that acts of terror warfare such as "making the civilian population or individual civilians the object of attack...shall be regarded as grave breaches." The same article also states that "grave breaches of these instruments shall be regarded as war crimes." Article 57 says that "those who plan or decide upon an attack shall...take all feasible precautions in the choice of means and methods of attack with a view to avoiding, and in any event to minimizing, incidental loss of civilian life, injury to civilians and damage to civilian objects," and they shall also "refrain from deciding to launch any attack which may be expected to cause incidental loss of civilian life, injury to civilians, damage to civilian objects, or a combination thereof, which would be excessive in relation to the concrete and direct military advantage anticipated."

and indirectly harming noncombatants is the widely accepted principle that we should strive to minimize the harm that results from war.

There is, however, at least one obvious alternative to the pragmatic view; for the legal distinction between directly and indirectly harming noncombatants roughly follows the contours of the Just War principle known as the Principle of Double Effect (hereafter PDE), and it seems quite likely that PDE was at least part of that distinction's original rationale.[2] It is natural to suppose, then, that the distinction can be grounded in PDE. Another possibility is that the distinction in question can be grounded in one of two close cousins to PDE: a principle defended by several moral philosophers and often called the "Means Principle" (hereafter MP), or a principle recently defended by Alec Walen and called by him the "Restricted Claims Principle" (hereafter RCP).[3]

The core idea of PDE is that harming (or at least killing) an innocent person is more difficult (and on some formulations, impossible) to justify if the harm is intended in the sense of being sought as an end, or as a means to an end, as opposed to being a mere foreseen side effect of pursuing some good end. The core idea of MP, on the other hand, is that harming an innocent person is more difficult to justify if the harm is a consequence of using that person as a means to achieving one's ends. Finally, RCP states that restricting claims are less weighty than claims that are not restricting, where a claim against a person S is restricting if and only if, should S respect that claim, S would be unable to achieve some good that S could achieve if the claimant were not present.

It is arguable that none of these principles applies to those noncombatants who, as a consequence of their participation in, or support for, an unjust war effort, can justifiably be harmed on grounds of defense. Nevertheless, all three principles clearly do apply to at least most of those noncombatants who qualify as "innocent bystanders," and, at least arguably, they all yield the conclusion that harming innocent bystanders directly is at least typically more difficult to justify than harming them indirectly. Thus, if most noncombatants in a nation engaged in war are innocent bystanders, and PDE, MP, or RCP is a valid moral principle, then the legal distinction between directly and indirectly harming noncombatants

---

2. The extent to which LOAC was in fact formulated to encode the moral principles of traditional Just War Theory is a matter of historical debate. See, for example, Davida E. Kellogg, "Terrorism and the Laws of War," *Military Review* (September–October 2005): 50–57. Kellogg says (53) that LOAC "is specifically intended to encode and enact the moral principles the Just War Tradition embodies."

3. Alec Walen, "Transcending the Means Principle," *Law and Philosophy* 33 (2014): 427–64. Gerhard Øverland defends a very similar view in "Moral Obstacles: An Alternative to the Doctrine of Double Effect," *Ethics* 124 (2014): 481–506.

appears to roughly track a moral distinction. I will refer to the view that such a moral distinction provides a reasonable basis for the legal one as "the traditional view."

The defender of the traditional view is burdened with two tasks. First, she must provide an adequate defense of PDE, MP, or RCP. Second, she must show that if the principle she defends is true, then it justifies the legal distinction between directly and indirectly harming noncombatants. My aim is to raise doubts about the possibility of successfully completing both tasks. This clears the way for the pragmatic view, and I conclude by refining that view so that it rests on a secure moral foundation.

For the sake of clarifying the structure of my argument, let us refer to formulations of PDE, MP, or RCP that imply that actions favored by the principle are *much* easier (say, at least twice as easy) to justify than actions disfavored by the principle as "strongly discriminating." And let us refer to other formulations as "weakly discriminating." In sections II–VI below I argue that strongly discriminating formulations of PDE, MP, and RCP are indefensible. I then argue that even if some weakly discriminating formulation of one of these principles is defensible, such a principle cannot provide an adequate basis for the legal distinction between directly and indirectly harming noncombatants.

I. PDE, MP, and Rights

Traditional formulations of PDE are strongly discriminating. On such formulations, there is an absolute prohibition against intending to take innocent life; but one can justifiably take innocent life if one does not intend the death in question (and one does not violate any other absolute moral prohibition) and (ii) taking that life is necessary to achieve good that is proportionate to the evil one produces. If it were true, a traditional formulation of PDE would be well-suited to serve as a basis for the legal distinction between directly and indirectly attacking noncombatants. Consider, however, one of Judith Jarvis Thomson's well-known trolley cases:[4]

Push. This is the case in which five lives are threatened by a runaway trolley and the only way someone (call her "Rescuer") can save those lives is to push a very large man ("Victim") off a bridge and onto the tracks below so that the trolley will strike him and, as a consequence of the drag created by the enormous

---

4. Judith Jarvis Thomson, "The Trolley Problem," in *Rights, Restitution, and Risk* (Cambridge, Mass.: Harvard University Press, 1986).

bulk of his body, come to a stop before it reaches the five. Rescuer chooses to save the five lives, and so Victim dies as a foreseen consequence of being struck by the trolley.

Let us assume that what common intuition tells us about this case is correct: Rescuer's killing Victim is unjustified and would remain so even if Rescuer saved ten or fifteen or twenty lives by killing Victim. This assumption threatens traditional formulations of PDE because in Push it appears that, strictly speaking, Victim's death is neither Rescuer's end nor the means by which she achieves her end and so is "unintended" in the relevant sense. Her means to saving the five includes pushing Victim off the bridge, Victim's being struck by the trolley, and his body's creating drag on the trolley; but any injury to Victim that results from her use of these means appears to be a regrettable side effect of the intended effects of her behavior. Because the benefits of pushing Victim off the bridge are substantially greater than its costs, traditional formulations of PDE wrongly imply that Rescuer justifiably kills Victim in Push.[5]

Notice, however, that in Push Rescuer uses Victim himself as a means to achieving her end; and on MP, that is supposed to be a morally salient feature of a case like Push, one that makes it more difficult to justify a killing in terms of benefits. (RCP also distinguishes between the two cases, but right now I want to focus on MP.) Consider, however,

Push II. To save the lives of five persons Rescuer must cross a very narrow bridge. Unfortunately, Victim is on that bridge, and Rescuer cannot get across in time to save the five unless she immediately pushes him off of the bridge. She does so even though she knows that, because he will land on the trolley tracks, Victim will be struck and killed by an approaching trolley.

Judging by discussions of similar cases in the literature, the common intuition here is that Rescuer's killing Victim is once again unjustified, and this in spite of the fact that she does not use Victim (or Victim's being struck or killed by the trolley) as a means to her end.

---

5. The literature on double effect contains several discussions of whether the defender of PDE can loosen her definition of "intended" so that some deaths, even though they are not, strictly speaking, intended, can, for the purposes of the principle, be counted as such because what is intended in the narrow sense is closely connected to the death in question. Even if such an approach rescues PDE from cases like Push, however, it cannot prevent other cases I discuss below (such as Push Car II and Landslide) from being used to undermine traditional formulations of PDE.

It seems clear that in Push II no less than in Push, Rescuer infringes upon the rights of Victim by acting on his body in a way that results in his death. Indeed, many of the actions that MP favors are infringements of rights and, as such, are very difficult to justify. Nevertheless, the proponent of a strongly discriminating formulation of MP would have us believe that those infringements upon rights that the principle discriminates against are, other things being equal, not only more difficult, but *much* more difficult, to justify than infringements upon rights that the principle discriminates in favor of. I see no reason to suppose that this is true. Judging by my own intuitions, it is *not* much more difficult to justify harmful behavior of the sort illustrated by Push than it is to justify harmful behavior of the sort illustrated by Push II. If we could say, for example, that if Rescuer's killing Victim in Push II would save ten lives, killing Victim would be justified, but her killing Victim in Push would remain unjustified even if she were to save twenty lives, then we would have intuition-based support for a strongly discriminating formulation of MP. My own intuitions inform me, however, that no such discrimination is possible, and I suspect that most others would agree.

Of course, even if I am right about that, we do not have a conclusive reason to reject strongly discriminating formulations of MP. Contemporary formulations of MP typically include an other-things-being-equal clause, thus insulating MP to some extent against counterexamples. Exploiting that clause, the defender of a strongly discriminating version of MP can respond to cases like Push and Push II by insisting that there is some moral factor present in Push II but absent in Push that closes the moral distance between them in terms of how difficult it is to justify killing Victim in those kinds of cases. Given the difficulty of proving a negative, that suggestion will be difficult to prove false. Nevertheless, Push and Push II are quite similar. Thus, unless one can identify the relevant moral factor that is allegedly present in Push II but absent in Push, at least the tentative conclusion must be that, because killing is not much more difficult to justify in cases like Push II than in cases like Push, we should reject formulations of MP that strongly discriminate between cases like Push and Push II.

II. Quinn's Defense of Double Effect

Not surprisingly, formulations of PDE and MP have been proposed that place Push II as well as Push among the actions that the principle discriminates against. Perhaps the best known of these is Warren Quinn's formulation of PDE, and I want to consider it in some detail.[6] Rescuer's behavior in Push is an example of

---

6. Warren Quinn, "Actions, Intentions and Consequences: The Doctrine of the Double Effect," *Philosophy and Public Affairs* 18 (1989): 334–51.

what he calls "harmful exploitation," and her behavior in Push II is an example of what he calls "harmful elimination."[7] In the former sort of case, a person x provides a second person y with an opportunity to achieve a certain end. (In Push, for example, Victim's presence on the bridge presents Rescuer with the opportunity to save the five.) Without x's consent, y exploits that opportunity and, as a foreseen consequence, infringes upon x's right not to be harmed. In cases of harmful elimination, on the other hand, x presents a threat or an obstacle to y's achieving a certain end. (In Push II, for example, Victim's presence on the bridge is an obstacle to Rescuer's saving the five.) Without x's consent, y eliminates that obstacle or threat and, as a foreseen consequence, infringes upon x's right not to be harmed.[8] Quinn proposes that in both kinds of cases, the inflicted harm is more difficult to justify in virtue of the role the victim plays in the agent's means-end reasoning. The agent does not merely foresee that her pursuit of her end will harm her victim; she "intends something for" her victim, something to which the victim does not consent and in virtue of which he is harmed. According to Quinn, that is what makes her behavior more difficult to justify.

Quinn's explanation of the apparent relevance of such intentions is broadly Kantian. He suggests that, other things being equal, the agent who intends something for his victims when he harms them treats them with greater disrespect than he would if he were to harm them without such an intention. In such cases, Quinn proposes, the agent "sees" his victims "as material to be strategically shaped or framed by his agency" (regardless of whether they consent to that shaping or framing). Thus, the agent's behavior is inconsistent with the Kantian ideal that "each person is to be treated, so far as possible, as existing only for purposes he can share." Quinn further proposes that (other things being equal) harmful exploitation is more difficult to justify than harmful elimination because the disrespect with which the agent treats his victim is morally more offensive. The suggestion appears to be that it is more disrespectful to treat others as mere resources to be exploited than to treat them as mere threats or obstacles to be eliminated.[9]

---

7. Ibid., 344.

8. Quinn does not explicitly say that an act that causes harm counts as harmful exploitation or harmful elimination only if the harm is foreseen. As shown by Fischer et al., however, Quinn's PDE is obviously mistaken if it is understood to apply to unforeseen harm. See John Martin Fischer, Mark Ravizza, and David Copp, "Quinn on Double Effect: The Problem of 'Closeness,'" *Ethics* 103 (1993): 707–25.

9. Quinn, "Actions, Intentions and Consequences," 348–51.

Quinn's attempt to reformulate and defend PDE so that it incorporates the core idea of MP is ingenious, but is his principle tenable?[10] Consider:

Push Car. Victim is in his car, and that car's being struck by the trolley would stop the trolley. Rescuer's car is behind Victim's car on a bridge over the tracks, and the only way for Rescuer to save the five threatened by the trolley is to use her car to push Victim's car off the bridge and onto the tracks below. Unfortunately, there is no time to warn Victim so that he can get out of his car before she pushes it. Thus, when she does push Victim's car onto the tracks to save the five, Rescuer foresees that Victim will be killed when the trolley strikes his car.

In this case Rescuer does not intend anything for Victim, for it is Victim's car that she uses to stop the trolley. Her behavior here, however, does not seem less wrong than her behavior in Push II or even Push. Perhaps some would disagree. I suspect, however, that almost no one would suppose that it is *far* easier to justify killing in a case like Push Car than it is to justify killing in cases like Push II or even in cases like Push. In all three kinds of cases there is an infringement of rights that makes it highly difficult to justify Rescuer's behavior by appeal to the good that it achieves and, unless my own intuitions are eccentric here, the suggestion that the justificatory burden is much greater in cases like Push and Push II than in cases like Push Car is clearly the wrong result.

Of course, there may be some moral factor in Push Car that is not present in Push or Push II that might be partly responsible for the size of the justificatory burden in cases like Push Car. Because Quinn's principle does require other things to be equal, the mere introduction of cases like Push Car does not conclusively show that Quinn's principle is false. Push and Push Car are highly similar, though, and so unless that alleged factor can be identified, my tentative conclusion must be that such cases raise reasonable doubts about Quinn's principle.

III. Recent Attempts to Improve Upon Quinn

Some moral philosophers have sought to refine PDE or MP by expanding Quinn's notion of harmful exploitation so that it encompasses your behavior in cases like Push Car. In a recent paper on the ethics of self-defense, Jonathan Quong defends

---

10. Jeff McMahan proposes an amendment to Quinn's formulation of PDE in "Revising the Doctrine of Double Effect," *Journal of Applied Philosophy* 11 (1994): 201–12. That amendment would not, however, enable Quinn's formulation of PDE to avoid the objections I raise below.

MP, arguing that to treat a person as a mere means encompasses using anything to which that person has a right (without his or her consent).[11] On Quong's view, Rescuer's behavior in both Push Car and Push II counts as harmful exploitation, and is especially difficult to justify, not because she uses Victim's body, but rather because she uses something else to which Victim has a right. In Push Car she uses Victim's car; and in Push II, she uses the space on the bridge that Victim had been using and hence had a right to continue to use.[12] (Recall that Rescuer needs to pass through that space to save the five.)

Quong's approach to defending MP does have the virtue of bringing a wide variety of the relevant cases under the single notion of harmful exploitation. However, this unification is achieved at the cost of undermining Quinn's attempt to identify a compelling rationale for thinking that harmful exploitation is especially difficult to justify. It is one thing to complain, "You used me!" but quite another to complain, "You used my car!" Because cars *are* mere resources to be exploited, there is nothing disrespectful in seeing them as such.

An even more serious problem is illustrated by the following kind of case:

Push Car II. Same as Push Car except that Victim does not own the car that Rescuer pushes. Against Victim's will, one end of a chain was attached to his wrist, and the other end was attached to the door of a third party's car.

On Quong's view, Rescuer's behavior in Push Car II is not harmful exploitation, for she does not use anything that belongs to Victim to save the five. If we assume that Victim is to the side of the car as Rescuer pushes the car from behind, she does not even use any space to which Victim was entitled. Perhaps not everyone will share my own intuition here, but even if some find Rescuer's behavior in cases like Push Car to be more difficult to justify than her behavior in cases like Push Car II, I strongly doubt that many will be inclined to say that her behavior in cases like Push Car is *much* more difficult to justify than her behavior in cases like Push Car II. Of course, there may be some moral factor in Push Car II that is not present in Push Car (or in Push or Push II) that might be responsible for the similarity in the justificatory burden in those two cases. Again, however, I cannot imagine what that variable might be.

Perhaps the following pair of cases is even more clearly a difficulty for Quong's view (assuming he is proposing a strongly discriminating principle):

---

11. Jonathan Quong, "Killing in Self-Defense," *Ethics* 119 (2009): 507–37.

12. Quong argues that one ordinarily has a right to the space one occupies, and I am inclined to agree with him on this point.

Boulder. Stopping the (unoccupied) trolley that threatens five lives requires Rescuer to roll a boulder down a hill so that it comes to rest at the bottom of the valley where the trolley tracks run. The boulder will provide an effective shield, preventing the trolley from reaching the five persons further down the line. The problem is that Victim is right in the path that the boulder must travel if it is to reach the tracks and stop the trolley. The boulder itself will roll right over him, and he will be killed as a consequence. Nevertheless, Rescuer rolls the boulder.

Landslide. Here stopping the trolley that threatens five lives requires Rescuer to cause a landslide so that rocks pile up at the bottom of the valley where the trolley tracks run. The rocks will provide an effective shield, preventing the trolley from reaching the five persons further down the line. The problem is that Victim is in the only available path for the landslide and will be killed by falling rocks. Nevertheless, Rescuer causes the landslide.

On Quong's view, Rescuer violates MP in Boulder, for there she needs to use the space occupied by Victim in order to rescue the persons on the track. In Landslide, on the other hand, Rescuer's behavior needn't violate MP, for we can assume that Rescuer does not use the space occupied by Victim because the rocks that hit Victim do not even reach the tracks. The cases are otherwise nearly identical. It seems quite clear, however, that Rescuer's behavior in cases like Boulder is not much more difficult to justify than her behavior in cases like Landslide. Thus, if Quong is understood to be offering a strongly discriminating formulation of MP, it appears that cases like Boulder and Landslide undermine his principle.

The basis for another possible development of Quinn's position can also be found in the literature on the ethics of self-defense. Arguing that the right to self-defense extends to killing persons attached to threats, Helen Frowe follows Gerald Lang in proposing that if, for example, someone is innocently aboard a runaway trolley that threatens to kill you, that person is part of a composite object that threatens to kill you and so you may kill him in self-defense (perhaps by firing a rocket at the trolley).[13] Applying Frowe's ideas to Push Car and Push Car II, one might propose that, in each of these cases, Victim is part of a composite object that Rescuer uses to stop the trolley, and so Rescuer's behavior is harmful exploitation in that Victim is harmed as a consequence of Rescuer's exploiting something of which Victim is a part.

---

13. Helen Frowe, "Equating Innocent Threats and Bystanders," *Journal of Applied Philosophy* 25 (2008): 277–90. Frowe credits Lang with the idea here, citing his unpublished manuscript.

Frowe's approach might enable Quinn to handle Push Car, but it will not have the desired result in Push Car II. For clearly mere attachment to an object that is being used is not sufficient for being part of a composite object that is being used. I can lean against, or even sit passively inside of, a crane as someone else uses it to lift something, for example, without being a part of any composite object that is used to lift something. Perhaps if something is attached to an object and also contributes to the end for which that object is used, it is then a part of a composite object that is used to achieve that end. It may be the case, for example, that even a fly sitting on a wrecking ball that is used to destroy a building would be part of a composite object that is used to destroy the building if in fact the mass of the fly contributes, however slightly, to the force of the ball's destructive impact with the building. In Push Car II, however, we may assume that whereas the car lands in front of the trolley and creates the necessary drag to stop it, Victim, although attached to the car by a chain, collides with the trolley in such a way that he makes no contribution at all to the forces that stop the trolley. We can even imagine that, when Rescuer pushes the car off the bridge, she foresees that the chain will come off Victim's wrist on the way down so that Victim is no longer attached to the car when the trolley hits both him and the car. Neither of these qualifications to Push Car II makes Rescuer's behavior seem any less wrong, but they do make it clear that Victim is not part of a composite object that Rescuer uses to achieve her end. Furthermore, even if I am mistaken and so in Push Car II Victim is part of a composite object that Rescuer uses, it is very clear that Victim is not part of a composite object that Rescuer uses to stop the trolley in Landslide. Thus, Lang's notion of a composite object does not extend the notion of harmful exploitation far enough to avoid the difficulties I have identified for strongly discriminating formulations of PDE and MP.

IV. The Restricted Claims Principle

Let us turn our attention to another cousin of double effect: RCP. In an ingenious attempt to find a principle that can more successfully accommodate common moral intuition than PDE or MP, Alec Walen proposes that "restricting claims are significantly less weighty than claims that are not restricting," where a claim against a person S is restricting if and only if, should S respect that claim, S would be unable to achieve some good that S could achieve if the claimant were not present. If "significantly more" here means or entails "much more," then Walen is proposing a strongly discriminating principle. Let us assume that this is his intent.

To handle cases like Push Car, Walen echoes Quong by narrowing the notion of a restricting claim against a person S so that it includes only those claims against S such that S's respecting the claim means that S cannot achieve some good that S could achieve if the claimant *and everything to which the claimant has a right* were not present. At least arguably, then, he can handle even a case like Push II because there Victim's claim can be seen as non-restricting if we assume that Victim has a right to the space he occupies. (It is difficult, however, to make sense of the question of whether Rescuer could save the five if the space occupied by Victim were not present.)

His view quite clearly fails, however, to accommodate cases like Push Car II and Landslide. Victim's claim against Rescuer is restricting in those cases, for if Victim and all that is his were not present, Rescuer would be able to save the five. Thus, it appears that a strongly discriminating formulation of RCP implies that Rescuer's behavior in cases like Push Car II and in cases like Landslide is much easier to justify than her behavior in cases like Push Car. Intuitively, that is the wrong result. Perhaps Walen could suggest that some restricting claims are as strong as some non-restricting claims, and that the restricting claim in Push Car II is an example of such a restricting claim. Still, until he also provides the criterion by which we can distinguish the stronger restricting claims from the weaker, Push Car II will remain a difficulty for his account.

RCP is also threatened by cases that do not threaten Quinn's formulation of PDE or Quong's formulation of MP. Consider:

Push III. The terrorist is about to execute five innocent persons and, so long as he stays safely inside his fortified bunker, there is nothing Rescuer can do to stop him. Fortunately, he would much prefer to do the execution outside the bunker and so Rescuer's plan is to shoot him when he comes out. Alas, the terrorist sees Victim on a nearby bridge and, worried that Victim might interfere with the execution, prepares for an indoor execution. The only way Rescuer can change his mind so that she can save the five is to immediately push Victim so that he falls off the bridge. (The terrorist will assume that Victim freely left the area and will decide once again to do the execution outside.) Rescuer pushes Victim even though she knows that Victim will fall in front of a trolley and be killed.

Here Victim's claim against Rescuer is restricting because if Victim and everything to which he has a right were not present, the terrorist would come outside and Rescuer would be able to shoot him and save the lives of the five hostages. Thus, unless Walen can qualify his view so that some restricting claims turn out to be as strong as some non-restricting claims, he must say that Rescuer's behavior in this sort of case is much easier to justify than her behavior in a case like Push or Push II or Push Car. Intuitively, that is once again the wrong result.

V. Alleged Support for a Strongly Discriminating Principle

Let us take stock. We have been assessing formulations of PDE, MP, and RCP that *strongly* discriminate against certain sorts of actions and in favor of others. I have not denied that the actions against which these principles discriminate are actions that are, in fact, very difficult to justify. The problem I have raised for each of these principles is that, when we are careful to hold other moral variables equal, actions that are strongly favored by the principle in question appear to be as difficult to justify, or at least nearly as difficult to justify, as actions that are strongly disfavored by the principle.

Nor can I think of any way to extend the notion of an intended effect, or the notion of harmful exploitation (or harmful elimination), or the notion of a restricting claim, so that PDE, MP, or RCP can overcome this difficulty. This may, of course, merely reflect a lack of ingenuity on my part; but at the very least, it remains to be shown that cases like Push Car II (or Landslide) cannot be paired with cases like Push or Push II or Boulder to undermine any strongly discriminating formulation of PDE, MP, or RCP.

It might be argued, however, that other pairs of cases do support the claim that some strongly discriminating formulation of PDE, MP, or RCP must be true. Walen tries to garner support for RCP by pairing a case that is essentially identical to Push with a case that is essentially the same as

Sidetrack. This is the case in which Rescuer prevents the trolley from striking and killing five persons by deflecting it onto a sidetrack with the foreseen consequence that it strikes and kills Victim.

Because in Sidetrack Victim's claim against Rescuer is restricting whereas in Push it is not, and because the common intuition in Sidetrack but not in Push is that Rescuer's killing Victim is justified, Walen believes that such cases provide intuition-based support for RCP.

It is doubtful, however, that the only morally relevant difference between Push and Sidetrack is that in Push the claim against Rescuer is restricting whereas in Sidetrack the claim against Rescuer is non-restricting. As Philippa Foot first noticed, one variable that appears to be playing a role in making it far easier to justify inflicting harm in cases like Sidetrack than in cases like Push is that Sidetrack is a case in which a threat is merely deflected, whereas Push is a case in which a threat is initiated. Deflecting harm seems to be a special sort of case: if one's aim is to prevent harm by shielding oneself or others from a threat, then the mere knowledge that the threat will thereby be deflected in the direction of an innocent bystander is not a reason to think that the balance of harm inflicted to harm averted needs to be high in order for one's actions to be justified.[14] It is not easy to say why that should be so, but we shouldn't try to force our intuitions about cases of deflection into the service of a strongly discriminating formulation of RCP.

Quinn relies on three pairs of cases to provide intuition-based support for his reformulation of PDE. One is the pair of abortion cases that has so often been used to illustrate PDE (a craniotomy case and a hysterectomy case). He describes the other two pairs as follows:

In the Case of the Strategic Bomber (SB), a pilot bombs an enemy factory in order to destroy its productive capacity. But in doing this he foresees that he will kill innocent civilians who live nearby. Many of us see this kind of military action as much easier to justify than that in the Case of the Terror Bomber (TB), who deliberately kills innocent civilians in order to demoralize the enemy. Another pair of cases involves medicine: In both there is a shortage of resources for the investigation and proper treatment of a new, life-threatening disease. In the first scenario doctors decide to cope by selectively treating only those who can be cured most easily, leaving the more stubborn cases untreated. Call this the Direction of Resources Case (DR). In the contrasting and intuitively more problematic example, doctors decide on a crash experimental program in which they deliberately leave the stubborn cases untreated in order to learn more about the nature of the disease. Call this the Guinea Pig Case (GP). In neither case do the nontreated know about or consent to the decision against treating them.[15]

I contend that none of Quinn's three pairs of cases provides a reason to suspect that some strongly discriminating formulation of PDE (or MP or RCP) is true. Presumably, he would concede that his pair of abortion cases provides no such reason, for he points out that some people feel that the intended killing of the fetus in the craniotomy case is "not much harder to justify" than the foreseen but unintended killing of the fetus in the hysterectomy case.[16] Moreover, using moral intuitions about abortion and killing in war to support any formulation

---

14. See Philippa Foot, "Morality, Action and Outcome," in *Morality and Objectivity*, ed. Ted Honderich (London: Routledge and Kegan Paul, 1985), 23–38. See also Gregory S. Kavka, "A Critique of Pure Defense," *Journal of Philosophy* 83 (1986): 625–33; and Samuel C. Rickless, "The Doctrine of Doing and Allowing," *Philosophical Review* 106 (1997): 555–75. Foot speaks of "diverting" a potentially harmful causal sequence rather than "deflecting" a threat.

15. Quinn, "Actions, Intentions and Consequences," 336.

16. Ibid., 350.

of PDE is methodologically suspect, for such intuitions are too controversial and too likely to be polluted by common practice, tradition, patriotism, and ideology to have much evidential value. Furthermore, if we consider cases of terror bombing and strategic bombing that are very similar to each other, I doubt that most of us do have Quinn's intuition that the strategic bombing would be "much easier to justify." Suppose, for example, that the *only* way to induce the enemy to surrender is to detonate an atomic bomb above a city, foreseeably killing tens of thousands of persons in the city below. Now compare two versions of the case. In the first, the bomb is detonated in order to kill the inhabitants of the city. The enemy is expected to surrender immediately in order to avoid further losses of life. In the second, the bomb is detonated over the city in order to destroy the enemy's weaponry (unbeknownst to its own civilian population, the enemy's leaders have distributed this weaponry across the city), and the loss of civilian life is foreseen but unsought. The enemy is expected to surrender immediately in order to avoid further losses of weaponry. Is it really true that these two acts seem morally far apart? I would need to see empirical evidence that the common intuition would be that the first act would be *much* harder to justify by appeal to the value of securing immediate surrender.[17]

Thus, it appears that insofar as Quinn's examples can be used to make a serious case for a strongly discriminating formulation of PDE, the success of that case depends on the contrast between GP and DR. Nor does this set Quinn apart: many writers have relied heavily on cases quite similar to GP and DR to provide intuitive support for PDE. Even Philippa Foot, in the course of arguing against PDE, concedes that in a pair of cases quite similar to GP and DR, it does seem to make a moral difference that the agent aims at the harm in the one case but not the other.[18] I think it important, then, to point out that the Doctrine of Doing and Allowing (DDA) can be used to explain the apparent fact that there is a substantial moral difference between GP and DR. Indeed, although he does not notice it, Quinn himself is committed to that conclusion. His work on DDA,[19]

---

17. Jonathan Bennett has argued that there is no moral difference between strategic and terror bombing. See his "Morality and Consequences," in *The Tanner Lectures on Human Values 1981 II*, ed. Sterling McMurrin (Salt Lake City and Cambridge: University of Utah Press and Cambridge Univ. Press 1981), part 3.

18. "The Problem of Abortion and the Doctrine of Double Effect," *Oxford Review* 5 (1967): 5–15; reprinted in Bonnie Steinbock and Alastair Norcross, eds., *Killing and Letting Die*, 2nd ed. (New York: Fordham University Press 1994), 266–79.

19. Warren Quinn, "Actions, Intentions and Consequences: The Doctrine of Doing and Allowing," *Philosophical Review* 98 (1989): 287–312.

although in my view flawed,[20] correctly ties the doctrine to intentions. In the most common sort of case, one does not do harm by merely failing to prevent harm. Quinn observes, however, that in cases where one does not act oneself, but intends the harmful action of something under one's control, one's behavior is closer in nature to doing harm. He illustrates the point with two cases: "Rescue III" and "Rescue IV." He describes Rescue III as follows:[21]

We are off by special train to save five who are in imminent danger of death. Every second counts. You have just taken over from the driver, who has left the locomotive to attend to something. Since the train is on automatic control you need do nothing to keep it going. But you can stop it by putting on the brakes. You suddenly see someone trapped ahead on the track. Unless you act he will be killed. But if you do stop, and then free the man, the rescue mission will be aborted. So you let the train continue.

He then describes Rescue IV:

Suppose...you are on a train on which there has just been an explosion. You can stop the train, but that is a complicated business that would take time. So you set it on automatic forward and rush back to the five badly wounded passengers. While attending to them, you learn that a man is trapped far ahead on the track. You must decide whether to return to the cabin to save him or stay with the passengers and save them.

He provides the following useful analysis of the moral difference between the two cases:

In Rescue III, but not in Rescue IV, the train kills the man because of your intention that it continue forward. This implicates you, I believe, in the fatal action of the train itself. If you had no control, but merely wished that the rescue would continue or if, as in Rescue IV, you had control but no such wish, you would not be party to the action of the train. But the combination of control and intention in Rescue III makes for a certain kind of complicity. Your choice to let the train continue forward is strategic and deliberate. Since you clearly would have it continue for the sake of the five, there is a sense in which,

---

20. Kai Draper, "Rights and the Doctrine of Doing and Allowing," *Philosophy and Public Affairs* 33 (2005): 253–80.

21. Quinn, "Actions, Intentions and Consequences: The Doctrine of Doing and Allowing," 299.

by deliberately not stopping it, you do have it continue. For these reasons your agency counts as positive.

What Quinn fails to notice, however, is that if his argument concerning the relevance of intentions to a proper understanding of DDA is correct, then the substantial moral difference between GP and DR can be explained in terms of that doctrine rather than PDE. For in GP the doctors intend the progression of the disease so that they can study it, but in DR the progression of the disease in those allowed to die from it is not intended. Thus, it turns out that Quinn's own work on DDA threatens his defense of PDE. For assuming that he is right about the role of intentions in DDA, we do not need PDE to account for the difference between GP and DR and hence that pair of cases provides no support for PDE. Furthermore, given that his point about the relevance of intentions to DDA can be adapted to most any formulation of DDA, we do not need to accept Quinn's interpretation of DDA to conclude that the contrast between GP and DR fails to provide genuine support for PDE (or MP or RCP). Of course, it is possible that PDE and DDA both identify moral variables sufficient to justify our moral intuitions about GP and DR, but the point is that, given the existence of a compelling account of those intuitions in terms of DDA alone, the fact that PDE also provides an account does not constitute positive support for PDE.

It may be objected that because I reject Quinn's interpretation of DDA I am in no place to use that interpretation as a weapon against PDE. I do not, however, reject the part of his account of DDA that I am wielding against PDE. His general point, although cashed out in terms of a defective formulation of DDA, is a good one. On most any interpretation of DDA, if you were to initiate the forward motion of the train in a case like Rescue III, knowing that it will run over and kill the man on the tracks, you would be doing harm. Quinn's insight is that letting the train move forward with the intention that it does move forward is morally akin to initiating its forward movement.

There are other sorts of cases that might seem to provide strong support for some formulation of PDE, MP, or RCP. Whether we create a police force, produce and sell pharmaceuticals, or build a major highway, it is foreseeable that in the long run completely innocent persons will be seriously harmed as a consequence of our actions. Sometimes police officers abuse their authority by engaging in acts of brutality, people foreseeably die in automobile collisions on any major highway, and most pharmaceuticals sometimes have deadly side effects for some users. In all such cases and many others, the harm we do to the innocent, though unintended, is completely foreseeable, and yet no one would suggest that we ought to avoid such behaviors altogether.

PDE, MP, or RCP might be used to explain why such behavior can be morally permissible in spite of its costs to the innocent; but once again there are alternative explanations that are at least as compelling. Most of those who are harmed by pharmaceuticals and highways voluntarily used them, and most of those who are exposed to the risks of an armed police force receive compensating benefits in terms of enhanced security. Furthermore, in many of these kinds of cases those who "inflict" the harm do not infringe upon rights at all, partly because they do not act on anyone's person or property in a way that results in harming them. To better appreciate this crucial point, consider the following two cases:

Coercion I: Jones, who happens to be standing beside you, wants to kill Smith, but Smith is a good distance from him and he is a poor shot. He knows, however, that you are an excellent shot. Accordingly, he provides you a gun and, aiming his gun at your head, demands that you shoot and kill Smith. You know that Jones will kill you if and only if you do not kill Smith. You choose to kill Smith.

Coercion II: Jones, who happens to be standing beside you, wants to kill Smith, but Smith is a good distance from him and Jones does not have a long-range weapon. He knows, however, that you have a long-range weapon. Accordingly, he aims his gun at your head and demands that you hand over your weapon. You know that Jones will kill you if and only if you do not hand over your weapon. You also know that he will kill Smith if and only if you do hand over your weapon. You hand over your weapon.

Many (including myself) have the intuition that you may save your own life in cases like Coercion II, but not in cases like Coercion I. RCP cannot be used to account for such intuitions because in both cases, Smith's claim against you is restricting. (If Smith were not present, you would not be coerced by Jones and so would be able to avoid being killed by Jones.) PDE and MP, on the other hand, do provide a way to discriminate between these cases. On my view, however, the correct way to discriminate between them is by reference to the fact that only in Coercion I do you infringe upon Smith's right of self-ownership, for only in that case do you act on Smith in a way that results in his death. In Coercion I, you enable Jones to act on Smith in a way that kills him, but you do not act on him yourself. Thus, his only relevant claim against you is a need claim that you not enable Jones to kill him by providing Jones with a gun. That claim, however, is defeated by your own need to provide Jones with a gun.[22]

---

22. A much fuller defense of this point can be found in Kai Draper, "Rights and the Doctrine of Doing and Allowing."

Perhaps I am overlooking some genuine, intuition-based support for a strongly discriminating formulation of PDE, MP, or RCP; but I am unaware of any cases that provide such support. We have seen that common intuitions about pairs of cases like Push and Sidetrack, GP and LR, or Coercion I and Coercion II, intuitions that might seem to provide support for a strongly discriminating formulation of one of these principles, can be explained in terms of other principles. Moreover, if PDE or one of its cousins is to receive the support of moral intuition, then it must be formulated in a way that reflects what intuition tells us about the extent to which Rescuer's behavior in a case like Push is more difficult to justify (in terms of the number of lives saved) than her behavior in a case like Push Car II; and I strongly suspect that most will be inclined to say that the former is at most a little easier to justify than the latter. Thus, it appears that if moral intuition provides any support at all for PDE, MP, or RCP, it supports only a weakly discriminating formulation of one of these principles.

VI. Is a Weakly Discriminating Principle Good Enough?

I do not deny that certain pairs of cases provide some support for the suggestion that some weakly discriminating formulation of PDE, MP, or RCP must be true.[23] Thus, even though (to my knowledge) no one has yet managed to formulate one of these principles in a way that does complete justice to common intuition, perhaps the prospects for doing so are bright enough to make it worthwhile to consider whether a weakly discriminating formulation could provide a basis for the traditional view. Let us suppose, then, that some weakly discriminating formulation of PDE, MP, or RCP is true. Can we now conclude that PDE, MP, or RCP provides an adequate basis for the legal distinction between directly and indirectly harming noncombatants?

I want to argue that the answer is no. Because the issue is largely an empirical one, however, I concede that my argument is inconclusive. What I suspect, though admittedly cannot prove, is that a weakly discriminating formulation of PDE, MP, or RCP will rarely if ever be relevant to military decision-making, and so there is little reason to use the laws of war to ensure that military decisions conform to such a principle. It is costly to enforce laws that criminalize behavior in war, and so only laws that provide substantial moral benefits are appropriate.

---

23. It is difficult to determine, however, whether such cases provide support for PDE and MP or for some principle useful for assessing degrees of viciousness but not degrees of wrongness. Intuitive support for PDE or MP would, as I have suggested above, require specifying some number such that if that number of persons were saved in each case, your behavior in Push would seem unjustified, but your behavior in Push Car II would seem justified.

My suspicion is based upon three considerations. First, a formulation of PDE, MP, or RCP that merely states that actions of one sort are easier to justify than actions of another sort will not be action-guiding at all and so, a fortiori, will not guide military decisions. This is not to say that PDE, MP, or RCP needs to be formulated in a way that precisely specifies how much easier it is to justify actions favored by the principle. Borderline cases are fine, but only if there are also clear cases. To be useful, then, PDE, MP, or RCP must, at least in conjunction with some other principle or principles, imply that within some specifiable range of numbers, your behavior in a case like Push Car II, but not in a case like Push, would be justified if the number of persons saved were to fall within that range. I for one am unable to identify any such range, and so I suspect that common intuition will at best justify a formulation of PDE, MP, or RCP that is virtually useless as a guide to conduct.[24]

Second, the typical military decision can be based only on very rough cost-benefit calculations. Thus, if a particular decision to indirectly harm noncombatants can be justified by appeal to the benefits that might be secured, then in all likelihood a weakly discriminating formulation of PDE, MP, or RCP will provide no reason to deny that a comparable decision to directly harm noncombatants would also be justified. If, conversely, a particular decision to directly harm noncombatants cannot be justified by appeal to the benefits that might be secured, then in all likelihood a weakly discriminating formulation of PDE, MP, or RCP will provide no reason to deny that a comparable decision to indirectly harm noncombatants would also be unjustified.

Third, the justificatory burden in a case like Push Car II seems quite heavy. A five-to-one ratio of lives saved to lives taken is not by itself an adequate justification. Nor, if I can trust my own intuitions, is a ten-to-one (or even a fifty-to-one) ratio. Thus, one might wonder whether it is realistic to suppose that such a burden would be met in war except in very rare cases. Can American military planners assert with any confidence, for example, that a series of attacks aimed at killing members of al Qaeda, but foreseeably killing several innocent bystanders as well, can be justified if more than a ten-to-one ratio of lives saved to innocent lives taken is required for justifiably killing the bystanders? I suspect not.

One final point: The legal requirement to avoid directly harming noncombatants is absolute, and a weakly discriminating formulation of PDE, MP, or RCP

---

24. It might be objected that even a principle that says merely that one sort of behavior is easier to justify than another sort could be useful because it would imply that in cases where one can achieve one's objective through either sort of behavior, one ought, other things being equal, to engage in the sort of behavior that is easier to justify. I suspect, however, that in war such cases are very rare.

can provide no basis for such absolutism. It might be objected that this only shows that I have been too quick to deny that there is intuitive support for a strongly discriminating formulation of one of these principles; for to many it does seem that murder is absolutely prohibited. I doubt, however, that it would seem to many that, for example, whereas your behavior in Push is murder and so would be morally wrong regardless of how many lives it saved, your behavior in Push Car II is not murder and so would not be wrong if a sufficient number of lives were saved. Thus, I see no reason to suppose that the line between murder and non-murder corresponds to any line drawn by PDE, MP, or RCP.

VII. The Pragmatic View

My conclusion thus far is that the case for the traditional view is weak. Our intuitions speak against strongly discriminating formulations of PDE, MP, or RCP, and there is reason to doubt that a weakly discriminating formulation of any of these principles would be relevant enough to military decision-making to provide an adequate basis for the legal distinction between directly and indirectly harming noncombatants.

Rejecting the traditional view clears the path for the pragmatic view, a view that I find promising. It is, of course, an empirical issue whether and to what extent criminalizing the direct killing of noncombatants reduces the costs of war, and so, as a philosopher, I am not in a position to provide a thorough defense of the pragmatic view. What I propose to do in this final section of my essay, however, is to refine the pragmatic view so that it rests on a tenable moral foundation.

It is quite common to suggest that the general rationale for the laws of war governing conduct in war is their potential to reduce the harm that results from war. This might seem commonsensical, but in fact it does not give justice its due; for the laws of war should aim not at reducing harm, but rather at reducing harm that is *not* justly inflicted. Let us call such harm "unjust harm."

To see my point here, consider the following hypothetical:

Kidnap. One hundred kidnappers have kidnapped and plan to murder fifty innocent persons. The only way to rescue the kidnapped individuals is through a military operation that will kill each and every kidnapper.

Surely it is justifiable to undertake the rescue mission even though twice as many persons will die as an immediate consequence of doing so. Nor do we need to appeal to speculative future benefits to justify the rescue. Perhaps killing the kidnappers would prevent them from committing additional crimes in the future. Perhaps killing them would deter others from committing similar crimes in the future. It doesn't really matter because the kidnappers are liable to defense. Hence, the rescue mission is justified even if the harm it inflicts greatly exceeds the harm it prevents. There is nothing wrong with preventing fifty murders at the cost of killing one hundred persons who would otherwise commit those fifty murders, and that is why it is so clear that the rescue mission would be justified.

As my example illustrates, the existence of enforcement rights (i.e., the right to defend oneself and others against unjust aggression, the right to take reparations, and the right to punish) entails that not all harm is equal. Justice is not opposed to inflicting harm insofar as one is merely exercising one's right to defend, take reparations, or punish. (The first of these three rights will, of course, play by far the greatest role in justifying violence in war.) Thus, the laws of war should aim not at minimizing harm per se, but rather should aim primarily at minimizing unjust harm, and the pragmatic view should be formulated as the view that the legal distinction between directly and indirectly attacking noncombatants is justified because it reduces the unjust harm that results from war.[25]

This places the pragmatic view on a firm moral foundation. Moreover, the pragmatic view is strengthened by this refinement in that it is more likely that the legal distinction in question reduces unjust harm than that it reduces harm. To see this, notice that one likely consequence of deterring direct attacks on non-combatants by criminalizing such attacks is that direct attacks on combatants will occur with greater frequency. Thus, on balance, it isn't obvious that criminalizing the former sort of attack reduces harm, as opposed to merely shifting harm from noncombatants to combatants. There is reason, however, to suppose that insofar as direct attacks on noncombatants are replaced by direct attacks on combatants, *unjust* harm is being reduced. For combatants who participate in unjust aggression are liable to defense; thus, subject to the restrictions on the right to defense (for example, necessity and proportionality), harming them to protect the potential

---

25. I say "primarily" partly because there may be some occasions on which one should inflict a lesser just harm for the sake of avoiding the infliction of a greater just harm. For example, if one can successfully defend the innocent by killing fewer, or guiltier, unjust aggressors, then, at least arguably, one should do so even if it would not be unjust to kill the greater number, or the less guilty.

Because even considerations of justice can sometimes be overridden by sufficiently weighty considerations of beneficence, there are also cases in which one should not inflict just harm. Indeed, if the position defended in this volume by David Rodin is correct, there can even be circumstances under which considerations of beneficence make it wrong to inflict just harm on aggressors in defense of their potential victims. Nevertheless, because beneficence so rarely comes into conflict with justice, and because it is generally inappropriate to enforce moral requirements that are not requirements of justice, I strongly doubt that the laws of war should ever impose sanctions for inflicting just harm.

victims of their unjust aggression is not unjust.[26] Consequently, the legal distinction between directly and indirectly harming noncombatants tends to shift the violence of war away from murder and toward discriminate acts of defense. Reducing the number of direct attacks on noncombatants by way of criminalizing such attacks is therefore a reasonable way to try to reduce the occurrence of murder in war even if it does not reduce the occurrence of killing in war.

It might be objected that even if harming noncombatants directly is usually unjustifiable, it is sometimes justifiable. Thus, criminalizing it has the potential to result in unjust punishments inflicted on those who justifiably harm noncombatants directly. I believe that this is a serious objection, but can be avoided if courts that prosecute war crimes recognize self-defense and necessity defenses in the relevant cases. Even those indicted for attacking noncombatants should have the opportunity for acquittal if they can show either that the noncombatants attacked were not innocent bystanders and were killed in a justifiable act of defense, or that they were killed because it was clear that the attack would prevent much greater harm to innocent persons than it would inflict.

I should emphasize that my argument here has not shown that the pragmatic view is correct. I cannot claim to have done the empirical work necessary to confirm that criminalizing harming noncombatants directly, while permitting harming them indirectly, actually does reduce unjust harm. Of course, there may be no way to provide conclusive empirical confirmation that the legal distinction in question has substantial net benefits. In international politics—indeed, in politics in general—we must often make educated guesses and hope for the best. Based on my limited knowledge, my own guess is that the legal distinction between directly harming and indirectly harming noncombatants can, with proper enforcement, serve a useful moral purpose by reducing the unjust harm that is almost always a consequence of war.

---

26. Many writers have questioned the relevance of the right of self-defense and other-defense to the ethics of war. See, for example, Judith Lichtenberg, "War, Innocence, and the Doctrine of Double Effect," *Philosophical Studies* 74 (1994): 347–68. My view is that such skepticism is unwarranted, but I do not defend that view here.

IV WAR'S BEGINNING AND ENDING

10 BEYOND THE PARADIGM OF SELF-DEFENSE?

ON REVOLUTIONARY VIOLENCE

Mattias Iser

Introduction

Until recently many people might have thought that the issue of justifying revolutionary violence was more or less obsolete. However, the "Arab Spring" and particularly the armed upheavals in Libya and Syria have proven the renewed urgency of this age-old question: under what circumstances are citizens justified in taking up arms against their government? In this essay I discuss a major challenge to the very idea of a justified revolution, which holds that—in analogy to acts of self-defense—it is always disproportionate to kill in defense of civil and political rights.[*]

After presenting the challenge as laid out by Richard Norman and David Rodin (section I), I refute it in four steps. First, I show that goods- or harm-centered accounts of self-defense neglect the crucially important dimension of (dis)respect (section II). Second, although our intuitions about individual self-defense provide the starting point for nearly all thinking about permissible violence today, it is often misleading to think about the justifiability of revolutions within the narrow confines of these intuitions. The paradigm of self-defense implicitly presupposes a just background order securing mutual respect. It is therefore ill-equipped to deal with political violence that attempts to erect such a political order, including fair procedures of decision-making and just law enforcement. Revolutions, I will argue, are

[*] I am grateful to Saba Bazargan, Anja Karnein, Jeff McMahan, and Sam Rickless for written comments on this essay. I have also profited from discussions at Goethe University Frankfurt, the Free University Berlin, Binghamton University, UCLA, and the annual meeting of the APSA in Washington, D.C. 2014.

not primarily defensive, although they are also about defending people's rights. Rather, they are transformative: revolutionaries aim at occupying the locus of power in order to change the basic structure of the society so as to effectively confer and protect legal rights (section III). Third, these two arguments lay the ground for a new approach that focuses on when the disrespect expressed by the regime's human rights violations becomes so severe as to allow for the transition from protest and civil disobedience to militant resistance. Starting from the narrowly defined causes for military humanitarian interventions, I argue that domestic revolutions can be justified by a broader range of rights violations (section IV). Fourth and finally, my proposed approach can also capture a phenomenon that the paradigm of self-defense remains blind to, namely the inherent dangers of revolutionary zeal (section V).

I. The Challenge: Civic and Political Rights as "Peripheral Rights"?

Usually, theories of permissible violence start with the analysis of a just cause, most prominently the defense against a wrongful harm. According to many accounts the criterion of proportionality is necessarily an integral part of the analysis of just cause: if we believe that a certain degree of violence constitutes a disproportionate reaction to a wrong, this wrong does not amount to a just cause for engaging in this kind of violence.

A very influential thesis put forward by Richard Norman (1995) and, in his wake, David Rodin (2003) maintains that killing in defense of one's civil and political rights can never be proportionate. Therefore, violations of those rights are always insufficient to provide a just cause for revolutions that will involve lethal violence. More precisely, both authors deal with what has been called "narrow" proportionality. According to a widely accepted proposal by Jeff McMahan, narrow proportionality concerns the degree of violence permitted against those who have rendered themselves liable, that is, who have no reason to complain about the violence they suffer. It is contested what exactly renders persons "liable" in this sense (see Iser 2013a, section 2), but there is unanimous agreement that a person who culpably attacks an innocent victim is liable. It is important, however, to note that such liability does not necessarily allow the victim to use *any* degree of defensive violence. The proportionality constraint on defensive violence is supposed to acknowledge that we owe respect to the humanity of the perpetrator as well. By contrast, considerations of "wide" proportionality also take into account the violence that is suffered by non-liable persons, the most common example being innocent bystanders (McMahan 2009, 19–20).

The thesis that killing in defense of one's civil and political rights can never be narrowly proportionate creates a major problem for any justification of violent resistance. According to this challenge even if all oppressed citizens were to consent to risking their lives in pursuit of freedom and equal recognition (and even if they need not kill any innocent bystanders), they would not be permitted to kill those who are preventing them from lifting the yoke of oppression.[1]

Norman and Rodin start from our intuitions in cases of self-defense and claim that any potentially lethal violence that protects a lesser good than life or bodily integrity is narrowly disproportionate. If you have to kill or severely injure an "aggressor" by defending yourself you have to think twice about how important the good or value is that you are protecting: is it really a "central" right worth killing for or merely a "peripheral" right? The main target of both authors is the view that one may lethally defend oneself against violations of property rights (Norman 1995, 128–29; Rodin 2003, 43–46). Thus, Norman provides the famous and powerful example of a mugger who threatens you with death if you do not hand him 50 pence. In this case, Norman argues, it would be disproportionate to kill the mugger in defense of this trivial sum (assuming that it is the only possible way of defending the 50 pence, that is, killing is necessary) (Norman 1995, 130). The harm we defend ourselves against should be "of the same order of magnitude" (Rodin 2003, 47) as the defensive measures we employ. It is not even permissible to defend your right by proportionate means thereby risking an escalation of the conflict that may require you to eventually kill the mugger.

It is certainly plausible that one should not kill in order to retrieve one's "pair of sunglasses" (ibid., 46) but things get messier when the authors reject "a general and undifferentiated right to kill in defence of one's *liberty*" (Norman 1995, 128, original emphasis; also Rodin 2003, 47–48). Although this sounds plausible for cases of rather trivial violations of liberty rights, both authors restrict the permissibility of defensive killing to the most extreme cases, namely kidnapping and slavery (Norman 1995, 128) or "wrongful lifetime incarceration, or some similarly grave infringement of liberty" (Rodin 2003, 48, similar Rodin 2014, 80).

Norman and Rodin use this line of argument in order to draw radical conclusions with regard to the permissibility of war and revolution. Thus, Norman claims that resistance against invasions that do not aim at mass murder or enslavement are not justifiable because "the aggressors will kill only because they are resisted. If there were no resistance, they could invade without having to take any

---

1. In a recent text Rodin has shifted the emphasis of his argument against the use of political violence to issues of wide proportionality, especially to special obligations of care we owe our nearest (Rodin 2014, 83–85). I am not able to deal with this argument within the confines of the present essay.

lives. It is precisely this resistance that has to be justified" (Norman 1995, 135). This argument of the "bloodless invasion," which reiterates Clausewitz's problematic idea that wars only start with the reaction of the defenders (Clausewitz 1832, 377), can easily be used to rule out nearly all cases of violent revolutions. Only regimes that engage in genocide or mass enslavement may justify armed resistance. Thus, both Norman and Rodin explicitly exclude the defense of national territory as well as the struggle for freedom and non-domination from the range of permissible ends of defensive violence because they regard them as "peripheral rights."[2] To support this claim, Rodin once again refers to our intuitions in cases of individual self-defense. Presumably, you are not permitted to kill "someone who sought to deprive you of important political freedoms, such as the right to vote or freely express your opinions" (Rodin 2003, 48). In what follows I will show why this view is mistaken.

II. Taking Respect Seriously

Many conceptions of self-defense, including those of Norman and Rodin, present us with a picture that is too reductive. Mostly, questions of proportionality are dealt with by comparing the goods or values involved in the particular situation. However, this exclusive focus on the good defended (or harm avoided) is misleading because it neglects two other dimensions, namely that of rights and, even more important, of the moral status of persons that has to be adequately respected. Such descriptions of the self-defensive situation, in other words, concentrate on possible harm but not on the wrong committed. For example, Rodin states that the "end of a defensive right will be defined as the good or value which a defensive action is intended to preserve or protect" (Rodin 2003, 35). By doing so, such an account necessarily remains deficient.

In order to validate this claim I will first introduce the three categories of goods, rights, and moral status before I show why it is important to distinguish several distinct ways in which—holding the harm caused constant—rights may be violated and disrespect expressed. This, I will argue, is an ineliminable part of what determines the severity of the wrong suffered.

Imagine that another person approaches you—either to take something away from you or to hurt or even kill you.[3] If you defend yourself, this can be analyzed along three different dimensions, namely (1) goods, (2) rights, and (3) moral status.

---

2. Jeff McMahan (2014) refers to attacks on such rights as "lesser aggression."

3. In the following passage I draw partly on material from Iser (2013a, 355–58).

(1) *Goods*: If you are attacked there is obviously a potential harm at stake that deprives you of some good. The endangered good can take many forms: it can be a wallet and its contents, your health, personal autonomy or even your life. All these goods are valuable as they serve your interests by either providing the pre-conditions of a good life or by constituting intrinsic features of it. This by itself provides you with a reason to ward off the attacker.

(2) *Rights*: Admittedly, both Norman and Rodin discuss whether we can defend ourselves against certain *rights* violations. What the notion of a right does in such a context is to indicate that the victim has a claim that is not paid due attention to.[4] However, both Norman's and Rodin's notion of a right does not carry independent weight in explaining the proportionality of one's defensive action. Both authors consider the proportionality of defending a right to x to be identical with the importance of x as a good. But this misses out on the meaning of rights. It is important to distinguish between rights as reasonable moral claims on others and the social fact of publicly acknowledged rights, be they social (in the sense of widely shared mores) or legal rights.[5] Having moral rights simply implies that I have a valid moral claim against others because of my status as a person. And this status, together with the moral rights springing from it, is inviolable (Nagel 2008, 107) in the following sense. Even if someone actually violated my rights because he wrongfully failed to acknowledge them, I would still "have" them. I would still have a reasonable claim that the violation should not have taken place.

In light of this ever-present possibility of others violating "inviolable" rights, publicly acknowledged rights—as codified, for instance, in positive law—serve two main functions, an instrumental and an expressive one. Let me explain both in turn. Public rights in the above sense have *instrumental* value because as socially accepted claims and especially as enforceable legal rights they secure goods in a way the mere existence of reasons backing our claims does not. Thus, such rights as social facts serve some interests of ours. We want to have a legal right to property because we value what we own and rely on it being effectively protected from any interference by others. We value the right to life because it is supposed to secure the life we cherish for its own sake.

This points to the difference between defending our wallet and defending our legal right to that wallet. If we defend our right to property we may do so because it not only secures our wallet but all our possessions. In this case, we do not only

---

4. In fact, if you do not have a right to x you may not defend it against others who have a right to it. If both parties do not have such a right, the permissibility to fight for x must rest, again, on other considerations than simply that it would be a good to you (or the others).

5. I am grateful to Saba Bazargan for urging me to elaborate on this point.

defend the particular good at stake, but the entire "protective umbrella" of the legal right to property. In extreme cases, we may even fear that a rights violation is not only signaling the denial of this specific right in a particular situation, but of our legal status as a rights-bearer as such. In an instrumental reading this would mean that we are in danger of losing the protection of all of our legal rights (even if we could still insist on having moral rights).

But in addition to these instrumental reasons, publicly acknowledged rights also have an *expressive* function. They do not simply protect our interests. Rather, they signify that it is generally understood that we can *reasonably demand of others* that they acknowledge them, that is, that they grant that we have a valid claim because our interests should be assigned a certain normative importance. This brings me to the dimension of moral status.

(3) *Moral status*: That our interests are publicly affirmed as giving rise to claim rights in this way signals something even more important, namely that we are recognized as persons who are owed a certain normative standing in the social world, that is, vis-à-vis other members of our community (Feinberg 1970, 251–53). Legal rights that are publicly affirmed by the community thus express attitudes of mutual recognition that are also conducive to every individual's sense of self-respect. However, that they are so conducive is not the reason why we want to have this status. Rather, it is the other way around.[6]

This distinction between the instrumental and expressive dimension of rights is ignored by recent accounts of self-defense. Rather, such accounts narrowly focus on the particular good at stake. Take the scenario by Richard Norman with which I began the discussion. The way Norman poses the problem, it is difficult to imagine *any* act of even mild violence that could be justified as a means of defense against the loss of 50 pence or even 500 pounds. This argument is certainly valuable in warning us of too easily embracing violent means. However, it neglects the intersubjective meaning of such disrespectful behavior. From this latter perspective, an attack on a person's moral rights can be read as calling into question or even denying his moral status, that is, disrespecting him.

What follows from this perspective for the issue of revolutionary violence? If we want to evaluate the importance of civil and political rights we do not only have to look at their instrumental function but also at their expressive role. If oppressed persons are struggling for legal rights hitherto not granted to them,

---

6. I have defended this view in more detail in Iser (2008, section 3.3.1). Thomas Nagel shares the same intuition when he writes that "what is good about the public recognition of such a status is that it gives people the sense that their inviolability is appropriately recognized. Naturally, they are gratified by this, but the gratification is due to the recognition of the value of the status, rather than the opposite—that is, the status does not get its value from the gratification it produces" (Nagel 2008, 109).

they may want these rights because they have instrumental value. Having a voice in political matters, for example, would allow them to influence political decisions. Entire groups may realistically hope to change policy outcomes. Thus, it makes sense for disadvantaged groups to struggle for an institutional setting that has better credentials in finding political solutions that are acceptable to all affected (see in more detail Iser 2008, section 3.3.2).

However, that is not the entire or even the main point of these struggles. They cannot be understood without also paying attention to their expressive significance. For instance, for a single individual the legal right to vote is mainly of symbolic value. This observation does not strip this right of its importance. Quite to the contrary, if an entire population strives for new legal rights—against, for example, its absolute monarch—what the members are demanding is public recognition of a specific aspect of their autonomous agency to which they have a moral claim.

Frequently, "some" moral status will not be appropriate. Thus, if members of a particular group want to be properly recognized by the rest of the citizenry, what they are demanding is often precisely not to be treated as "second-class citizens" (Taylor 1992, 37) but to be addressed as equals.[7] Such *equal* respect, which constitutes the normative core of modern morality, has to be distinguished from a common usage in which "respect" denotes something quite different, namely respect for the qualities of a particular person's character. It has been proposed that the former should be termed "recognition respect" whereas the latter should be labeled "appraisal respect" (Darwall 1977). Appraisal respect resembles esteem in that specific properties of a person, rather than the general fact of being a person, are valued (see also Iser 2013b, section 2.2). In the following, I will use the term "respect" to denote the attitude of recognition respect with regard to the *equal* moral standing of persons and their rightful demands. I hereby assume that such egalitarianism is what morality requires (for a more detailed justification, see Iser 2008, section 3.2.1).

III. Why Self-Defense Is Misleading: On the Transformation of a Political Order

In light of the foregoing distinction between two dimensions of rights, their instrumental and expressive aspects, it is seriously misleading to turn, as Norman and Rodin do, to intuitions familiar from the context of individual self-defense

---

7. I am grateful to Sam Rickless for insisting on the distinction between recognition of moral status and of *equal* moral status. For examples of the historical differentiation between no, some (second-class), and equal status, see Benhabib (2006, 34).

when thinking about violent revolutions. There are two main reasons for this. First, the picture of self-defense that fuels our moral intuitions already presupposes the existence of a just background order secured by effective law enforcement. Once one explicates these implicit assumptions (section 3.1), one realizes that, second, the paradigm of self-defense is ill-equipped to deal with political violence that tries to erect such a political order in the first place—including fair procedures of decision-making and just law enforcement (section 3.2).

a. What Is Missing in Self-Defense: Making the Implicit Explicit

The literature about self-defensive violence is tellingly devoid of any discussion of expressive elements. For instance, many authors assume that a potential victim should use violence only as a last resort and should flee the scene if trivial goods are at stake, that is, should try not to risk an escalation. However, it is often simply presupposed that the state's monopoly on violence is effectively protecting the victim. Thus, the individual's right to defend himself is needed only in cases of emergency. By contrast, the option of fleeing the scene is not so easily available to the police. It is the right and perhaps even the duty of the police to risk escalation even if some constraints apply here as well. Thus, if the police confront a burglar and tell him to surrender, he might open fire. It is the prerogative of the police to escalate the situation in this way and even to respond with their weapons—as long as they pay due attention to considerations of wide proportionality. If the burglar, by using his gun, endangers the lives of officers or bystanders he can be shot. The responsibility of having escalated the situation lies clearly with him.

How can one explain this difference with regard to our intuitions about narrow proportionality? We have to remember that the police do not only protect individual citizens. Law enforcement is society's main tool of distancing itself from crime and of reaffirming the law, which is—after all—one of the main institutional expressions of the societal recognition order. Whereas individual victims might waive their right to defend themselves, such inaction of the police would have to be regarded as silently standing by while the law is being violated. This is especially salient with regard to the potentially humiliating effects on the victim. Just consider the symbolic meaning of the police simply watching an assault on members of a minority.

All this does not rule out the possibility that in many cases police action may be widely disproportionate and in some cases even narrowly so. But it is a reminder that police action is not only instrumentally necessary but also *expressive* of the community's condemnation of the criminal act. These expressive considerations are strikingly missing from the reading of self-defense that Norman and Rodin propose. This reading can account neither for some instrumental aspects (deterrence) nor for the entire expressive dimension (condemnation) of police work and punishment. It rather presupposes them all along.

b. Transformation Instead of Defense

All these expressive aspects of law enforcement are also absent, however, in a severely unjust political order. If the institutions and laws do not express norms of mutual respect neither does what the police, courts, or correction facilities are providing. It has thus rightly been observed that revolutionary movements often start with the desire that ongoing injustices finally receive their deserved punishment (Haque 2013), not to speak of the hope that the police finally work for the benefit of the population. But that a society is in such a deplorable state is primarily due to political—and most important, legislative—decision procedures that are not fair or accountable enough to express respect for the moral status of their citizens. In such a situation a revolution's goal is not merely the warding off of some aggression (as in the case of national self-defense or a rather narrow view of the goal of humanitarian interventions), that is, a return to a just situation ex ante. Rather, its end has to be the radical transformation of the status quo.

After all, unjust state institutions and laws do not only violate but, what is more, frequently deny the existence of moral rights; and this is clearly a more aggravated form of disrespect.[8] Take, again, Norman's case of the mugger. Here, it is only the mugger who disrespects your property right by violating it. Thus, although you lose the 50 pence for good, you do not lose your legal right to the 50 pence (you can never lose your "inviolable" moral right anyway, although it may be violated). If you go to the police the officers will acknowledge that you still

---

8. In order to be able to say that institutions express disrespect one has to presuppose a peculiar intentionality on their side, which is possible only if we conceive of them as (part of) corporate agents. See for such a view Iser (2015, 30) and François Tanguay-Renaud's contribution to this volume (esp. 3–5). Tanguay-Renaud discusses the possible ramifications of such a view of the state for its and its individual members' liability to attack. While the state's liability can justify some kinds of attack (such as violations of its territorial sovereignty or damage to its property, 12–13), he concludes, I believe correctly, that the only factor that can ground an individual's liability to be seriously harmed is this individual's actions or omissions (22–23). For a permissive view of when members of unjust regimes may permissibly be coerced and even seriously harmed because they culpably do not live up to their moral duties—and more specifically the natural duty to support just institutions—see Richard Arneson's contribution to this volume (esp. 4–5, 10–11). However, he does not ground this permission in the fact that those individuals render themselves liable. Rather, he offers a moralized reading of a lesser evil justification (3, 13–14). By contrast, two differing arguments for the necessary intertwinement of both forms of justification are provided by Jeff McMahan's and David Rodin's contributions to this volume, respectively.

have the legal right to your property as well as full legal standing. Your legal right has been violated, but it has not been taken away. It is an entirely different matter once we deal with a legal order that does not grant you such rights. In contrast to a single mugger the state strips you of your legal right, not only of a good (hereby violating your right). In fact, there are two possible cases: either a (new) government permanently takes away your formerly granted legal right to X or you live in a political order that never granted you such a right to begin with although it should. Normatively both cases are on a par. However, empirically resistance is much more likely to arise in the former because people react more readily to a loss than to not receiving something, even if what they are lacking is due to them.

A revolution does not only defend an already accepted legal right. It also claims and tries to effectively establish legal rights that are withheld but morally deserved.[9] Thus, the end of a legitimate revolution is best captured by reference to the basic structure of a society, to use a term introduced by John Rawls. The term "basic structure" denotes "the way in which the major social institutions distribute fundamental rights and duties and determine the division of advantages from social cooperation" (Rawls 1971, 6). The injustice of a basic structure might be long-standing or the sudden result of a new government's action. The latter is, for example, the case when military juntas overthrow a democratic government, get rid of the constitution, and effectively erect a new basic structure.

The paradigm of individual self-defense is not well equipped to cover the importance of such an institutional order in both its instrumental and expressive dimensions. Instrumentally, a basic structure has by its very nature long-lasting and pervasive effects on all individuals in that society. Expressively, it assigns specific forms of status by granting or denying certain legal rights. Individual attacks, however, are by definition local as well as temporary with regard to their consequences. Furthermore, although they may (but do not have to) express utter disrespect, they can never humiliate as deeply as an unjust, for example racist, basic structure. It is because of this significance that Rawls compellingly argues that the natural duty to support and further just institutions is the "most important" one (ibid., 293).[10]

---

9. Revolutions might sometimes attempt not only to change the legal order but the entire cultural value system, hereby trying to establish social rights in the sense of more respectful attitudes in informal settings. However, as will become obvious below, violent political revolutions are often too blunt an instrument to achieve such social progress.

10. It is true that nobody can ever take away your equal moral status or dignity as this is connected with your agency, period. However, unfortunately, this Stoic idea does not do away with the wrong against those victims who are robbed of their legal rights and may, as a consequence of this, suffer extremely humiliating treatment, potentially causing a severe disruption of their world- and self-trust (see Scarry 1985; Margalit 1996, 115–19, 145).

This gives rise to another fact often overlooked in discussions of domestic resistance that follow the paradigm of self-defense. The "aggressor" is not merely the particular agent of an institution *as an individual* even if she violates the victim's moral rights. Rather, it is the institution itself. From this it follows that in order to "ward off" the attack of the institution you have to transform it. You may have to ward off the agent executing the institution's demands temporarily first, but logically it is only of secondary importance.[11] Yet how disrespectful does a society have to be in order to justify violent resistance?

IV. Just Causes of Revolutionary Violence: Human Rights and Disrespect

It is important to introduce at least a threefold differentiation of possible reasons for resistance: we may, first, talk about the basic structure being unjust; second, about a government abusing its power within (but not changing) a "nearly just" basic structure; and third, specific governmental decisions (be it directives or laws) that are deemed to be unjust although, again, the basic structure remains "nearly just" and the government acts within its legitimate bounds (Rawls 1971, 310, 319–23).[12] Because neither the last nor even the second option has the impact necessary to justify violent revolution, in what follows I will concentrate on the first.

Lethal means may be permissible as a last resort in one's struggle against *institutions* that are guilty of an unnecessary and *grave* denial of persons' moral status. The term "institutions" signifies the entrenched quality of the humiliation. Admittedly, the qualifier "grave" is inherently vague. Both qualifications are supposed to lay to rest the worry that any expression of disrespect, even just a trivial one, could trigger justified violence, perhaps even lethal violence. This would indeed be absurd.

---

11. As an expressive corollary, within an unjust society the members who suffer discrimination feel humiliated by the society, not only and not even primarily by the agents of the governing institutions. Certainly, these agents might add disrespect by treating the members who are suffering discrimination even worse than the regulations demand, but they certainly do not have to do so. If they act according to the rules, they still disrespect the addressee—but "only" as agents of the institution. Institutions can disrespect people (see Iser 2013b, section 1.2).

12. For a slightly different distinction of reasons for revolutionary action see already Locke (1690), namely illegitimate appropriation of authority by external conquest (ch. 16) or domestic usurpation (ch. 17) on the one hand and tyranny on the other. The latter signifies the replacement of legitimate laws by the arbitrary will of those in power, either by the "prince" (the executive who also takes part in legislative decision-making) procedurally undermining the rightful powers of the parliament (legislature) or by either of both political bodies substantially violating the citizens' moral rights (chs. 18 and 19).

Let me also note that I readily grant that we cannot grasp the severity of a certain instance of institutional disrespect without also considering the dimension of the goods that are at stake. As we face a continuum from severe humiliation to phenomena with regard to which it is highly controversial whether they are disrespectful (such as certain redistributive policies), quite a few theories of recognition have focused on negative experiences of clear *dis*respect by looking at violations of the most basic rights to bodily integrity. In fact, the normative expectation of being treated with respect becomes especially obvious once we look at extreme forms of humiliation in which specific (groups of) persons are symbolically excluded from humanity—and sometimes treated like animals or mere objects as a consequence. Violations of life and limb rights thus also play an important part in a recognitional account of the kind I am offering.

Not surprisingly, the human right to bodily integrity (and the goods hereby protected) is internationally accepted as giving legitimate permission for military humanitarian interventions if it is violated on a massive scale, namely, to quote the UN *High-level Panel on Threats, Challenges and Change*, if one faces "mass murder and rape, ethnic cleansing by forcible expulsion and terror, and deliberate starvation and exposure to disease" (High-level Panel 2004, s. 201, 56). Such systematic and widespread rights violations are taken to clearly signify a regime's forfeiture of its sovereignty rights. Humanitarian interventions thus defined seem to fit the paradigm of defense of others.

Yet several things should be noted. First, although military humanitarian interventions were—in the beginning—conceived of as swift "in and out" operations, many have come to realize that they demand much more than just defensive force, namely often transformative efforts. In order to be successful they have to engage in "state building" that is supposed to enable a genuinely fair political process in which the population can freely determine its future fate as well as the erection of impartial and effective law enforcement institutions.

Here, political violence is not seen as a replacement for a fair political process but as creating the preconditions for such a political process in the first place. This, however, brings such humanitarian interventions in closer proximity to the idea of regime change as the external equivalent of domestic revolutions.[13] Second, if these extreme human rights violations on a massive scale give external powers the right or even the duty to intervene by military force, then those who have to suffer these rights violations surely have a right to fight against the government too. Since in the case of domestic revolutions there is no normative barrier that is erected in order to protect nations against potentially neo-imperial intrusions from outside hereby

---

13. On the relationship between revolutions and humanitarian interventions, see Buchanan (2013).

securing the international legal system, it is at least initially plausible—although it would still have to be argued in more detail—that violent domestic resistance can be justified with reference to less fundamental human rights violations, all other things being equal (see also Walzer 1977, 89). But how much less fundamental?

Let us look, for example, at John Rawls's list of human rights in his *Law of Peoples* that—as a "political" conception—is explicitly designed to determine when external actors may permissibly intervene in a sovereign state. In this list Rawls uses John Locke's triad of life, liberty, and property before adding a fourth element, namely that of equality, understood in a rather minimal way (Rawls 1999, 65). If only implicitly, Rawls seems to assume a normative hierarchy, starting with securing human life, especially from arbitrary attacks (be they lethal or "merely" injurious) and torture. Still very minimal are those liberty rights that Rawls integrates as a second element. However, they do not entail equal liberty (ibid., 79) but only "freedom from slavery, serfdom, and forced occupation, and to a sufficient measure of liberty of conscience to ensure freedom of religion and thought" (ibid., 65). And although he includes a reference to "formal equality" (ibid.) this does not explicitly prohibit severe forms of discrimination due to ethnicity, race, or gender (critical with regard to the latter, see Buchanan 2004, 129). Rawls also does not mention the *equal* right to conscience or the right to publicly voice one's opinion. Finally, in Rawls's as well as in many other accounts, the right to democratic participation does not even figure within the catalog of those rights that would justify outside military intervention. This is often the case because it is perceived to conflict with the right to collective self-determination that might include a decision against democratic government (see Cohen 2010, 349–72; Beitz 2010, 174–86).

However, *within* domestic societies struggles for democratic rights have not only been one of the main pillars of legitimate revolutions but are also expressions of collective self-determination and not an obstacle to it. Thus, all *political conceptions* that tailor their list of human rights to their role in international politics, namely by singling out just causes for humanitarian interventions, miss the importance of a broader spectrum of human rights for the justification of domestic resistance and revolution.[14]

In fact, I want to claim that all mentioned forms of severe inequality manifest disrespect that may potentially justify violent resistance *as a last resort* because persons simply do not have to endure living under such conditions. Thus, frequently in history it was not necessarily denied that those under discussion were humans, but rather that they had equal moral standing and this denial led to an inferior

---

14. Rawls admits that there is a distinct class of "constitutional rights" or "rights of liberal democratic citizenship" (ibid., 79) but he does not clarify what role they may play for the justification of domestic revolutions.

legal status. Instead of being approached as adults, women and people of different color, for instance, were regarded as second-class citizens not capable of responsibly reproducing and shaping the social norms of their communities. If such denigrating attitudes are institutionalized in law it may be justifiable to resort to lethal violence against clearly demarcated liable persons.

The above considerations are still relatively vague—and for a reason. The severity of disrespect cannot merely be deduced from the moral rights violated or even explicitly denied by a regime. Rather, in each instance the reasons *why* their legal observance or even institutionalization is not granted need to be analyzed. In order to illustrate this point let us start, again, from a simple individualistic case. Beyond all harm car theft also expresses a form of disrespect. I say "a form" of disrespect because we have to distinguish different ways in which one's moral status can be violated by theft. It makes a salient difference why such rights are violated. Did A merely happen to be the accidental object of a crime (as in the case of a car theft in an anonymous street) or was he the purposeful target of a rights violation?[15] If the latter is the case, it is important to know why: perhaps A would be the one least harmed (for example, because he is particularly rich). Or he is an especially easy victim. Or, normatively most problematic, he is thought of as not possessing this particular right—or even no rights at all—because he belongs to a specific group Y or has property Z that allegedly explains his having unequal or even no moral status at all. The last possibility is the clearest case of disrespect although presumably the harm suffered in this instance, the loss of a car, remains exactly the same. Such an interpretation in terms of disrespect is especially adequate if B does not violate A's rights only once, but does so repeatedly (similarly, see Coady 2008, 85–86).

As already argued above, such a continuous or even permanent negation of another's right clearly indicates misrecognition of another's moral status and is most effectively achieved by unjust state institutions or laws. However, here again it matters *why* the political order represented by its government does not adequately recognize moral claims. Differences are to be located on two levels. First, governments may under-fulfill granted legal rights, may grant them but may not do enough to effectively prevent such rights violations, may even legally allow them to happen or, finally, actively violate rights themselves (see Pogge 2008, 47–48, also 65–73).[16] Second, if governments violate moral rights it matters

---

15. I discuss this case in more detail in Iser (2013a, 372–73).

16. These different kinds of "rights violations" should, again, not be confused with the mere lack of goods. If a government has to save money and thus stops providing some public goods that it used to supply its citizens with, the latter lose some goods. But if they did not have claim rights to such goods, we cannot speak of an injustice.

whether they do so universally or whether they target a specific group. And even in the latter case it makes a crucial difference whether those granted fewer legal rights are ascribed at least a certain form of honor (as in the case of women in patriarchal societies, although this honor might be ideological in sustaining structures of unjustified domination) or whether they are clearly denigrated as inferior. In all these cases governmental institutions commit serious wrongs. But although I would argue that women in a patriarchal society are disrespected, those groups openly humiliated as inferior suffer under an even more severe form of disrespect. One of the most obvious cases of the latter is the South African apartheid regime, which manifested extreme denigration. Such humiliation clearly justifies violent resistance *as a last resort*.

Frequently, though, lethal violence is neither a last nor even an effective resort. A peculiar mixture of honoring and disrespecting a certain group, such as might be the case with women in patriarchal societies, may hold the promise that one can transform this belief system. Additionally, when the victims are confronted with an ideology deeply ingrained in the entire society, violence might also prove to be an ineffective tool. It has to be remembered that violence in itself can never create conditions of mutual recognition. It can only remove obstacles toward realizing a state of affairs in which such recognition might be more easily achievable.[17] However, if a more just society was already feasible and, for example, prevented merely by a small group of racists, violence might—under certain circumstances— be an effective and proportionate means to achieve that better society.

Paradoxically, although the possible just causes are greater in the case of do-mestic resistance, the two criteria of proportionality and probability of success might often make insurgency harder to justify than military interventions by out-side forces. We merely have to assume, not unrealistically, that the intervening forces are much more powerful than domestic resistance, and especially so if the latter is constituted by an oppressed minority. This may be counteracted by the fact that outside interventions can make it harder to establish a just society after the war. In general, the goal of transforming a basic structure poses much higher obstacles in terms of a probability of success than acts of self- or other-defense.

The demand the criterion of probability of success imposes on justifications of violence becomes especially pressing when the outcome of the revolution—or even the likelihood of its success—cannot be known. And this is nearly always the case. After all, the normative rationale for the criterion of probability of success is to minimize unnecessary harm. If one cannot predict that a revolutionary

---

17. However, women using violence might by the very act of doing so undermine many of the stereotypes that cement their subordinate role, such as being essentially passive, caring, or un-determined.

movement will succeed in overthrowing an oppressive regime, there is the danger of no good being within reach.

If there is only a very low probability, the criterion holds that no harm should be inflicted or suffered to begin with. If, under such circumstances, one still wants to justify a revolution the emphasis must shift—at least partly—to its expressive dimension, namely that it manifests freedom. In this vein Hannah Arendt writes: "Long before those who were involved in them could know whether their enterprise would end in victory or disaster, the novelty of the story and the innermost meaning of its plot became manifest to actors and spectators alike" (Arendt 1963, 19).[18] The importance of such expressive elements in revolutionary violence entails problems of its own, though.

V. Expressive Violence and Revolutionary Zeal

Because revolutionary violence ideally strives for a more just social and political order it contains an expressive dimension. The very act of fighting for principles of justice affirms those principles (as police action and punishment would do in a fully just society). Thus, the means employed by the insurgents should not symbolically undermine the goal pursued. Frequently, this creates problems for the insurgents as they have to balance instrumental against expressive considerations ("What will prove militarily successful? What is normatively justifiable in light of the better, more just, order we seek to establish?"). But unfortunately, such revolutionary violence is—as all forms of allegedly legitimate violence—also subject to paradoxes that haunt it.

First, the powerful emotion of indignation combined with the idea of having justice on one's side may lead the revolutionaries to mistakenly demonize their opponents. Even if they correctly perceive the political order as utterly unjust (and it is worth mentioning that they might greatly exaggerate that injustice), they may—due to their rage searching for some outlet—focus on particular (groups of) individuals who are either not responsible at all or not sufficiently responsible to justify violence against them. Thus, they may succumb to the grave mistake of personalizing rather anonymous institutions and structures. After all, the indignant subject does not only see his opponent as a strategic nuisance—as might be the case if violence just serves the purpose of power maximization—but frequently pictures him as the representative of everything that is oppressive. As

---

18. A purely expressive use of violence, however, can only be justified in the rarest of circumstances. The Jewish uprising in the Warsaw Ghetto is one of them. I elaborate on the specific and rare conditions in which such expressive violence is legitimate in my *A Theory of Legitimate Violence: A Recognitional Account* (book manuscript in preparation).

all revolutions show, the indignation that fuels them contains a strong retributive aspect. In the case of Mohamed Bouazizi's self-immolation, which triggered the "Arab Spring," people at his funeral shouted: "Farewell, Mohamed, we will avenge you. We weep for you today. We will make those who caused your death weep" (BBC 2008). As people are not willing to endure the injustices inflicted on them any more, they do not only, instrumentally, want those injustices to stop but they wish all injustices suffered in the past to be accounted for. Either violence is then a means of transformation to achieve a new political order in which the perpetrators can finally be brought to justice in a procedurally fair way (Haque 2013) or—much more problematically—revolutionary violence is thought to be a form of punishment itself. This may be the case because people either do not entertain the hope of reaching a new and more just order or because they want to take immediate revenge without the procedural precautions of fair state retribution.

This danger is aggravated, second, by the fact that insurgents often lack the procedures to reach decisions that are sufficiently deliberated upon. Sometimes they explicitly reject such procedures because they self-righteously believe themselves to be epistemologically superior (heightened by groupthink that is sometimes due to operating underground). In such cases they may make arbitrary decisions, arbitrariness being the very opposite of justice.

Finally, there is a dangerous component entailed in all forms of violence and thus also in revolutionary violence, namely what I label its "hedonistic" dimension. Because violence—and the dangers that come with it—can heighten one's sense of self as well as of agency, it is able to provide pleasure. A poem by Césaire quoted in Frantz Fanon's *Wretched of the Earth* poignantly depicts the excitement of finally resisting violently. In this poem a rebel recounts to his mother an attack in which he took part:

> It was a November night. . . . /And suddenly clamors lit up the silence,/we had leapt, we the slaves, we the manure, we beasts with patient hooves./ We were running like lunatics; fiery shots broke out. . . . We were striking. Sweat and blood cooled us off. We were striking amidst the screams and the screams became more strident and a great clamor rose toward the east, the outbuildings were burning and the flames sweetly splashed our cheeks. (Fanon 1963, 46)

The rebels are presumably the ones shot at whereas they only strike. It is not quite clear who is screaming—the rebels or their former masters, although the entire tone of the text indicates the latter. It is, however, certain that the rebels, for the first time, experience themselves as agents who act in solidarity with their comrades and that this provides them with an existential delight. As understandable as such sentiments are given a long history of oppression and humiliation, this short passage also highlights the dangers involved in an expressive use of violence. The "cooling" blood may, after all, stand for the experience of the exceptional that regularly allows violent adolescents to gain a specific "adrenaline kick" from their violence (see, e.g., Nunner-Winkler 2004, 53). Such excitement is also able to diminish one's sense of boredom. Not all frustrating experiences—for example, of not feeling that one's life matters—are due to disrespect; they can also be signs of a life that is simply experienced as empty. Violence can fill such an inner void at least to a certain extent. This brings it in close proximity to a drug that allows the user to escape reality.[19]

The possibility of such experience presupposes either what I have referred to as demonization above or a denial that one is fighting humans who deserve respect. Thus, it is also not very surprising that the victims the rebels strike down do not seem to have any recognizable faces amid all those anonymous "screams" becoming "more strident." Such unruly "pleasures," if firmly embedded as ensuing habits in a "culture of violence," might undermine the revolutionary goal of achieving a more just and peaceful society that, after all, demands virtues of civility and compromise. Whoever sanitizes their account of legitimate violence from these "dark sides" runs the risk of taking normative justifications already as the whole where other motives distort the supposedly legitimate actions. Yet this would not be in the interest of a critical theory of legitimate violence. Thus, it is important to bear Michael Walzer's skeptical remarks in mind: "The mark of revolutionary struggle against oppression, however, is not this incapacitating rage and random violence, but restraint and self-control" (Walzer 1977, 205). Such "restraint and self-control" necessitate not only a clear view of the most important considerations of when violent resistance can be justified but also an awareness of its inherent dangers.

The arguments provided in this essay are supposed to illustrate that it becomes much less plausible to refer to our intuitions stemming from the legal context of individual self-defense when considering the narrow proportionality of violent revolutions. Rather, if one takes into account the meaning of certain

---

19. For these reasons nonviolent resistance has frequently been proposed as a strategy that is less dangerous for the agent and might, under certain circumstances, even be politically more effective. Both violent and nonviolent forms of resistance manifest what Nancy Sherman in her contribution to this volume describes as at the same time "an act of defiance" and an "act of resilience" (6). In such cases the resisters do not only want to express their agency but solidarity with each other. They might also try to morally address their oppressors, appealing to their sense of justice or at least decency. Sherman provides the fascinating and multifaceted example of the "moral protest" (5) by inmates of the Nazi concentration camp Theresienstadt (Terezin) who performed Giuseppe Verdi's *Requiem* every night (4–7).

actions and, more important, institutions, it is not quite so clear that a "corollary of the requirement of necessity is that there is a general duty to retreat from an aggressor, if it is possible (that is to say, readily feasible) to avoid harm in this way" (Rodin 2003, 40). Plausible as this might initially sound, in some cases retreat is not an option. This is so when the very end of one's action, instrumental as well as expressive, is to stand up against injustice, and to defend one's position of equality. In those cases retreating would undermine exactly this end.

BIBLIOGRAPHY

Arendt, Hannah (1963). *On Revolution*. London: Penguin, 2006.
BBC (2008). "Tunisia Suicide Protester Mohammed Bouazizi Dies," http://www.bbc .co.uk/news/world-africa-12120228.
Beitz, Charles (2010). *The Idea of Human Rights*. Oxford: Oxford University Press.
Benhabib, Seyla (2006). *Another Cosmopolitanism*. New York: Oxford University Press.
Buchanan, Allen (2004). *Justice, Legitimacy, and Self-Determination: Moral Foundations for International Law*. Oxford: Oxford University Press.
Buchanan, Allen (2013). "The Ethics of Revolution and Its Implications for the Ethics of Intervention." *Philosophy and Public Affairs* 41, no. 4, 291–323.
Clausewitz, Carl von (1832). *On War*. Princeton: Princeton University Press, 1984.
Coady, C. A. J. (2008). *Morality and Political Violence*. Cambridge: Cambridge University Press.
Cohen, Joshua (2010). *The Arc of the Moral Universe*. Cambridge, Mass.: Harvard University Press.
Darwall, Stephen L. (1977). "Two Kinds of Respect," *Ethics* 88, no. 1, 36–49.
Fanon, Frantz (1963). *The Wretched of the Earth*. New York: Grove Press, 2004.
Feinberg, Joel (1970). "The Nature and Value of Rights." *Journal of Value Inquiry* 4 no. 4, 243–57.
Haque, Adil Ahmad (2013). "The Revolution and the Criminal Law." *Criminal Law and Philosophy* 7, no. 2, 231–53.
High-level Panel (2004). *A More Secure World: Our Shared Responsibility. Report of the High-level Panel on Threats, Challenges and Change*, http://www.un.org/en/ peacebuilding/pdf/historical/hlp_more_secure_world.pdf.
Iser, Mattias (2008). *Empörung und Fortschritt. Grundlagen einer kritischen Theorie der Gesellschaft*. Frankfurt: Campus (English translation forthcoming, New York: Oxford University Press).
Iser, Mattias (2013a). "Recognition and Violence—The Challenge of Respecting One's Victim." *Revue Internationale de Philosophie* 265, 353–78.
Iser, Mattias (2013b). "Recognition." *The Stanford Encyclopedia of Philosophy* (Fall 2013), edited by Edward N. Zalta (Stanford: Stanford University Press), 1–35, http://plato.stanford.edu/archives/fall2013/entries/recognition/.

Iser, Mattias (2015). "Recognition Between States? Moving Beyond Identity Politics." In *Recognition in International Relations: Rethinking a Political Concept in a Global Context*, edited by Christopher Daase, Caroline Fehl, Anna Geis, and Georgios Kolliarakis, 27–45. Basingstoke: Palgrave Macmillan.

Locke, John (1690). *Two Treatises of Government*, edited by Peter Laslett. Cambridge: Cambridge University Press, 1960.

Margalit, Avishai (1996). *The Decent Society*. Cambridge, Mass.: Harvard University Press.

McMahan, Jeff (2009). *Killing in War*. Oxford: Oxford University Press.

McMahan, Jeff (2014). "What Rights May Be Defended by Means of War?" *The Morality of Defensive War*, edited by Cécile Fabre and Seth Lazar, 116–55. Oxford: Oxford University Press.

Nagel, Thomas (2008). "The Value of Inviolability." In *Morality and Self-Interest*, edited by Paul Bloomfield, 102–13. Oxford: Oxford University Press.

Norman, Richard (1995). *Ethics, Killing and War*. Cambridge: Cambridge University Press.

Nunner-Winkler, Gertrud (2004). "Überlegungen zum Gewaltbegriff." In *Gewalt*, edited by Wilhelm Heitmeyer and Hans-Georg Soeffner, 21–61. Frankfurt: Suhrkamp.

Pogge, Thomas (2008). *World Poverty and Human Rights: Cosmopolitan Responsibilities and Reforms*, 2nd ed. Cambridge: Polity.

Rawls, John (1971). *A Theory of Justice*, rev. ed. Cambridge, Mass.: Harvard University Press.

Rawls, John (1999). *The Law of Peoples*. Cambridge, Mass.: Harvard University Press.

Rodin, David (2003). *War and Self-Defense*. Oxford: Oxford University Press.

Rodin, David (2014). "The Myth of National Self-Defence." In *The Morality of Defensive War*, edited by Cécile Fabre and Seth Lazar, 70–89. Oxford: Oxford University Press.

Scarry, Elaine (1985). *The Body in Pain: The Making and Unmaking of the World*. Oxford: Oxford University Press.

Taylor, Charles (1992). "The Politics of Recognition." In *Multiculturalism: Examining the Politics of Recognition*, edited by A. Gutmann, 25–73. Princeton: Princeton University Press.

Walzer, Michael (1977). *Just and Unjust Wars: A Moral Argument with Historical Illustrations*, 3rd ed. New York: Basic Books, 2000.

11 WAR'S ENDINGS AND THE STRUCTURE OF JUST WAR THEORY

Seth Lazar

Introduction

The messy and drawn-out conclusions to the recent wars in Iraq and Afghanistan have forced philosophers to consider a dimension of war's morality that they had largely ignored. Most Just War theory focuses on *jus ad bellum* and *jus in bello*—justice in the resort to war, and its prosecution, respectively. In the last decade, *jus post bellum* has been added, focusing on the aftermath of war.[1] But in recent work David Rodin and Darrell Moellendorf have argued that this tripartite division is not exhaustive: we need a fourth category, governing the termination of conflict. Moellendorf calls this *jus ex bello*, Rodin *jus terminatio* (I will follow Moellendorf).[2] In Rodin's formulation, *jus ad bellum* governs the transition from peace to war and *jus in bello* governs conduct in war; while *jus ex bello* governs the transition from war to peace, and *jus post bellum* governs conduct in the postwar peace.[3]

This essay presents two responses to this valuable rethinking of the structure of Just War theory. First, it examines the function of these Latinate prepositional subcategories, arguing that while they play a useful

---

1. See, for example, Gary J. Bass, "Jus Post Bellum," *Philosophy and Public Affairs* 32 (2004): 384–412; Brian Orend, "Jus Post Bellum," *Journal of Social Philosophy* 31 (2000): 117–37; Carsten Stahn and Jann K. Kleffner, *Jus Post Bellum: Towards a Law of Transition from Conflict to Peace* (The Hague: T.M.C. Asser Press, 2008).

2. D. Moellendorf, "Justice and the Assignment of the Intergenerational Costs of Climate Change," *Journal of Social Philosophy* 40 (2009): 204–24; David Rodin, "Two Emerging Issues of Jus Post Bellum: War Termination and the Liability of Soldiers for Crimes of Aggression," in Stahn and Kleffner, *Jus Post Bellum*, 53–76.

3. David Rodin, "Ending War," *Ethics and International Affairs* 25 (2011): 359–67, at 359–60.

heuristic role, to understand the morality of war we need to deploy deeper and subtler distinctions. Second, it draws attention to an under-theorized aspect of the morality of war, which is particularly but not exclusively salient for war's endings: the role of negotiation in armed conflict.

I. The Structure of Just War Theory

Just War theory in the Western tradition has, over the course of a long and complex history, come to rest on a set of principles purported to govern the initiation and conduct of wars. The standard *ad bellum* principles are just cause, last resort, proportionality, reasonable prospects of success, legitimate authority, public declaration and right intention; the *in bello* principles are necessity, proportionality and distinction.[4] Both the distinction between *ad bellum* and *in bello*, and each of these specific principles, have deep roots in Just War theory's history, and they dominate contemporary popular thinking about the morality of war (especially in public political discourse, and in theological pronouncements on war's morality).[5]

Analytical philosophers working on Just War theory have, over the last twenty years, subjected this simple orthodoxy to radical scrutiny.[6] This has included normative challenges—such as disputing the view that *in bello* judgments can be made without reference to *ad bellum* standards, and questioning the validity of some candidate principles. It has also made possible an underlying structural challenge—that the principles governing resort to war apply throughout a conflict, such that each day that we take up arms, we must be sure that the *ad bellum* principles are satisfied. Even combatants whose side resorted to war justifiably might be contributing to an unjustified phase of their conflict, or to securing an unjustified objective.

Surprisingly, however, this implicit structural challenge has not translated into a wholesale critique or rejection of the categories of traditional Just War theory. We still divide our analyses into discussions of *jus ad bellum* and *jus in bello*, and we still commonly deploy the traditional principles—even when they have been convincingly demonstrated to collapse into one another. There is an

---

4. For an orthodox reading, see A. J. Coates, *The Ethics of War* (Manchester: Manchester University Press, 1997). For the history, Gregory M. Reichberg, Henrik Syse, and Endre Begby, *The Ethics of War: Classic and Contemporary Readings* (Oxford: Blackwell, 2006).

5. See, for example, Edward M. Kennedy, "Statement of Senator Edward M. Kennedy on Iraq," *Congressional Record—Senate* 153, no. 14 (July 17, 2007): 19290–19292. Also available at http://www.democraticunderground.com/discuss/duboard.php?az=view_all&address=389x1412463.

6. See especially Cécile Fabre, *Cosmopolitan War* (Oxford: Oxford University Press, 2012); Jeff McMahan, *Killing in War* (Oxford: Oxford University Press, 2009); David Rodin, *War and Self-Defense* (Oxford: Clarendon, 2002).

analytical inertia that ties us to this conceptual map, despite the many ways in which its shortcomings have been revealed.

One symptom of this inertia is that instead of subjecting the established categories to sustained critique and revision, we supplement their shortcomings by conceiving new categories on the same model. This is most noticeable in the literature on *jus post bellum*, in which philosophers commonly set about identifying principles analogous to those of *jus ad bellum* and *jus in bello*, to govern the aftermath of conflict.[7] And it is also a feature of the new literature on *jus ex bello*.

My goal in this section is not to criticize specific formulations of *jus ad bellum*, *jus in bello*, *jus ex bello* or *jus post bellum*. It is instead to push back against that conceptual inertia, and advance the revisionist project of the analytical turn, by asking just what philosophical purpose these categories serve—and whether there are any other distinctions to be drawn in the morality of war, which might be philosophically more significant.

My first proposal is that we should explicitly affirm that the categories of ad/in/ex/post are merely useful heuristic devices for directing our attention to a specific subject matter: they do not identify normatively significant and distinct sets of principles. To some degree, the category of Just War theory itself is the same: it directs our attention to evaluating the morality of a particular human practice: warfare. One way to think about the morality of war is to divide it up into sub-practices, and ask about the morality of each of those; and dividing the practice of warfare into sub-practices of initiating, fighting, and ending wars is a logical approach.[8] Of course, we could just as well divide up armed conflicts into different sub-practices—for example attack and defense; ceasefires and deterrence; direct attack and diversions. But initiation, conduct, and ending form a jointly exhaustive triad, and they are sufficiently distinct from one another that we cannot infer conclusions about one sub-practice from facts about the others. A war's being permissibly initiated, for example, does not entail it will be permissibly fought or ended; nor does impermissibility at the outset entail wrongdoing in prosecution and termination.[9] Practitioners and policy-makers forced to consider

---

7. E.g., Orend, "Jus Post Bellum."

8. My own view is that the aftermath of warfare takes us beyond the scope of Just War theory proper—indeed that it is wrong to look at war's aftermath through the Just War theory lens—but nothing rests on that here.

9. Some recent theorists of war's morality might initially dispute the latter observation—much of the revisionist critique of Walzerian Just War theory has been construed as an assault on just this thesis of the independence of prosecution from initiation (in Walzer's terms, one can fight an unjust war justly). However, few would deny that combatants in a war that was impermissibly initiated can sometimes find themselves contributing to a subsidiary just cause, such that they are prosecuting the war permissibly. See Fabre, *Cosmopolitan War*; McMahan, *Killing in*

the morality of an actual or potential war must clearly consider whether each of these sub-practices is permissible; and if they permissibly initiate, fight, and end their war, they can surely say that their war as a whole was permissible.

However, in the interests of avoiding conceptual confusion, the ad/in/ex triad should have no more substantive role in our account of war's morality. The principles governing initiation, conduct, or ending are not unique to their respective phase; nor do the contexts of starting, fighting, or ending wars give different valence or weights to principles that apply in other contexts.[10] This should be uncontroversial for most contemporary analytical Just War theorists. What we need to do now is to ask whether there are any more useful divisions that can be drawn in the just war landscape—ways of organizing our thinking that can shed more light than can a simple heuristic checklist. In particular, it will help to separate out conceptual distinctions that might otherwise be subsumed under the *ad bellum/in bello* distinction, but which are better considered independently. The first concerns the level of analysis at which we operate; the second is a contrast between different kinds of moral reason. I will discuss each in turn.

Let us stipulatively define warfare as mass conflict in which at least one side is an organized collective. This definition has two important features: first, its assumption that for conflict to count as war, it must pass a threshold of magnitude; second, its claim that at least one belligerent in war is an organized collective. This does not presuppose some controversial account of collective agency, or falsely imply that only states can fight wars. Instead it simply contrasts warfare and the conflict one might find in a Hobbesian state of nature, among disorganized aggregates of individuals—a "war" of all against all. This is a descriptively different phenomenon, and we do well not to assume that the principles governing Hobbesian anarchy are the same as those relevant to war proper.

Warfare's scale, and the organized, collective nature of at least some of the participants, are such that there is a stark division between the capacities of participating agents. Only a select cadre of political and military leaders has the power to determine whether a war as a whole will be initiated, fought, and ended. Subordinate commanders and individual combatants have the power to determine whether they participate, and perhaps whether those under their command

---

War; David Rodin and Henry Shue, introduction to *Just and Unjust Warriors: The Moral and Legal Status of Soldiers* (Oxford: Oxford University Press, 2008); Michael Walzer, *Just and Unjust Wars: A Moral Argument with Historical Illustrations* (New York: Basic Books, 2006).

10. In this respect, *jus ad bellum/in bello/ex bello* may be different from Just War theory, which one might think both engages unique moral principles, and gives its own valence and weight to principles that do apply outside of war. Showing this is a substantial project in its own right, however.

participate, but they can do little to influence whether the war as a whole begins, continues, or ends.

This means we should apply our Just War principles at two distinct levels of analysis. First, we can consider the war as a whole, as political and military leaders think of it, when deciding whether to initiate/continue/end a war.[11] Second, we can think of the actions and operations that constitute the war, as their relevant agents must think of them, given that they have the power only to control their own participation, and perhaps those under their command. Notice that political and military leaders will also have to make decisions about their own participation, and indeed about individual actions and operations. The difference is that they also get to make decisions governing the war as a whole. Notice also that the ability to make decisions governing the war as a whole is not simply attached to some office, but rather is contextually dependent. Situations might arise where some subordinate commander (or even, less plausibly, some individual combatant) can make a decision that decides the fate of the war as a whole. In such cases, while their rank might declare them subordinate, the circumstances render them more powerful than their purported leaders.

We can synecdochically label these different levels of analysis "Command Ethics" and "Combatant Ethics," respectively. Command Ethics governs the morality of war as a whole, Combatant Ethics governs the morality of specific actions and operations within the war. Command Ethics governs the war as a whole in two distinct senses. First, it can mean the whole war effort, construed in a forward-looking, or prospective sense, at a given point in time. This covers when political and military leaders must decide, at some given point in time, whether to initiate, continue, or end a war as a whole. But the "war as a whole" can also mean the whole war, construed diachronically from start to end. Thus we might say that, at some given point in the conflict, the political and military leaders of one belligerent were prospectively justified in fighting at the bar of Command Ethics, but that their war as a whole, construed from start to end from the perspective of history, was morally wrong. In this essay I focus on the synchronic sense of Command Ethics; the perspective of history is not, I think, as practically relevant.[12]

It might be tempting to use the *ad bellum/in bello* distinction to capture the same basic divide between analysis of the war as a whole and of individual actions and operations that compose it. But although it is undoubtedly convenient to

---

11. Notice that "the war as a whole" refers only to the war effort as pursued by one belligerent. It does not mean the war as a whole, including the war efforts of all belligerent parties.

12. Notice that the prospective/diachronic contrast cuts across the objective/subjective (or fact-relative/belief- or evidence-relative) contrast.

repurpose existing labels in this way, it is nonetheless conceptually confused. First, we cannot reduce the question of resort to war to the domain of Command Ethics. Each subordinate commander and individual combatant must also consider whether his own resort to war is justified—this is one of the central insights of revisionist Just War theory.[13] Second, we should not confine Command Ethics to focusing only on the *resort* to war. This is the key insight of theorists of *jus ex bello*, such as Rodin and Moellendorf.[14] The question of whether the war as a whole is justified must be answered not only when considering whether to initiate conflict but also continuously throughout. When the war as a whole is no longer justified, it must be brought to an end. The key distinction is between the levels of analysis at which we operate—the war as a whole, or its constituent actions and operations. We will only confuse matters by using categories that direct our attention to specific sub-practices within the practice of warfare.

Adopting this conceptual shift would be invaluable in clarifying one recent debate. Much has been written on the question of whether the *jus in bello* is independent of the *jus ad bellum*—whether one can fight permissibly in a war that was impermissibly begun.[15] The originally controversial, but now (at least among philosophers) orthodox view is that only those fighting for the side that satisfies *jus ad bellum* can fight permissibly; if your side went to war impermissibly, then no matter how scrupulously you seek to observe the standards of justified conduct, all of your actions are condemned.

Throughout this discussion, however, it has been recognized that his side having permissibly *initiated* a conflict is not directly relevant to the permissibility of a combatant's actions now. More relevant is whether he is fighting for a side whose war as a whole is permissible *now*, and that is not determined by whether the war as a whole was permissibly initiated. That his side started the war permissibly is undoubtedly a good thing, and may be evidence that its war as a whole is now permissible, but there may be countervailing factors—perhaps the war began in legitimate national defense, but its goals have now expanded to include territorial aggression; or perhaps it appeared proportionate at the outset, but now we know that the suffering it will cause is simply too high. Indeed, whether the combatant's actions are permissible does not even depend on whether the war as a whole is justified, right now. For, even if the war as a whole is permissible, the combatant's action might serve some subordinate objective that renders it impermissible;

---

13. See especially Fabre, *Cosmopolitan War*; McMahan, *Killing in War*; David Rodin and Henry Shue, eds., *Just and Unjust Warriors*.

14. Darrel Moellendorf, "Jus Ex Bello," *Journal of Political Philosophy* 16 (2008): 123–36; Rodin, "Two Emerging Issues."

15. For example, Rodin and Shue, *Just and Unjust Warriors*.

and even if the war as a whole is impermissible, the combatant's actions might serve a subordinate objective that renders it permissible. None of this is controversial among revisionist Just War theorists. And yet the debate is still framed as though it were about the dependence of *jus in bello* on *jus ad bellum*. But when we get our concepts clear, we see that the proclamation that compliance with *jus in bello* is dependent on compliance with *jus ad bellum* is as unhelpful as the contrary thesis, defended by Michael Walzer, that the *jus ad bellum* and *jus in bello* are independent of each other.[16] Certainly, sometimes the fact that one's side impermissibly initiated the conflict, combined with the fact that one's actions contribute to that impermissible whole, will entail that one cannot fight permissibly. But there are other cases where what matters is not whether the war was permissibly begun, but whether it is permissible, as a whole, *now*, and others still where the evaluation of the war as a whole is irrelevant to the evaluation of this particular action—where Combatant Ethics is wholly independent from Command Ethics—because the action contributes to a subordinate aim whose justification does not depend on the status of the war as a whole. The real insight of Walzer's critics is that the justification of combatants' use of force in war (the topic of Combatant Ethics) is inseparable from the outcomes to which that use of force contributes. This is only obscured by retaining Walzer's *ad bellum/in bello* distinction.

The interplay between Combatant and Command Ethics is a rich seam for mining insights into the morality of war, but I will comment on just one more before turning to another important, but often overlooked, distinction. One set of particularly interesting questions concerns how to understand necessity and proportionality in wartime. Both constraints are structured around the consequences realized by an action. But should the salient consequences be only those that are causally attributed to the specific action or operation, or should they be tied into the consequences of the whole military endeavor of which that action is part? Some operations might fail to satisfy necessity, for example, when considered in isolation, but might satisfy a collective necessity standard, as applied to the war as a whole. Conversely, in other cases each operation might satisfy necessity, but the war as a whole might fail to do so.

In other areas of morality and practical reason we typically recognize a contrast between positive, justifying reasons on the one hand, and negative reasons, or constraints, on the other. Positive practical reasons count in favor of an action, while negative reasons count against. The absence of a negative reason—its failure to apply—can be a necessary condition for permissibility, but does not count

---

16. Walzer, *Just and Unjust Wars*, 21.

in favor of the action being evaluated. Consider, for example, the action "drive to work." A negative reason against doing so is my lacking a driver's license. Indeed, arguably it is a necessary condition of my permissibly driving to work that I should possess a license. Nonetheless, the fact that I have one gives me no positive reason to drive to work—it does not count in favor of my doing so.

As with the contrast between Command and Combatant Ethics, one might again be tempted to use the *ad bellum/in bello* contrast to draw out this distinction between justifying reasons and constraints. The *jus ad bellum* might be taken to govern what justifies going to war, while the *jus in bello* would govern how one may fight a war that is justified. Again, this way lies only confusion. Restricting the category of justifying reasons to those that apply to the resort to war, and that of constraints to those that apply to the conduct of war, ignores the fact that there are clearly both positive reasons and constraints that apply both to the evaluation of the war as a whole and to that of particular actions within the war. Indeed, sometimes the same reasons apply: the necessity constraint applies both to particular actions within the war and to the war as a whole, for example.

Properly separated from the *ad bellum/in bello* distinction, the contrast between justifying reasons and constraints can help shed further light on the central controversies in contemporary Just War theory. As noted above, one of the revisionists' main contentions has been that soldiers fighting a war that did not satisfy *jus ad bellum* cannot now fight in accordance with *jus in bello*.[17] There is an asymmetry between just and unjust combatants (where that means, respectively, combatants on the side that satisfied *jus ad bellum*, and combatants on the side that did not satisfy *jus ad bellum*). But if we analyze the moral reasons facing combatants into justifying reasons and constraints, this conclusion (that unjust combatants cannot fight in accordance with the *jus in bello*) might need to be modified. It is quite possible that there are constraints on the actions and operations taken by combatants that can be satisfied even by those who lack sufficient justifying reasons to render their conduct permissible. For example, the principle of noncombatant immunity holds that combatants ought not to intentionally attack noncombatants. Recognizing the symmetrical application of a constraint such as this is consistent with arguing that, in Combatant Ethics, unless your actions contribute to an objective that gives sufficient justifying reasons for the harm that you do, you cannot fight permissibly.

There is a place in contemporary Just War theory for the concepts of *jus ad bellum*, *jus in bello*, and *jus ex bello*, but that place is limited. They usefully direct our attention to the specific sub-practices that compose the practice of warfare.

---

17. For example, McMahan, *Killing in War*, 15.

These sub-practices raise distinct questions, which can be answered independently. We should allow them no grander role than this, however; when seeking to structure our thinking about the morality of war, instead of using *jus ad bellum* and *jus in bello* as placeholders for more fundamental conceptual divisions, we should focus on those divisions themselves—such as that between the war as a whole and its constituent parts, and that between justifying reasons and constraints. But these are just examples—a first attempt to rethink the structure of Just War theory from first principles. We need contemporary Just War theorists to direct the same critical attention that they have trained on Just War theory's central normative precepts onto the structure that it presupposes. If doing so vindicates the traditional categories, then we have vindicated a grand tradition; if it does not, then we will have slipped its shackles.

II. Just Negotiation

Warfare is the use of organized mass violence to compel an adversary to make political, territorial, human, or economic concessions. Its violence and coercion are inherent. But violence is not the only means by which belligerents seek to draw concessions from one another, and coercion is not the only tool in hand. Wars are also structured, from beginning to end, by negotiations and the option of negotiating. When starting, fighting, and indeed ending wars, the possibility of negotiation plays a crucial role in calculations of necessity. If the option of negotiation is available, then fighting is permissible only if the marginal moral costs are justified by the marginal moral benefits. This delivers the traditional Just War principle of last resort, but it is also salient for the prosecution of wars, when negotiation of ceasefires, truces, and other constraints are utterly crucial. And of course unless one side's predominance allows it to impose an unconditional surrender, peace after war will always be based on negotiation.

My goal in this section is to start the process of thinking through principles for just negotiation in war. Negotiation is almost as integral to warfare as the use of mass violence ("almost," because a war without any negotiation is possible, though these days unlikely), and the silence of contemporary Just War theory on this topic is an important omission. I will proceed by identifying what I take to be the normative underpinnings of just negotiation, before setting out a preliminary discussion of some plausible principles. First, however, it is important to address skeptics who might think the project doomed from the outset.

Few will deny that, outside of war, the practice of negotiation is governed by norms. Some will think that these norms should be thinly conceived—we should not strengthen our hand by either force or fraud. Others will propose much thicker norms—we should offer only terms that we would accept if we did not know which side of the deal we would end up on. But in war, some forms of force and fraud are the basic tools of military strategy, while enemies are unlikely to be inclined to imagine themselves in the adversary's position. Is it perhaps unrealistic, or even inconsistent, to expect negotiators in military contexts to observe similar constraints?

Moreover, our standard means of thinking through the ethics of negotiation typically presuppose that the negotiating parties start out from a morally neutral standpoint. But in war this is obviously not always the case. Often one of the parties will have been fighting impermissibly; often they all will. Negotiations among them might look like agreements reached among Mafiosi, or between good guys and bad.

These are undoubtedly reasons for caution, and also to regard the constraints of just negotiation as overridable. But there remain powerful normative foundations for a set of principles of just negotiation, and the principles themselves have strong intuitive appeal. I will focus on three distinct normative foundations for just negotiation, focused on trust, vulnerability, and the natural law principle that *ex injuria jus non oritur*.

The first point is simple. The suffering, destruction, and wrongdoing endemic to war cannot be overstated. Minimizing that suffering, destruction, and wrongdoing is a crucial imperative. It is not the only imperative—sometimes it can be overridden—but it is obviously and profoundly important. Unless on the annihilation of one side, peace must be based on negotiation. And for negotiation to succeed, it is necessary for the opposing belligerents to attain a minimal degree of trust in one another. This is true both of political leaders and of combatants; obviously unless compelled by force, the leaders will not accept or adhere to agreements unless they trust each other. And whatever their political leaders agree to, combatants will lay down their arms only if they can do so safely, without leaving themselves or their communities vulnerable to lethal threats or persecution. We should not be overambitious. Our goal is not to forge out of warfare a deep communion between the former adversaries. We are aiming only at that minimal quantum of trust that allows you to turn your back on your enemy without believing he will strike when you do. Even this much trust can make peace possible. We achieve and sustain this trust by adhering to the principles of just negotiation.

Peace depends on trust, trust depends on good faith. To invite and then betray this trust is perfidious, a sign of bad faith, and a sin against peace. There are powerful consequentialist objections to perfidy—it undermines peace not only now but also in the future. International law condemns *in bello* perfidy so roundly because it threatens to undermine the whole system of normative regulation of armed conflict. If some people abuse these norms to their own advantage— "inviting the confidence of an adversary to lead him to believe that he is entitled to, or is obliged to accord, protection under the rules of international law applicable in armed conflict, with intent to betray that confidence"[18]—they undermine the trust and reciprocity on which the system of regulation is based. The same goes double for perfidy in war termination: if some states and combatants abuse the trust that defeated states and combatants show in them, others will learn their lessons, and fight until annihilated. Why accept peace terms when you can't trust your adversary to observe them? Perfidy in war termination undermines not only a particular peace, but the prospect of peace after war in general.

But the wrong of perfidy, and the countervailing importance of good faith, are not reducible to their bad consequences. Lying and breaking promises are ordinarily wrong, but in some cases more wrongful than in others. When one contracting party is, through their contract, especially vulnerable to the other, relying on the other's good faith to preserve them against weighty harms, then breaching the contract is especially invidious.[19] To expose themselves so severely is to make a great leap of faith, so there is a lot of trust to betray. These vulnerabilities generate responsibilities: when others are vulnerable to my actions, I need to take care not to inflict undue harm, and not to take advantage of their vulnerability. Again, adhering to the principles of just negotiation is a means of avoiding exploiting the vulnerability that inevitably attends seeking a negotiated end to a violent conflict.

Finally, ending war means creating a new territorial and political settlement. The underlying principle governing the terms that can legitimately be sought is that right cannot arise out of injustice: the operating objective of warfare should be to restore rights that were justly held before the war, not to create new rights.

Together, these normative underpinnings push back against the skepticism voiced above. However great the differences between negotiations in wartime and practices of negotiation in other contexts, and however deep the adversaries' commitment to thwarting their foes, there must be constraints on how we negotiate, because without those constraints, we cannot engender the trust necessary to secure peace without outright victory; we will exploit our adversaries' vulnerabilities, and make them regret the risk they took in coming to the negotiating table; and we will propagate territorial and political settlements that have their roots in injustice. Undoubtedly these reasons together do not ground absolute constraints on just negotiation, but they do seem sufficient to reject the thesis that, in this area of the practice of warfare, Just War theory is uniquely silent.

---

18. Article 37.1 of additional protocol I, part III, section I in Adam Roberts and Richard Guelff, *Documents on the Laws of War* (Oxford: Oxford University Press, 2000), 442.

19. Compare Robert E. Goodin, *Protecting the Vulnerable: A Reanalysis of Our Social Responsibilities* (Chicago: University of Chicago Press, 1985).

Assuming the success of the foregoing argument, what principles govern negotiation in war? Full discussion of these is beyond the scope of this essay, but at least four immediately suggest themselves: first, "good faith," which governs the spirit with which negotiations are begun and carried out; second, "safe quarter," which focuses on the safety of the participants during negotiation; third, "no new rights" constrains the terms that can be sought and legitimately agreed on; and finally "compliance" governs adherence to negotiated agreements. I will discuss each briefly in turn.

The idea of good faith[20] is that you should enter negotiations because you intend to achieve a fair peace, not because you intend to use the process as a means of securing military advantage. It is a necessary condition of the parties to a negotiation trusting each other that each believes that the other is negotiating in good faith. But negotiating in good faith also inevitably renders you vulnerable to the adversary; hence their negotiating in bad faith not only undermines trust but also exploits your vulnerability.

Safe quarter means not harming the negotiators. If belligerents cannot trust their adversaries to respect the special status of peace negotiations, then few wars will end short of outright defeat for one side. This would obviously be calamitous. To offer the adversary's negotiators protection, only then to kill them, is perfidy in the classic sense, and an intrinsically execrable betrayal of trust and vulnerability.

The principle that victory in war can ground no new rights constrains the terms that can legitimately be demanded of the adversary. It reflects the contemporary view that warfare must only ever be a means to defend preexisting entitlements, not to establish new ones. Classical Just War theorists often had a quite different view. For example, Grotius argued that "any one whatever, engaged in regular and formal war, becomes absolute proprietor of every thing which he takes from the enemy: so that all nations respect his title."[21] Provided you can enclose or secure the stolen land with permanent fortifications, or hold the captured vessels in dock for twenty-four hours, you are entitled to keep whatever territory you can seize.[22] Political power comes with territorial control: "by conquest, a prince succeeds to all the rights of the conquered sovereign or state; and if it be a commonwealth, he acquires all the rights and privileges, which the people

---

20. My discussion of good faith draws on Hugo Grotius, *The Rights of War and Peace: Including the Law of Nature and of Nations* (Westport, Conn: Hyperion Press, 1979), 3.XIX–XX.

21. Ibid., 3.VI.ii. In these chapters Grotius describes what justice permits in the termination of conflict; he later advocates moderation on grounds of charity. That said, he still affirms that bare possession of territory after war is a sufficient grounds for retaining it (3.XX.xii).

22. Ibid., 3.VI.iv.

possessed."[23] And of course with territorial control and political power come entitlements to booty, in particular to pay for the services of professional soldiers: "as a compensation for this loss of time, and this personal danger, it is but reasonable they should have a share of the spoils."[24]

This view of war termination is remarkably indifferent both to the perverse incentives it creates, and to the great moral tragedy of war. Warfare cannot be a ground for new entitlements. Wars not only involve untold suffering but they are also imbued with wrongdoing and injustice. There is no way to fight a morally pure war, in which all the suffering we inflict is regrettable, but not wrongful. Warfare is an unavoidably and massively duty-breaching, rights-violating endeavor.[25] These duties may only be breached when other, stronger duties override them; rights may only be violated to prevent imminent violations of proportionately serious rights. Victory in war may not be used to ground new rights, but only to defend, or to enforce, those we already have.

This principle constrains justified and unjustified belligerents with equal force. Obviously unjustified belligerents are not entitled to demand the spoils of their military aggression; but even a justified belligerent may not use victory for territorial expansion or resource extraction, or interference in the political arrangements of the defeated adversary that is not warranted by the necessity principle.

---

23. Ibid., 3.VIII.

24. Ibid., 3.VI.xiv.

25. In his essay for this volume, Richard Arneson takes issue with my earlier defense of this thesis (Seth Lazar, "The Responsibility Dilemma for *Killing in War*: A Review Essay." *Philosophy and Public Affairs* 38 (2010): 180–213). I address several arguments similar to Arneson's in my reply to Strawser and McMahan, "Liability and the Ethics of War," in *The Ethics of Self-Defense*, ed. Christian Coons and Michael Weber (New York: Oxford University Press, 2016), 292–304. For present purposes, suffice it to note that Arneson ultimately agrees with my claim that lesser evil justifications have a much greater role to play in the ethics of war than McMahan and others typically allow:

> Perhaps the crucial reason why it is morally permissible to attack and kill enemy soldiers when they are prosecuting an unjust war and one is fighting for a just cause in opposing them is that killing enemy soldiers in these circumstances makes a contribution to winning the just war, and in the case at hand, the moral stakes in this conflict are very high. The crucial point is not that the enemy soldiers have made themselves liable to be killed but that their right not to be killed is overridden by the bad consequences of respecting their right.

I entirely agree with this view: it is the kind of position I imagined when I wrote about "rejecting the ideal of the rights-respecting war" (p. 213 of that essay). I also agree with Arneson's footnote 17, in which he observes that the revisionist take on the ethics of war leaves less standing in the conventional morality of war than McMahan and others have claimed.

What about if the conflict unavoidably leads to the collapse of one side's institutions of governance, or if the collapse of those institutions precipitated the conflict—does that not generate a right, even perhaps an obligation on the part of the victor, to fill the power vacuum? It does not. The right to govern themselves remains with the individuals whose government has fallen. The victors and the international community might have an obligation to help rebuild the institutions necessary for legitimate governance, which might entail limited rights to govern in the interim, but they are rights held in trust, and for a limited period only.

What about rights to compensation—are these not new entitlements grounded in the war? Focusing on compensation after war is probably a bad way to direct limited resources. However, even where compensation is justified, this right is not grounded in victory at war. The very idea of compensation is that something to which one had a right before the war has been damaged or destroyed, and the other party has a duty to make good that loss, and restore you to the status quo ante. What grounds your right to compensation is the antecedent right that was violated in war.

What if the objective of the conflict is to secure rights that were not respected before—for example, self-governance that had hitherto been frustrated by a colonial power? This too should not be viewed as a right grounded in victory in war, but as the realization of a right that was frustrated by the enemy, giving rise to the war. If there are justified wars of national liberation, then the rights that they result in are not the product of the victorious war, but were its cause.

What if an unjust aggressor has succeeded in capturing territory, and will accept peace only if their entitlement over that territory is accepted by the defeated party, and indeed the international community? Grotius argued that "solemn war" gives "validity to every promise, which may be conducive to its termination, so that if either party, through an ill-grounded fear of further calamities, has, even against his will, made promises unfavourable, or acceded to terms disadvantageous to himself, such an engagement will be binding." The reason being that if belligerent powers were not entitled to "alarm each other…into submission upon the most unequal terms," "wars, which are so frequent, could never have been brought to a conclusion, an object so much for the interest of mankind." While I agree that even unfavorable terms must sometimes be accepted, and adhered to—the principle of compliance demands that much—I reject Grotius's belief that states are entitled to use military leverage to impose whatever terms they choose. But this is because I deny Grotius's further belief that warfare is a legitimate means of establishing new entitlements over, for example, territory and resources. Thus I think the terms that can be offered to a defeated party are constrained by this "no new rights" principle, so they should never be in a position where they have to accede and adhere to an entirely unpalatable peace treaty.[26]

Of course, in practice unjustified belligerents will habitually demand recognition of political and territorial gains to which they are not entitled. They would therefore be compounding their wrongful war with wrongful negotiation—since they were prepared to kill without justification, it is hardly surprising that they would negotiate in the same way. But the fact that the constraint is often ignored is not evidence that it does not apply—it merely indicates another dimension of the unjustified belligerents' wrongdoing.[27]

One might complain that contemporary territorial and political boundaries were themselves almost all forged in injustice—does my principle mean that none of these can be viewed as legitimate? Clearly not; but the entitlement is not grounded in the unjust acts through which those borders were established, but rather in the subsequent history and the character of the institutions developed thereon. There is a statute of limitations on the injustices that grounded contemporary states' institutions, which mean that their subsequent history can legitimate unjust beginnings. This does not mean, however, that those beginnings were not unjust, or that these histories can be used as a model for future state-building.

What if two states went to war over previously unoccupied land—following the discovery of a habitable planet, for example, to which no people have any prior entitlement? Does not victory in this case ground rights to control the conquered territory? Perhaps the claim that victory in war cannot ground new rights results from the contingent fact that, in the world as it actually is, all territory has already been claimed by some state. But if there were some terra nova, could we acquire rights to it through conquest of competing claimants? I think we could not. To each according to his threat advantage, as Rawls noted, is not a plausible principle of justice, and is not a plausible principle for the allocation of "manna from heaven," as this terra nova would be. This is clear enough in interpersonal cases. Suppose an indivisible chunk of manna falls from the skies, and lands between you and me. We then jointly initiate a fight, which I win. My victory does not ground a right to that manna. Prima facie, each of us is no more or less entitled to the manna after the fight than before. Perhaps, if you attacked me, when I was offering a fair decision procedure (that we toss a coin, say), then your aggression might mean you lose your claim to some chance of getting the manna. But then

---

26. Grotius, *The Rights of War and Peace*, 3.IXX.xi.

27. As David Rodin notes, this means that there is often something morally problematic about a negotiated end to armed conflict, since it allows unjustified belligerents to make use of advantages wrongly gained. See Rodin, "The War Trap: Dilemmas of *Jus Terminatio*," *Ethics* 125 (2015): 674–95.

the ground of my claim to it would not be my victory in the fight with you. Rather, by attacking me, the only other person with any antecedent claim on the manna lost that claim. If there were a third person who could receive the manna, who neither attacked nor defended me, but was a bystander to our fight, then she and I would have equal claims to the manna when you are defeated.

Of course, interpersonal analogies cannot be applied to interstate conflicts without critique, but equally we need some reason why these basic insights should be thought false at the international level. It is undoubtedly true that the prudential logic of international affairs means that sometimes other states have to recognize legal rights to territory acquired through conquest. But these are legal rights only; any moral rights are acquired only through the passage of time, and the legitimate expectations of the inhabitants.

The final principle is compliance; this is the mirror image of good faith. Good faith is about acting with the intention of reaching a legitimate peace settlement, and compliance is about adhering to the settlement. It is necessary for trust, and to avoid exploiting the vulnerability of the other party to the deal. The duty to comply, however, is grounded in a principle of reciprocity: if the adversary breaches the terms of the peace agreement, and acting in kind satisfies the necessity constraint, then the duty to comply no longer applies.

Conclusion

The recent focus on the termination of armed conflict can yield valuable results for Just War theory. The introduction of *jus ex bello* is the least significant of those, however; indeed the whole system of dividing the field into these prepositional subdomains, while useful as a heuristic for practitioners and policy-makers, too often obscures the more fundamental divisions that make up the structure of Just War theory. Two important contrasts are, first, between the levels of analysis at which our evaluation is applied—whether to the war as a whole, or to individual actions and operations within the war—which I call the difference between Command Ethics and Combatant Ethics. And second, between the positive justifying reasons that count in favor of fighting, and the constraints that must either be satisfied or overridden for fighting to be permissible. The real fruit of the new focus on war termination is not the introduction of more Latin into Just War theory, but revelation of the need to supplement our existing Just War principles with norms to govern the negotiations that structure war's endings.

12 MORAL RECOVERY AFTER WAR

THE ROLE OF HOPE

Nancy Sherman

I. Two Faces of Hope

Returning service members often carry the weight of their war in messy moral emotions that are hard to process and sometimes hard to feel. Some of these emotions can get sidelined in clinical discussions of posttraumatic stress (PTS),[1] when the stressor is narrowed to exposure to life threats in the face of unpredictable danger, and symptoms are streamlined to hyper-vigilance, numbing, and flashbacks.[2] The examples of this kind of PTS are familiar, real, and sometimes harrowing. They are a reminder of soldiers' exquisitely honed reflexes and observational skills highly adaptive in war, but often maladaptive at home: soldiers still on hyper-alert can run to take cover at sudden loud noises or swerve fast off the road to avoid surface irregularities that downrange mark implanted bombs; some, good at compartmentalizing for mission focus,

---

1. There has been a push within some sectors of the military to remove the "D" for "disorder" in PTSD—in order to destigmatize the phenomena. (Amputees, after all, suffer limb injuries, not leg disorders.) According to a 2008 RAND study nearly 20 percent of Iraq and Afghanistan veterans screened positive for PTSD. (Tanielian and Jaycox 2008)

A summary critique of epidemiological studies, from the National Center for PTSD, put the figure in 2008 closer to 10–18 percent, http://www.ptsd.va .gov/professional/newsletters/research-quarterly/V20N1.pdf, accessed June 14, 2013.

The Department of Veterans Affairs recently released a report showing that 30 percent of the Iraq and Afghanistan veterans treated at the VA hospitals and clinics have been diagnosed with PTSD. See http://www.publichealth.va.gov/docs/ epidemiology/ptsd-report-fy2012-qtr3.pdf, accessed June 14, 2013. Also, http:// www.thedailybeast.com/articles/2012/10/21/nearly-30-of-vets-treated-by-v-a-have-ptsd.html, accessed June 14, 2013.

2. For an important, now classic study of PTSD, see Herman 1992.

do the same at home, withdrawing from family and friends, feeling safe only with battle buddies who have lived and breathed their war; others return to the pitch of the battlefield in flashbacks that smell, sound, and feel like the real thing, and that can unleash real and lethal aggression. As one senior military psychiatrist, Charles Hoge, puts it, "Under prolonged stress, the stress 'thermostat' is reset."[3] Recalibrating the physio-psychic thermostat back to what is conducive to healthy living in a peaceful civilian environment can be for some no small challenge, even if for many the transition is without trauma.

But the idea of resetting thermostats is limiting. In recent years, a number of military psychological researchers and clinicians have pressed to expand the clinical focus and recognize the prevalence and distinctiveness of a dimension of psychological stress that is *moral*—hence the notion of "moral injury" and its emotions and interventions.[4] Some argue that prolonged exposure techniques standardly used to desensitize and extinguish fear responses may have little effect in addressing crippling moral doubt or survivor guilt.

Still what often goes unremarked in that research is the ubiquity (and, sometimes, naturalness, fit, and commingling) of moral emotions such as guilt, shame, resentment, disappointment, empathy, trust, and hope *outside* the clinical arena. These can be a part of healthy processing of war, and part and parcel of ordinary practices of holding persons responsible.

Though this is not a traditional subject for philosophers of war (whose primary focus remains on justification of norms of war), it is, of course, a standard focus in philosophical moral psychology, notably in work begun by P. F. Strawson in his classic study of reactive attitudes, and in a literature that has followed and is growing.[5] Strawson's seminal idea is that reactive attitudes are constitutive of moral responsibility, and not a side effect of some independent, underlying belief in responsibility.[6]

With 2.4 million US service members returning from a decade of war in which many have served long, multiple deployments in complex and challenging

---

3. Hoge 2010, xiv.

4. See especially Litz, Stein, Delaney, Lebowitz, Nash, Silva, and Maguen 2009; Maguen and Litz 2012; Nash, Krantz, Stein, Westphal, and Litz 2011; Shay 1994, 2002; and Lansky 1995, 2003a, 2003b, 2004, 2005, 2007, 2009.

5. Strawson 1993; Watson 2004; especially "Responsibility and the Limits of Evil: Variations on a Strawsonian Theme" in Wallace 1996; Darwall 2006; Walker 2006; Macnamara 2011; Hurley and Macnamara 2010; Martin 2008, 2010, 2011; and Smith 2005.

6. Watson 2004, 220. Earlier moral psychologies, like Aristotle's, standardly link certain emotions, such as resentment or shame, with blame, and so with moral responsibility for attitude and conduct, but not in the radical way that Strawson does. See Aristotle (1984) *Nicomachean Ethics* (hereafter NE) II.7 (1108b1), NE III.1 *Rhetoric* (hereafter Rh). II.2, II.6, II.9.

partnerships, a philosophical discussion of reactive attitudes toward self and others in the context of war is timely. Even if not a part of military ethics per se, it is certainly a part of ethics relevant to the military. And that the issues span more general concerns in moral psychology is a welcome way of bringing the moral psychology of soldiering into more mainstream philosophical discussion.

My broad interest in this essay is moral repair, loosely understood as building up healthy moral relationships within self and with others, after war.[7] More specifically, here, I consider hope in persons (inter- and intrapersonal) as a distinct kind of moral attitude that focuses our attention and energies on pockets of good will in self or others, and on occasions for aspiration and investment.[8] As such, it opposes indifference, and too, tendencies toward numbing that can go hand and hand with the harboring of deep suspicion and distrust. This kind of hope is paradigmatically forward-looking, and plays an important role, I suggest, in social and intrapsychic moral reintegration after war. But I am also interested in hope for outcomes, and the kind of agency it can involve, and how the two kinds of hope support each other.

II. Defiant Hope

I want to set the tone and begin to explore the contours of hope with an example that is from war, but is not about its combatants. The example draws from the documentary movie *Defiant Requiem*, about the Nazi camp of Terezin (in Theresienstadt, outside Prague), and the Jewish inmates singing for their life through performances of Verdi's *Requiem*. The movie documents conductor Murry Sidlin's recreation of that *Requiem* recently in the extant walls of Terezin.[9]

As is well known, many of the inmates at Terezin were accomplished artists and musicians, performers, conductors, and composers. And one, Raphael Schächter, a talented pianist and opera-choral conductor, captured by the Nazis in 1941, brought with him just one piece of music, Giuseppe Verdi's demanding chorale work, his 1874 *Requiem*. During the internment and with some complicity of the guards, the prisoners gathered nightly in the dank basement of the compound,

---

7. For further development of the emotions of moral injury and repair after war, see, my recent book, *Afterwar: Healing the Moral Wounds of our Soldiers* (Sherman 2015). For related essays, see the discussion of self-empathy in Sherman 2014a and Sherman, 2016; of subjective guilt in Sherman 2010, especially, chap. 4; and Sherman 2013; of trust and self-trust, in Sherman 2014b.

8. In thinking about hope, I am indebted to conversation with Adrienne Martin, especially with regard to Martin 2013. For other work on hope that has influenced my thought, see Margaret Urban Walker (Walker 2006), Jonathan Lear (Lear 2006), and Philip Pettit (Pettit 2004).

9. http://www.defiantrequiemfilm.com, accessed September 8, 2013. I attended a showing of the film at the Washington Jewish Community Center, May 6, 2013, after which Murry Sidlin spoke.

around a piano, and learned the complicated choral parts of the Latin requiem, with Schächter holding the only copy of the score. They sang, with hope against hope, to change minds, to have the Nazi leadership hear the humanity of their voices and rescind their death sentence. That hope became increasingly futile, as one death train after another rounded up Jews and took them onto death marches or Auschwitz. And when that happened, they would reconstitute their chorus, over and over, with winnowing and frail population, and repeat the defiant act of hope. The Nazi brass eventually did come to hear the chorus in a culminating performance on June 23, 1944; it was entertainment for them, but for the singers and Schächter it was survival of the soul. And as Sidlin implied in remarks at a showing of the documentary in Washington, D.C., the refrain in the *Requiem*, "*Dies Irae*," that the "day of wrath" would come, was ironically for these Jews, unpracticed in the rituals of Latin masses, a moral protest that they could deliver face to face to their torturers, concealed through art. It was their retribution.

But singing the *Requiem* also expressed their hope. And hope with two interrelated facets. The prisoners sang to express hope *for* a future outcome or eventuality—to be saved, rescued, and redeemed, whether by God's hand or human hand. And that hoped for outcome nourished some as food, despite desperate hunger, as one survivor of the chorus recalled. Singing to be saved brought back to life near-corpses.

But another aspect of their hope, far more galvanizing, I suspect, was the hope they had *in* one another and the aspirations they placed *in* their humanity. By singing together, after backbreaking days of labor and beaten servitude, they raised their voices and followed an extremely complex musical score. They worked on their parts, put them to memory, and saw mirrored in one another high humanity. They kindled hope in one another and in themselves, in their potential to rise above the most subjugating circumstances and to not just survive, but to thrive, in a sliver of a way, for a sliver of time, as artistic and spiritual souls. In the very act of choral singing, in answering a soloist's vocal call with responses and intricate recants, they reciprocally *addressed* and *recognized* one another, and in this context, *acknowledged* one another's hope in humanity. Moral address was woven in the interaction and communicated as part of the choral activity. Perhaps, too, they had hope *in* the Nazi leadership that their art would awaken their own humanity. But I can't imagine that this energized as much as the reciprocal hope they placed in one another, a calling out to each (through music) of the potential of the other's humanity, and an echoing back, in acknowledgment, that she has been appropriately recognized. Singing Verdi's *Requiem* to one another, night after night, was an act of defiance, but also an act of resilience, a way of being buoyed by a commonwealth of humanity, at work in recreating a piece that must have been appreciated by the performers as itself an exquisitely fine and noble expression of humanity.

This is a powerful example of the promise of interpersonal hope, even in futile conditions. Hope can be about eventualities—"non-normative hope," following Adrienne Martin's usage; but it can also be about aspirations we hold on behalf of persons—"normative hope," as she calls it. And in some cases, though not all, part of the point of addressing others with hope is that the recipients might take up the values or principles deemed worthwhile and aspired for on their behalf. Thus, on my view, hopefulness is not an optimistic temperament or behaviorally trained positive attitude, but a desire for what we believe are uncertain outcomes where that hopefulness gives us a certain cognitive resolve to put projects and plans in place (in the case of non-normative hope), or a normative, aspiring attitude with regard to worthwhile ends we set for ourselves or others (in the case of normative hope). Hope can serve as a "scaffold" for normative change.

Aristotle makes clear this last point at the beginning of the *Nicomachean Ethics*. His remarks also go some way toward showing the intermingling of normative and non-normative hope. He reminds us that we don't accurately attribute happiness (*eudaimonia*) to a child, but in calling him "happy," invest hope in him that he will become that:

> It is natural, then, that we call neither ox nor horse nor any other of the animals happy; for none of them is capable of sharing in such activity [of reason and its excellences]. For this reason also a boy is not happy (*eudaimōn*); for he is not yet capable of such acts, owing to his age; and boys who are called happy are being deemed happy by reason of the hopes (*dia tēn elpida*) we have for them.[10]

Calling the child "happy" *misattributes* to him the developed rational capacities requisite for character excellence (or virtue) and which, when exercised properly, with the experience of years and adequate external goods, constitute happiness. But the misattribution can be pedagogical: "deeming" or "congratulating" the child as happy sets a goal worth aspiring toward and begins to "bootstrap" (or "scaffold") the requisite development and behavior for it. It gives the child "a job" and the parents a job, and encourages a two-way set of emotion-inflected behaviors that will communicate assessments in making progress on that job. Hope and disappointment, the parent's and the child's own, and in turn, responses to each

---

10. NE I.10 1099b33-1100a3, using revised Oxford translation throughout, with slight alteration here, changing "being congratulated" to "being deemed."

other's reactive uptakes and "updates"[11] in the face of various interim goals, will populate the path. These are back and forth volleys—mirrorings and challengings—that are the familiar stuff of interpersonal engagement from childhood up.[12]

Given that hope for happiness in Aristotle's lexicon is not just hope for successful outcome (to conceive of happiness that way would be "a very defective arrangement," he insists, that would mistakenly "entrust to chance what is greatest and most noble"),[13] the hope he points to here is *primarily* normative—that is, hope *in* the child that he will undertake the right "kind of study and care," as Aristotle puts it, requisite for realizing a flourishing and happy life.[14] To be sure, the Stoics will "call" Aristotle on just this point, arguing that he has fudged on the issue and still left too much to externals and luck.[15] Virtue is sufficient for happiness, they insist, following Socrates. There is something to this charge, and perhaps, for our purposes, what it shows is that *hope for* happiness, for an Aristotelian and probably for most of us, slides between *hope in* one's agency and reason (and that of others), and *hope for* a hospitable world in which we exercise our individual and shared agency. Normative and non-normative hope mix and mingle. The point is a familiar one, especially in war. Good commanders place express hope in their troops, that they will embrace the rules of engagement and the skill bases necessary for good and just fighting. But they also hope that they will *fare well* in addition to *do well.* And the wisest among them will hope that in doing well, they will have the resources to accept *and* internalize judicious discriminations of responsibility.[16]

With this as background, I want to continue with the following topics.

In section III, I consider non-normative hope through a soldier's narrative. This kind of hope has an obvious role in moral repair, and important connections with hope in persons. In section IV I return to hope in persons—normative hope—exploring the kind of moral address involved, with interviews from soldiers providing the central cases. In section V, I turn to hope in self, with focus on a Marine spouse's hope in her husband and its role in bootstrapping his hope in himself.

---

11. I thank Trip Glazer for this term.

12. For patterns of attunement and misattunement between child and caregiver, see Stern 1985.

13. NE 1099b22.

14. NE 1099b18.

15. For further discussion of Stoic positions, see Sherman 2005.

16. This is not to suggest that such line drawing is ever easy or intuitive. For notions of responsibility in the context of balancing risks in force protection and protection of noncombatants, see Luban 2014. He suggests the plausibility of a strict liability view of accepting risks (and hence, acquiring responsibility) in cases where soldiers cause danger to noncombatant civilians.

III. Hope for Outcomes

Returning service members sometimes tell me that they feel like they have lost meaning and purpose in their lives. Some desperately miss the sense of being part of something much larger than themselves in the way that a war effort is; others miss the fast operational tempo of missions that can intensify that sense of purpose and belonging.[17] Some long for the respect and status earned in uniform, as Eduardo ("Lalo") Panyagua does, a twenty-something Marine corporal who rose out of the Los Angeles barrio and its gangs to serve three deployments in Iraq and Afghanistan, in his last, in charge of thirty-five Marine and Afghan National Security forces outside Marja, in extremely dangerous and demanding engagements from November 2009 through June 2010.[18] Though a corporal, in this last mission, he essentially filled the billet of a sergeant. Lalo is just not sure he can find that kind of standing in civilian life. In his case, the loss is profound, the despondency, at times, unbearable, and the hunger for replacement meaning palpable. Others come home missing limbs, and some have severely disfiguring facial scars or brain injuries that severely challenge a notion of good functioning after war. For some, unhappiness as despair—the sense that reality falls short of longed-for ideals and that one can't close the gap—descends.[19] Recent spikes in suicide rates within the military point to real and urgent concerns here.[20]

This is where hope can get a foothold.[21] Paradigmatically, substantive hope looks with desire (or perhaps with its own special kind of motivation) to the future, with its possibilities but uncertainties, and in normative cases, to self and

---

17. This is not to downplay the boredom in war. For an interesting discussion and panel in which I participated, see http://videos.huffingtonpost.com/the-boredom-of-war-517827695, accessed June 19, 2013.

18. Lalo is the husband of a former Georgetown student of mine, Donna Hernandez, whose story I tell below. I have interviewed both on several occasions, during 2012–14. I have their permission to tell their stories.

19. See Sarah Buss (Buss 2004) for this notion, though she claims such unhappiness is, at root, irrational.

20. On this, see the Rand Report, "Losing the Battle," http://www.cnas.org/files/documents/publications/CNAS_LosingTheBattle_HarrellBerglass.pdf. For a recent report suggesting that deployment to war zones is not a major factor in the rise in military suicides (and for criticism of the report), see http://www.nytimes.com/2013/08/07/us/deployment-factors-found-not-related-to-military-suicide-spike.html?_r=0, accessed October 20, 2013.

21. For resilience and positive thinking initiatives in the Army, see Martin Seligman's designed Army-wide resilience training program, "Comprehensive Soldier Fitness," discussed in Seligman 2011; Seligman and Fowler 2011; and Reivich, Seligman, and McBride 2011. For critiques of Seligman's positive psychology approach, see Held 2004; Ehrenreich 2009; and http://www.psychologytoday.com/blog/dangerous-ideas/201103/the-dark-side-comprehensive-soldier-fitness, accessed July 25, 2013.

others, and to positive differences each can make in a life.[22] Hope presumes that possibilities (however bare) and people are *open* to one, and that prospect can galvanize energy. Hope presumes a kind of "possibilism"[23] that can stabilize focus and fortify resolve.

Philip Pettit develops the idea: "To form the hope that something is the case or that I or someone else will manage to make it the case, I have to invest that scenario with a level of confidence" that may exceed "the confidence of my actual belief in the prospect and with a degree of stability that will certainly exceed the stability of my actual belief."[24] In this sense, hope is a form of *pragmatic* rationality. It redirects attention and desire and imaginative planning to possibilities that a more fact-processing, probability-assessing, evidence-seeking mentality might reject:

> Forming the hope that a particular scenario will eventuate, or at least eventuate in the event of your taking a certain initiative, is a way of handling the hurly burly of belief. It frees you from the bleakness of beliefs that wax and wane unpredictably in level of confidence. It gives you firm and friendly coordinates in an uncertain and uncompanionable world. To have hope is to have something we might describe as cognitive resolve…Without hope, there would often be no possibility for us of asserting our agency and of putting our own signature or stamp on our conduct. We would collapse in a heap of despair and uncertainty, beaten down by cascades of inimical fact.[25]

---

22. By *substantive* (non-normative) hope I mean to exclude trivial hopes, such as figure in the expression "I hope it won't rain today" or "I hope he catches his train," though I don't have good ways of drawing a hard line between these usages and weightier ones aside from context. My primary interest is in hope that mobilizes focus and practical agency, as will become clear shortly. Here, too, I recognize that there are genuine and substantive ways of hoping where a notion of agency (or agential investment) seems out of place—such as future directed hopes that do not involve effort (hoping that certain legislation passes but essentially being passive about it) or past directed hopes, where practical agency is out of place (for example, hoping that Hitler died a miserable death). (On this, see Martin 2011.) Still, I am thinking of *hope paradigmatically* as a kind of agential investment.

23. Albert Hirshman's term, discussed in Cass Sunstein, review of *Worldly Philosopher: The Odyssey of Albert O. Hirschman*, by Jeremy Adelman, *New York Review of Books*, May 23, 2013, http://www.nybooks.com/articles/archives/2013/may/23/albert-hirschman-original-thinker/?pagination=false, accessed July 2, 2013.

24. Pettit 2004, 159.

25. Ibid., 160.

On this picture, hope is deeply connected with practical agency; as it is some- times put, hope is a form of "agential investment."[26] In this regard, it is distinct from *mere* or *idle* wish, such as for the impossible or near impossible—"for im- mortality," as Aristotle says.[27] And, too, it is distinct from wishful thinking—at least in the way Freud sometimes understands the latter, as a "turning away from reality," with wishful fantasies "regarded as a better reality."[28] For similar reasons, the notion of wish fulfillment, in the sense of satisfaction fully hived off from the constraints of reality, does not capture the meaning of hope either. To be sure, substantive hopes typically involve a kind of ego satisfaction, in the sense of a desire for one's own thriving or *eudaimonia*.[29] And these kinds of hopes may be expressed in the constructions of fantasy and its narratives, as mediums for prac- tice and for trying out future possibilities.[30] I expand upon this shortly. But the point for now is that that fantasy can be an important way of *engaging* reality and not of retreating from it into a fully separate, disconnected track.

To explore some of these intuitions, consider Dan Berschinski, an Army vet- eran whom I have interviewed several times in the past few years.[31] He embodies a sense of hope and the kind of investment of agency, imagination, and grit that hope often involves.

On August 18, 2009, Dan Berschinski, then a twenty-five-year-old first lieu- tenant from West Point, in command of an infantry platoon in Kandahar, Afghanistan, stepped on a bomb while trying to retrieve the remains of his unit

---

26. For an overview and critique of agential investment views, see Martin 2011, in which she argues that hope is not a special form of motivation, though a common way of expressing hope is through fantasies that "can influence motivation both rationally...and nonrationally," 171. So in the end, she accommodates typical cases that express the motivational character of hope. Her worry is that viewing hope as itself a special form of motivation or effortful investment is too restrictive, and cannot accommodate the sort of counterexamples where hope is genuine but *passive*, whether with respect to the future or past; for example, hoping that certain legisla- tion passes but putting no effort into advocacy and support, or hoping that Hitler died a mis- erable death, where agential effort just makes no sense. (On this see Martin 2011.) Still, the kind of hope I am interested in here is *paradigmatically* agential and motivational, whether constitutively so or as a matter of concomitant, typical expression.

27. "Choice cannot relate to impossibles,...but there may be a wish even for impossibles, for example, for immortality. And wish may relate to things that could in no way be brought about by one's own efforts." NE 111b20-25.

28. See Freud 1974 SE XIV, 233, see also SE XIV, 244, 316–18, 324–25; SE XI, 50–51.

29. See Nussbaum 2001, 31–33 on this view of some emotions and their connection with *eudaimonia*.

30. For more on the role of fantasy in hope, see Martin 2011; Lear 2006.

31. I spoke to Berschinski and his family several times in 2012–13. I have their permission to tell their stories.

observer. A botched-up medevac left Dan bleeding profusely, and his family was pretty sure he was not going to make it alive out of Afghanistan. In the end, he was stabilized enough to be put on a plane to Landstuhl Regional Medical Center, though too fragile to actually leave the plane. Within a week, he was flown to Walter Reed Hospital (in Bethesda, Maryland), where his parents awaited him. Bob and Susan Berschinski were warned that if he somehow pulled through, the hemorrhaging would likely result in severe brain damage. Dan miraculously did pull through, with no trace of traumatic brain injury. As Susan said to me, "Once they brought him out of the coma, it was rapidly apparent *he* was still there."

But his body wasn't all there. He had lost nearly half of his skeleton and the joints that held it together, now so much dust in the Afghan desert:

> My guys found a boot…mostly intact actually, and they said to me later that they played rock-paper-scissors to see who would have to stick their hand inside the boot to see if there was any flesh inside. But there wasn't. It was empty.…I don't know what happened.

When Dan came to, he knew much of his body was gone, but under a protective white sheet, he couldn't really take in the damage, and his parents kept up a brave face. "He was a mess…There was not a place on him that you could touch that didn't hurt," said Bob. After more than a dozen operations, and being pinned together by an exoskeletal frame to stabilize his remaining limbs, Dan officially became a double above-the-knee amputee, with a reconstructed left arm and hand, minus a pinky. But critically, he was missing a right hip joint. With that much skeletal damage, and profound socket challenges for securing a good fit with the most customized prostheses, it was fairly clear that Dan would never walk again. Without sit bones, he even had trouble sitting in a wheelchair without sliding off.

The evidence confirmed that prognosis. Others in the Army had suffered his kind of injury, but no one had walked again.

But then a shard of hope emerged. Dan soon learned of one "successful" (that is, ambulatory) missing hip, above-the-knee amputee. Andre Kajlich, a civilian living in Seattle, was hit head-on by a train while studying chemistry in Prague for six months. Ten years later, Kajlich now walks with two prosthetic legs and a single cane. A YouTube video shows his jerky movements and falls going down stairs without quad muscles. But it also shows that he clearly walks.[32] And he not only walks, but he is a world-class paratriathlete.[33]

---

32. http://www.runnersworld.com/runners-stories/losing-his-legs-made-him-stronger-than-ever, accessed July 2, 2013.

33. See http://www.walkingwithnewlegs.com/Andre_Kajlich.html, accessed July 2, 2013.

Kajlich soon became an emulatory model for Dan, providing evidence that walking with his meager skeleton was humanly possible. And that possibilism set in motion a *project* of hope, not unlike a complex master plan with embedded initiatives, collaborative and individual.[34] Those initiatives included consultations that brought Kajlich to Walter Reed, to discuss his case with Dan and other similarly injured vets. But gruelingly, for Dan, it involved two and a half years of intense physical and occupational therapy at the rehabilitation gym on Walter Reed's campus, and a deep immersion into the mechanics, fit, and usage of prosthetics. Dan became expert in the metrics of gait, stride, and balance and more basically, in "wearing legs": how to keep stumps comfortable inside a silicon sleeve and carbon socket all day; how to get a good fit in the morning, when the stump is thin and not yet swollen from rub and wear; how to maneuver and feel comfortable wearing the heavy belt needed to hoist up the leg that is missing its hip bone and socket. All this was in aid of making possible an independent and ambulatory lifestyle.

Dan's case illustrates well Pettit's notion of the pragmatic rationality of hope. We can speculate that in the course of his recovery, Dan puts the counterevidence and low probabilities, the examples of "unsuccessful" similarly injured military guys that would stand between him and ambulation, to the side. They become background information, though presumably still accessible at some level. True, in taking up this stance of hope, he restricts exposure to evidence, but only in the way that many emotions do, by narrowing our focus to certain patterns of salience that then dispose us to building "epistemic landscapes" that cohere with those patterns of salience.[35] In this sense, hope is not systematically different from other emotionally laden ways of seeing.

Dan, like many vets, carries a mental calculation of where his war injuries fit relative to those others suffer. He has it easy, he thinks, compared to arm amputees or veterans who suffer severe brain damage. But he has it a lot harder than below-the-knee amputees: they're mere "single" or "double" "paper cuts," as he affectionately calls them. Also, he doesn't take for granted that he is a veteran with a college education *behind* him, and that he has strong resources in a loving and upper-middle-class family and supportive girlfriend.[36] "All that helps," he says. "Others aren't as lucky." These considerations factor into Dan's hope. His hope is ardent, but it isn't blind.

---

34. Bratman 1987.

35. Goldie 2005, 99; Brady 2007. Also see Hurley and Macnamara 2010 for considerations on reactive attitudes *as* emotions and not beliefs, and background to this in Sherman 1997, 39.

36. They both began attending Stanford Graduate School of Business in fall 2013.

There is one final strand of this sketch of non-normative hope to tease out. And that is the role of imagination and its motivational dimensions.[37] I suspect, at some level or other, Dan fantasizes that he is like Kajlich, and that someday he will be able to do the things that Kajlich can do. To use Adam Smith's term, he "trades places in fancy" with Kajlich. And in the space of imagination, Dan is able to practice and anticipate constructively, "pre-rehearse" as the Stoics would say, what a possible future reality might look like, and so avoid the paralysis of idle fears and the futility of empty hopes.[38] Kajlich's precedent means that Dan does not have to have *radical hope*—imagine from scratch, so to speak. I have in mind here Jonathan Lear's portrayal of Plenty Coups, the Crow leader, who must and does imagine (through the interpretations of dreams and fantasies) a totally novel way of thriving for himself and his people in the face of the annihilation of Crow culture with the death of the buffalo.[39] Crow concepts of courage and virtue that depend upon the warrior life of hunting buffalo no longer have application; radical hope and radical fantasy are required to create new thick content for virtue if a people are to flourish again. Dan's conceptual and moral challenge is not as great. Still, in a related way, imagination, fantasy, and interpretations make concrete his hopes, and help to shape and revise plans that are expressions of his hopes.

Dan trades places with Kajlich, but I suspect Kajlich also "trades" places with Dan. Through a biographical, retrospective narrative of what it was like to take his first, post-accident steps, he puts himself in Dan's "shoes" and closer to Dan's current frustrations and challenges. This also puts him in a position of investing *hope in* Dan (aspiring on his behalf), which, presumably, helps inspire Dan's own hope in himself. At this point, we move from talking about non-normative hope to normative hope—the hope we have *in* others and *in* oneself.

IV. Hope in Others

Dan's hope, in this reconstructed narrative, is for an eventuality that he can walk. But that hope is interlaced with normative hope. He invests hope *in* the medical and therapy staff at Walter Reed and in the institution that supports its rehabilitative gym;[40] he puts hope *in* the civilian contractors who make and fit prosthetics

---

37. For more on the role of imagination and hope, see Martin 2011.

38. I describe this kind of mental practice in Sherman 2005, esp. 117, 145 in connection with Seneca and Cicero's writings.

39. Lear 2006. For a review essay on the book, see Sherman, 2009.

40. Known as the "M.A.T.C" (Military Athletic Training Center), and referred to by one of my interviewees and double amputee, Army Lieutenant Colonel Greg Gadson, as the "Gold's gym for guys missing things."

for veterans; he puts hope *in* his immediate circle of friends and family; he puts hope *in* Congress in myriad ways—to authorize adequate allocations for veteran spending, to deliberate wisely about future military and humanitarian engagements, to support worldwide rights for persons with disabilities.[41] And he puts hope *in* the American electorate to put the right people into office to make these decisions. Equally, he puts hope *in* American business and education leaders to create opportunities for veterans, like himself, to be reintegrated into the workforce and to return to school and training programs. And others invest hope *in* him—his therapists, coaches, mentors, fellow amputees at the rehab gym, his family, girlfriend, peers, and so on. And he invests in himself in ways that are mutually reinforced by his investments in others and their investments in him. Normative investments underlie his hopes for himself (and others) to be able to function well after military service in war.

Normative hope is a form of normative address: we call upon a person to reach, or at least strive toward, some ideal or standard. As with trust, the anticipation falls short of confident belief and involves exposure to some vulnerability and risk-taking. One could be disappointed; the target might not take up the call; or she may recognize that she is being hoped in, counted on, so to speak (to use the language of trust), and acknowledge back that she has been appropriately recognized, but still not fulfill the aspirations invested in her or wholeheartedly take up the challenges. To return to Aristotle, our sons and daughters may not do what is required of them to meet the challenges implicit in our hopes. We may hope in them on credit, so to speak, but then be disappointed.

In the *De Beneficiis*, Seneca rehearses a colorful example of the call-and-response trope of recognition and acknowledgment in the case of benefaction and the return of gratitude. His example is prescient as a sketch of the reiterative looping characteristic of reactive attitudes and the need for a good interactive fit of call and response in successful uptake. Doing a kindness and being reciprocated with gratitude is like a game of catch. You should know to whom you are throwing the ball. The passage bears quoting at length:

> I would like to take up an analogy which our own Chrysippus drew with a game of ball. It falls to the ground through the fault either of the person throwing it or of the person receiving it, while it only remains in play by passing, properly thrown and caught, from one pair of hands to the other. A good player needs to send it off differently to a tall partner than a short one. The

---

41. As in the United Nations treaty for disabled rights which the Senate recently rejected, http://thehill.com/blogs/global-affairs/un-treaties/270831-senate-rejects-un-treaty-for-disabled-rights-in-vote, accessed July 23, 2013.

same principle applies to a favour. Only if properly accommodated to both the persons involved, bestower and recipient, will it leave the one and reach the other as it should. Again, if the game with a trained and practised player, we shall be bolder in throwing the ball. No matter how it comes, his hand will be ready and quick to drive it back. Against an untrained novice, we shall not throw it so hard or so vigorously but be more relaxed, aiming the ball right into his hands and simply meeting it when it comes back. We should use the same procedure when doing favours....As it is, we very often make people ungrateful and welcome the idea that they should be so, as though our favours could only be great if we cannot be thanked for them....How much better and more considerate it would be to see to it that recipients too have a part to play, to welcome the idea that you could be thanked....[42]

Obviously, doing someone a good turn is best geared to what that recipient needs and is capable of using. As Seneca goes on to suggest, giving books to a country bumpkin or a heavy coat to someone in summer will not count as a wise pass likely to be caught with enormous gratitude by the recipient![43] Similarly, trust given to someone who has signaled no competence or interest in the domain in which one is asking her to be trustworthy is not a wise exposure of vulnerability, nor a likely way to scaffold deeper trust in that person.[44]

But hope in others is somewhat different from trust. We may not fully trust persons and their readiness to receive us appropriately, but we still may hope in them, and in an even more robust way than trust, hope that our hope in them makes them responsive to our call. Thus, hope in others can presume a clearly developmental stance. We want to move a recipient along and hope he will rise to the challenge and catch the ball. Still, we are often willing to accommodate somewhat—throw the ball, with the recipient's limits in mind—all the while still trying to get him to catch. And where we simply can't engage the other properly (or are met with deep resistance), we may enlist others' help to throw the ball for us.

To make this concrete, consider the following narrative, one among many conversations I have had recently with a dozen or more women service members. (Most of the women have asked that their names be withheld.)[45]

---

42. Seneca, *On Favours*, II.17.3–6 in (Cooper and Procopé 1995). For related analogy based on the looping back of the mutual reciprocations of the Three Graces, see *On Favours* 1.3.8 in (Cooper and Procopé 1995).

43. For an earlier discussion of Seneca on emotional expression in benefaction and gratitude, see Sherman 2006; and Sherman 2004.

44. I develop these ideas in the case of trust in Sherman 2014a.

45. I conducted these interviews in June 2013.

An elite pilot, "Roberta," with a distinguished record of academic laurels and military awards, is told to her face by her new commander that despite her promotion to a highly coveted senior job on his base, he "fought against" her going there and would continue to do everything he could to undermine her appointment. As she put it, using the lingo of her "brothers" on base, her very presence was "disrupting the status quo" and "tearing down heritage and tradition."[46] In her case, she turned to a male mentor to help break into the "bro network," and plead her cause. There was no way that her new boss could recognize directly *from her* that her hope in him to accept her on equal footing with her male peers was legitimate and something he had moral reason to commit to. He had to hear that through different channels. It is not even clear that he *recognized* the moral call in the end, and may only have felt pressured for political reasons to act in conformity with regulation and policy. To revert to Seneca's metaphor, this is a case where an individual (Roberta) is already in a game of ball, so to speak, but can't get successful uptake from the recipient. And when she finally does, only through the intervention of another player, the "successful" catch may reflect changed behavior more than changed attitude.

In this case, Roberta's hope presumably devolves to disappointment. But her disappointment in the commander is compatible with any resentment she might feel toward him, or indignation her mentor feels toward him.[47] The resentment or indignation has as its evaluative content that she has been demeaned and degraded by her commander, forced to work in a hostile environment where he encourages sexist values protective of the old military as a male-only club. Any resentment, were she to express it directly to him, would hold him strictly accountable for his behavior. Her disappointment, in contrast, has as its evaluative content that she is let down by his impoverished leadership and by his failure to recognize her bid to him (or that made on her behalf) to take her military service seriously and on an equal footing with any male's.

One more clarification is important here. It might be thought that the disappointment that results from the frustration of normative hope is a tamped down version of resentment. We hold back, suppress the full force of our blame or resentment, and show or feel only a milder version of it. I don't think this gets it right, even though on occasion we may *replace* our resentment with disappointment, in deference either to the youth and inexperience of the moral "progressor," or the difficult challenges, external or internal, a target faces in meeting

---

46. Preserving "heritage and tradition," is also code, she adds, for protecting "pornography in on-line briefs and pinup posters on the wall."

47. There can be a "double attitude," as Adrienne Martin puts it (Martin 2013). I thank her for conversation on this issue.

aspirations. But even in such cases, we are taking up a different normative stance in disappointment than we are in resentment. In the first case, our aspirations on behalf of someone are frustrated and we feel let down; in the second, we feel violated, transgressed, toyed with, and hold a target responsible for the transgression. Moreover, disappointment, in others or self, needn't be inherently a mild emotion. It can be felt as profoundly and intensely as the most bitter kind of resentment or guilt. And it can cripple and paralyze and lead to the bleakest kind of despair. The difference between disappointment and resentment is qualitative, not scalar.

V. Hope in Self

We have been focusing on hope and disappointment in others. But many who return from war are dogged by profound disappointment in themselves, in the sense that they somehow have fallen short of ideals of what it is to be a good soldier. Sometimes the disappointment stems from an over-idealized sense of good soldiering, or an intolerance for good and bad luck in war. In a related way, some may feel (subjective) guilt that doesn't track strict culpability or wrongdoing. In some of these cases, there may be causal but not moral responsibility at work—such as when an individual is the proximate cause of a nonculpable accident. In other cases, merely surviving when a buddy doesn't, without in any sense being the agent or cause of that buddy's death, unleashes deep guilt.[48]

In this final section I want briefly to turn to the corrective dimension of self-hope as a reply to overly harsh self-address. Hope in self can update earlier reactive uptakes. And we can be bolstered in that self-hope through the hope of others in us.

But first, it might seem a stretch to think of self-reactive attitudes as moral addresses. After all, in the self-reflexive case, we don't have to *express* the attitudes to *disclose* them to ourselves. And so, if address is primarily *expressed* attitude, then the idea of moral address to self seems strained. Moreover, the background notion of call and response in speech acts again points to the idea of public, and paradigmatically, oral address and response. The model isn't an easy fit for private, normative self-review.

But this is too literal a read of moral address. Even in second-personal cases, we still may hold each other *responsible* without holding *accountable*, where the latter involves, in addition, imposing sanctions that only make sense when our

---

48. I discuss these cases in Sherman 2010, chap. 4; and Sherman 2013. Also, Sherman 2015.

blame or reproach is communicated.[49] Moreover, insofar as evaluative attitudes are *emotions* that draw us in or rivet attention,[50] an important part of moral address, which is to get someone to pay attention to you, is already at work in the self-reactive case. All this, of course, is to put aside the fact that we often do openly express emotions to ourselves, in talking to ourselves, in singing to ourselves, in journaling, in screwing up our face muscles, and in scores of other communications. Some of these communications may need decoding and unmasking, but when we are done, they are the beginning of interpretive narratives, again, which we *tell* ourselves.

But to return to the question with which I began: in what sense can self-hope act as a corrective update on harsher reactive attitudes we hold toward ourselves, particularly when those attitudes—of guilt, shame, or self-disappointment—are not entirely apt, and are the cause of deep anguish? Self-forgiveness, self-empathy, and self-compassion all can play a role.[51] But so, too, can normative hope. Insofar as hope invests aspiration rather than normative demands for strict compliance, we begin by giving ourselves some latitude in the face of significant internal and external challenges we may face. We take up the progressor's stance, not the perfectionist stance of a sage, to use the Stoic idiom. For some, this will involve recognizing the limits of agency in the face of luck and embedded existence. And this willingness to tolerate luck may combine with the resources of hope to engage imagination, in order to be able to rethink and re-narrate traumatic or nagging scenarios in a less "stuck" and less self-punishing way. So, in time, a Marine may come to imagine those who have died under his watch as *in fact* not condemning him. Or he may no longer imagine himself exposed, under another's critical gaze, in a way that compromises self-presentation and brings on shame.[52] In short, new possibilities open up in how we hold ourselves responsible and how we view others as holding us responsible.

Consider again Marine Corporal Lalo Panyagua. One incident leaves him wracked with guilt. He was in Marja in charge of twelve Marines, living and traveling in tight quarters, out of an armored vehicle. Although the same age as some of his troops, he was paternal toward them, "his kids," he calls them, whom he "taught and trained" how to use lethal force and restrain it. The area they traveled was thick with enemy insurgents and laced with mines. It had become his habit to

---

49. Macnamara emphasizes this point in Macnamara 2011.

50. Or conversely, "emotionally significant objects and events capture and consume attention" as Michael Brady puts it (Brady 2009, 423).

51. For the role of self-empathy in moral healing, see Sherman 2014b.

52. For an exploration of this view of shame, see Velleman 2001.

warn each Marine, before exiting the vehicle, to carefully check his footing for explosives. One time, though, he forgot to repeat the warning. A Marine exited the vehicle, stepped on a mine, and was instantly blown to pieces. Four years later, the guilt and self-reproach have not abated.

Lalo's wife, Donna, is critical to Lalo's project of self-hope. He is a moral progressor in her eyes, and his own project of hope in himself leans heavily on her implicit and explicit hope in him. Still the journey has not been easy.

With little transition time, Lalo returned from his third tour, in Afghanistan, to a stateside base where he became a combat guy at a desk job, surrounded by most who had not gone to war and a commander who viewed him as a malingerer for taking time off for his medical appointments. It was Donna who got him to seek psychotherapy (to see "the wizard," as he puts it), two years after his return and a pileup of frightening incidents—including his flinging her out of bed across a room as he relived a battle scene flashback, holding her at knifepoint one night when she startled him during a thunderstorm, assaulting strangers who looked to him like they might harm her. She has since taken away his knife. He has taken up archery in its place: "He can't really hurt me with a bow and arrow!" she laughs.

Donna is good at compartmentalizing, and since childhood, excelling in her studies has been her sanctuary and salvation. But she also has a sustained vision of Lalo as someone who is absolutely lovable—"everyone falls in love with Lalo," she has said to me several times, meaning not just that he charms, but that he is worthy of her love, and that of others. Estimations of worth and goodness, of course, needn't have anything to do with estimates of a person's *psychological* capacities to overcome crippling and harsh guilt or accept the limits of agency and what is beyond one's control.

But *admiring* another's goodness or capacity for hard work in the service of important and worthwhile ends *may* have such an influence. And Donna knows well and deeply, in a way that Lalo can forget, just how good a Marine he is and how he surpassed expectations in every mission he was assigned. When he wore his regalia, at her request, at their wedding when they eloped when she was a freshman, and at her graduation from Georgetown this past year, she was reminding him of his honors and his capacities. She is trying to reconnect him with his capabilities and his confidence in them.

These are public addresses of sorts *to* him of her hope *in* him. They are nudges, offerings of content for introjection that will renourish his own self-images. They are attempts at tempering and updating his self-blame for being a leader who lost troops. Of course, uptake, especially in this kind of case, can be partial and primarily a performance,[53] outer posturing of normative hope, perhaps in showing up

---

53. For Stoic lessons on the difficulty of inner change, see Cicero's critique of Stoic doctrine in connection with his own grieving (Sherman 2005, 132, 143–49).

for psychotherapy appointments, say, but resisting the hard work and trust alliance with a therapist required to really invest in the possibility of therapeutic change. But just as a therapist's finely expressed trust in a patient can elicit trustworthiness,[54] so, too, can a partner's artful and finely attuned hope in one bootstrap one's own. Donna is able to do this for Lalo.

Lalo's self-hope, in this case, mirrors Donna's hope in him. It would be hard to spend any time with them and not see that quickly. They have invested in each other's futures, in her education and in his healing from war. She is a survivor of war, no less than he, and he has hopes one day of having a strong college education. They partner, in part, by trading places.

We human progressors are engaged in complicated moral and psychological interactions. We elicit change in response to each other's aspirations, as well as our own. For a returning veteran, recognizing that another has invested hope in you can be deeply corrective and healing. It can nourish overall hope in self and sustain hope for projects that rekindle a sense of meaning and purpose after war.[55]

BIBLIOGRAPHY

Aristotle. (1984). *The Complete Works of Aristotle: The Revised Oxford Translation*, ed. Jonathan Barnes. Princeton: Princeton University Press.

Brady, M. S. (2007). "Recalcitrant Emotions and Visual Illusions." *American Philosophical Quarterly* 44: 273–84.

Brady, M. S. (2009). "The Irrationality of Recalcitrant Emotions." *Philosophical Studies: An International Journal for Philosophy in the Analytic Tradition* 145: 413–30.

Bratman, M. (1987). *Intentions, Plans, and Practical Reasons*. Cambridge, Mass.: Harvard University Press.

Buss, S. (2004). "The Irrationality of Unhappiness and the Paradox of Despair." *The Journal of Philosophy* 101: 171–200.

Cooper, J. M., and J. F. Procopé. (1995). "Seneca: Moral and Political Essays." *Seneca: Moral and Political Essays*. Cambridge: Cambridge University Press.

Darwall, S. (2006). *The Second-person Standpoint*. Cambridge, Mass.: Harvard University Press.

Ehrenreich, B. (2009). *Bright-Sided: How the Relentless Promotion of Positive Thinking Has Undermined America*. New York: Metropolitan.

---

54. For an excellent discussion of trust and growing trustworthiness, see (Jones 2012).

55. I am grateful to Trip Glazer for his invaluable research assistance in the final stages of preparing this essay. I am also deeply indebted to the Guggenheim Foundation for their generous fellowship support 2013–14 and to Georgetown University for its support of my research during the fellowship.

Freud, S. (1974). *Standard Edition of the Complete Psychological Works of Sigmund Freud*. Translated by J. Strachey. London: Hogarth.

Goldie, P. (2005). "Imagination and the Distorting Power of Emotion." *Journal of Consciousness Studies* 12: 127–39.

Held, B. (2004). "The Negative Side of Positive Psychology." *Journal of Humanistic Psychology* 44: 9–46.

Herman, J. L. (1992). *Trauma and Recovery*. New York: Basic Books.

Hoge, C. (2010). *Once a Warrior Always a Warrior*. Guilford, Conn.: Globe Pequot.

Hurley, E., and C. Macnamara. (2010). "Beyond Belief: Toward a Theory of Reactive Attitudes." *Philosophical Papers* 39: 373–99.

Jones, K. (2012). "Trustworthiness." *Ethics* 123: 61–85.

Lansky, M. R. (1995). "Shame and the scope of Psychoanalytic Understanding." *American Behavioral Scientist* 38: 1076–90. doi:10.1177/0002764295038008004.

Lansky, M. R. (2003a). "The 'Incompatible Idea' Revisited: The Oft-invisible Ego-ideal and Shame Dynamics." *The American Journal of Psychoanalysis* 63: 365–76. doi:10.1023/B:TAJP.0000004741.67949.3f.

Lansky, M. R. (2003b). "Modification of the Ego Ideal and the Problem of Forgiveness in Sophocles' Philoctetes." *Psychoanalysis and Contemporary Thought* 26: 463–91.

Lansky, M. R. (2004). "Trigger and Screen: Shame Dynamics and the Problem of Instigation in Freud's Dreams." *The Journal of The American Academy of Psychoanalysis and Dynamic Psychiatry* 32: 441–68.

Lansky, M. R. (2005). "The Impossibility of Forgiveness: Shame Fantasies as Instigators of Vengefulness in Euripides' Medea." *Journal of the American Psychoanalytic Association* 53: 437–64. doi:10.1177/00030651050530021701.

Lansky, M. R. (2007). "Unbearable Shame, Splitting, and Forgiveness in the Resolution of Vengefulness." *Journal of the American Psychoanalytic Association* 55: 571–93.

Lansky, M. R. (2009). "Forgiveness as the Working Through of Splitting." *Psychoanalytic Inquiry* 29: 374–85. doi:10.1080/07351690903032090.

Lear, J. (2006). *Radical Hope: Ethics in the Face of Cultural Devastation*. Cambridge, Mass.: Harvard University Press.

Litz, B., N. Stein, E. Delaney, L. Lebowitz, W. P. Nash, C. Silva, and S. Maguen. (2009). "Moral Injury and Moral Repair in War Veterans: A Preliminary Model and Intervention Strategy." *Clinical Psychology Review* 29: 695–706.

Luban, D. (2014). "Risk-Taking and Force Protection." In *Reading Walzer*, edited by I. Benbaji and N. Sussman. London: Routledge.

Macnamara, C. (2011). "Holding Others Responsible." *Philosophical Studies* 152: 81–102.

Maguen, S., and B. Litz. (January 13, 2012). "Moral Injury in Veterans of War," http://www.ptsd.va.gov/professional/newsletters/research-quarterly/v23n1.pdf, accessed March 6, 2012.

Martin, A. M. (2008). "Hope and Exploitation." *Hastings Center Report* 38: 49–55.

Martin, A. M. (2010). "Owning Up and Lowering Down: The Power of Apology." *Journal of Philosophy* 107: 534–53.

Martin, A. M. (2011). "Hopes and Dreams." *Philosophy and Phenomenological Research* 83: 148–73. doi:10.1111/j.1933-1592.2010.00422.x.

Martin, A. M. (2013). *Normative Hope* (previously titled *Gratitude, Disappointment, and Normative Hope*). Young Ethicist Prize, RoME (Rocky Mountain Ethics Conference), University of Colorado, Boulder, 2012.

Nash, W. P., L. Krantz, N. Stein, R. J. Westphal, and B. Litz. (2011). "Comprehensive Soldier Fitness, Battlemind, and the Stress Continuum Model: Military Organizational Approaches to Prevention." In *Caring for Veterans with Deployment-related Stress Disorders*, edited by J. I. Ruzek, P. P. Schnurr, J. J. Vasterling, and M. J. Friedman, 193–214. Washington, D.C.: American Psychological Association.

Nussbaum, M. C. (2001). *Upheavals of Thought: The Intelligence of Emotions*. Cambridge: Cambridge University Press.

Pettit, P. (2004). "Hope and Its Place in Mind." *Annals of the American Academy of Political and Social Science* 592: 152–65. doi:http://ann.sagepub.com/archive/.

Reivich, K. J., M. E. P. Seligman, and S. McBride (2011). "Master Resilience Training in the U.S. Army." *American Psychologist* 66: 25–34. doi:10.1037/a0021897.

Seligman, M. E. P. (2011). *Flourish: A Visionary New Understanding of Happiness and Well-being*. New York: Free.

Seligman, M. E. P., and R. D. Fowler. (2011). "Comprehensive Soldier Fitness and the Future of Psychology." *American Psychologist* 66: 82–86. doi:10.1037/a0021898.

Shay, J. (1994). *Achilles in Vietnam: Combat Trauma and the Undoing of Character*. New York: Touchstone.

Shay, J. (2002). *Odysseus in America: Combat Trauma and the Trials of Homecoming*. New York: Scribner.

Sherman, N. (1997). *Making a Necessity of Virtue: Aristotle and Kant on Virtue*. Cambridge; New York: Cambridge University Press.

Sherman, N. (2004). "Virtue and Emotional Demeanor." In *Feelings and Emotions: Interdisciplinary Explorations (The Amsterdam Symposium)*, edited by A. Manstead, N. Frijda, and A. Fischer, 441–54. Cambridge: Cambridge University Press.

Sherman, N. (2005). *Stoic Warriors: The Ancient Philosophy Behind the Military Mind*. New York: Oxford University Press.

Sherman, N. (2006). "The Look and Feel of Virtue." In *Norms, Virtue, and Objectivity: Issues in Ancient and Modern Ethics*, edited by C. Gill, 59–82. Oxford: Oxford University Press.

Sherman, N. (2009). "The Fate of a Warrior Culture: Nancy Sherman on Jonathan Lear's Radical Hope (Harvard: 2006)." *Philosophical Studies: An International Journal for Philosophy in the Analytic Tradition* 144: 71.

Sherman, N. (2010). *The Untold War: Inside the Hearts, Minds, and Souls of Our Soldiers*. New York: W.W. Norton & Company.

Sherman, N. (2013). "Guilt in War." In *On Emotions*, edited by J. Deigh. New York: Oxford University Press.

Sherman, N. (2014a). "Recovering Lost Goodness: Shame, Guilt, and Self-Empathy." *Psychoanalytic Psychology* 31: 217–33.

Sherman, N. (2014b). "He Gave Me His Hand but Took My Bow: Trust and Trustworthiness." In *Combat Trauma and the Ancient Greeks*, edited by P. Meineck and D. Konstan. New York: Palgrave Macmillan.

Sherman, N. (2014c). "Self-Empathy and Moral Repair." In *Emotions and Values*, edited by S. Roeser and C. Todd. Oxford: Oxford University Press.

Sherman, N. (2015). *Afterwar: Healing the Moral Wounds of our Soldiers* New York: Oxford University Press.

Sherman, N. (2016). "Moral Injury, Damage, and Repair." In *Our Ancient Wars*, edited by V. Caston and S.-M. Weineck. Ann Arbor: University of Michigan Press.

Smith, A. M. (2005). "Responsibility for Attitudes: Activity and Passivity in Mental Life." *Ethics* 115: 236–71.

Stern, D. (1985). *The Interpersonal World of the Infant*. New York: Basic Books.

Strawson, P. F. (1993). "Freedom and Resentment." In *Perspectives on Moral Responsibility*, edited by J. R. Fischer and M. Ravizza. Ithaca: Cornell University Press.

Tanielian, T. J., and L. Jaycox. (2008). *Invisible Wounds of War: Psychological and Cognitive Injuries, Their Consequences and Services to Assist Recovery*. Santa Monica: Rand.

Velleman, J. D. (2001). "The Genesis of Shame." *Philosophy and Public Affairs* 30: 27–52.

Walker, M. U. (2006). *Moral Repair: Reconstructing Moral Relations After Wrongdoing*. New York: Cambridge University Press.

Wallace, R. J. (1996). *Responsibility and the Moral Sentiments*. Cambridge, Mass.: Harvard University Press.

Watson, G. (2004). *Agency and Answerability*. New York: Oxford University Press.

INDEX